2012年第1期（总第2期）

NON-TRADITIONAL SECURITY STUDIES

非传统安全研究

浙江大学非传统安全与和平发展研究中心
塔里木大学非传统安全与边疆民族发展研究中心 编

CONTENTS

目　录

学术争鸣

《非传统安全与当代世界》译丛书评

非传统安全相关学科研究综述

非传统安全研究

2012 年第 1 期（总第 2 期）
浙江大学非传统安全与和平发展研究中心
塔里木大学非传统安全与边疆民族发展研究中心 编

Non－traditional Security Studies

(founded in 2010)

Tel：(86) 571－8820 8518
Fax：(86) 571－8820 8518
Address：Room 411－1，Xiyi Building，Zijingang Campus，Zhejiang University，Hangzhou，310058，P. R. China
Email：nts@ zju. edu. cn

Editor－in－chief：YU Xiaofeng
Publisher：Intellectual Property Publishing House
Distributor：Xinhua Bookstore

编 者 按

余潇枫　甘均先

2011 年 11 月在北京召开的“中国与跨大西洋国家：应对全球安全挑战”慕尼黑安全政策会议核心小组会议，把“能源、资源与环境：新安全标准?”设为重要议题之一。本期的海外专稿《在“人类世”中转变能源思想》是对能源安全议题的重要反思。该文第一作者梅飞虎（Maximilian Mayer）曾参加浙江大学非传统安全与和平发展研究中心于 2011 年 10 月召开的“第四届海峡两岸能源经济学术研讨会”，现文是在会议发言《在“人类世”中反思能源安全》的基础上的拓展。作者通过对“人类世”概念的讨论，试图阐明环境安全的观念对于人类世纪的作用，并尝试用“人类世”这个概念来重新理解能源安全，以超越对于安全概念传统论述的困局。

对于非传统安全威胁而言，重要的不仅仅在于发现，更重要的还在于如何应对与治理。非传统安全治理可以分为三个层次。从宏观的国际层次来看，非传统安全治理需要国际社会的协作；从中观的国内层次来看，非传统安全治理需要中央政府的政策权衡；从微观的社会民众层面上看，非传统安全治理需要包括个体、非政府组织等在内的共同参与。同时，治理不仅需要行为体的参与，还需要考察治理的绩效，以决定是否执行后续政策。本期主要选编了四篇关于非传统安全治理的论文，他们分别从不同角度探讨了非传统安全治理。

崔顺姬的《东亚非传统安全问题新趋势与治理新思路》，回顾了 2011 年发生在东亚的重大非传统安全事件。她给出了三种解决途径：综合性路径，利用多种手段组合解决问题；可持续性路径，为安全治理提供可持续的操作平台；以人为本的路径，重视对弱势群体安全的保护。

李开盛的《国际非政府组织与非传统安全治理》，分析了国际非政府组织在救灾、减贫、环保等方面的重要作用。他指出了非政府组织天然的优势与劣势——优势在于非政府组织投入非传统安全治理的意愿和动力强烈，劣势在于非政府组织可以使用的资源很少。

甘均先、毛艳的《中国的非传统安全合作与外交能力建设》，分析了 2011 年与中国有关的国际非传统安全合作的新特征，以及中国应对非传统安全问题的新思维。他认为中国应该在国际非传统安全合作上继续转变思维，注重议题操作、沟通言说和信息传播三方面的外交能力建设。

胡税根、徐元帅的《中国政府非传统安全应对能力评估研究》，对中国政府在“5・12”大地震中的应对进行了评估。他借鉴了企业管理的方法，建立了一个由 7 大指标和 25 个二级指标组成的评估模型。他的论文从管理学的角度来分析非传统安全治理，给我们带来了有益的启示。非传统安全治理也亟需更多的学科外智力支持。

作为中国与非传统安全为主题的理论思考，原华荣、王凌艳的《人口数量与中国发展安全》一文值得一读。该文分析了人口规模对于中国可持续发展的重要意义。他们将“生态环境安全”“资源安全”“社会安全”“国土安全”等作为中国“发展安全”的主题，并认为“人口数量安全”是“发展安全”的核心。由于人口数量影响到“种际平等”“代际平等”“种内平等”，如何控制人口数量就成了人口安全的核心。基于人口与资源的比重大小，他们认为，未来的世界强权将是那些“较少人口享受较多资源”的国家，如美国、俄罗斯、加拿大、澳大利亚和巴西等，尤其是俄罗斯具有最大的发展潜力。从人口数量与资源分配的角度来分析国家发展的潜力是本文主要的特征，但是一个国家的文化底蕴、科技实力也是国家发展的重要变量。本文的结论是否正确，需要读者自主作出判断。

本期的“学术争鸣”摘引了王逸舟、王义桅和陈世瑞的最新研究成果。王逸舟认为中国外交应该从“无为”走向“有为”，他提供了一种“创造性的介入”的视角，即温和地、渐进地修正国际体系的规则和规范。王义桅对中国崛起提出了一种新的观念——“包容性崛起”，即西方与中国等发展中国家相互包容的发展观。包容性崛起要求中国与西方国家“利益共赢”“权利共享”“责任共担”“价值共享”。陈世瑞从“混沌理论”的角度分析了非传统安全治理。他将非传统安全问题呈现出的特征如复杂性、扩散性、动态性、跨国性视为混沌现象的非线性特征，由此他提出“混沌管理”，介入非传统安全的自组织过程，控制非传统安全威胁“混沌发生”的条件和规模，改变其动态行为来化解危机。

本期还选刊了一组《非传统安全与当代世界》译丛的书评。朱锋分析评论了布赞的《国际安全研究的演化》，他探讨了布赞安全研究的特色，并认为中国应该建立自己的多元化安全研究议程。余潇枫对阿查亚的《人的安全：概念与应用》和《安全化困境：亚洲的视角》进行了评论，针对前一本著作，他认为以人为本是非传统安全研究的基本价值观；对于后一本著作，他认为安全化理论的亚洲视角深化和超越了安全化的传统路径。

海外专题

Attuning Concepts of Energy Security to the Anthropocene*

Maximilian Mayer and Peer Schouten

Abstract: This article draws on the notion of the Anthropocene in order to ask what it means for conceptions of security that the environment is an effect of human agency. Accepting that the Anthropocene is not only a geological era, but also a concept that carries an urgent normative connotation, we explore two of its implications for our understanding of energy security. Firstly, we cannot leave the externalities of pursuing energy security out of the picture. Most attempts to rethink energy security for the 21st century do not live up to this criterion. Because fundamental insecurity persists despite successful attainment of traditional energy security, we reconsider the premises upon which energy security is based. The first implication is that the factuality of the 'modern' separation between mankind and nature is breaking down, such breaking down uncover a contested web of relations, which, however, is not reflected in the ontology underpinning energy security. Second, we need to take one step beyond discursive understandings of security. To conceptualize security as discourse and, subsequently, energy security as a discursive political agenda, is to adopt the language of 'radical constructivism' and to treat energy and climate security as 'merely' socially constructed. Poststructural views comfortably remove from sight the many externalities. The implication of taking the Anthropocene condition seriously is then also methodical: we must treat security not associally constructed but rather as also built up from—and threatened by—the very material elements and collective actions that are mobilized and assembled in its pursuit. An adequate conception of energy security needs to incorporate the material processes by which we attain that security. To move beyond the discursive we consider energy security as an *assemblage*, constituted by and dependent on both hybrid elements that are both 'social' and 'material' at the same time—rather than being a social construct divorced from 'nature'.

Key Words: Anthropocene, Energy Security, Environment Security

This article draws on the notion of the Anthropocene in order to ask what it means for conceptions of security that the environment is an effect of human agency. While an increasing part of humanity enjoys the fossil fuel-based improvement of living standards, such internationally renowned bodies as the Intergovernmental Panel on Climate Change (IPCC) have called attention to the challenge those emissions from consumption of natural resources present to global ecosystem (Lubchenco, 1998). Another manifestation of the same dilemma is the 2010 Gulf Coast oil spill, which President Barack Obama called 'the worst environmental disaster America has ever faced' (The White House, 2010). It resulted directly from that

* This is a shortened and revised version of Maximilian Mayer and Peer Schouten: "Energy Security and Climate Security under Conditions of the Anthropocene", a chapter from *Energy Security in the Era of Climate Change* edited by Luca Anceschi and Jonathan Symons (Palgrave Macmillan, 2012); reproduced with permission of Palgrave Macmillan.

nation's hunger for affordable mineral resources. We ask, therefore, how is it possible that the security of nations depends on oil consumption on the one hand (Litfin, 2003), while Politicians speaks of 'waging a battle' against an 'oil spill that is assaulting our shores and our citizens' on the other? Or, in more general terms, how can we come to terms with the fact that the pursuit of energy security causes widespread *in*securities?

Tackling this dilemma in an insightful way, Simon Dalby (2009) has hailed the notion of the Anthropocene as a new paradigm for global politics. The Anthropocene, a term imported from earth sciences, refers to a new geological period in which human actions have such an impact that we need to fundamentally rethink our relationship to the environment (Crutzen & Stroemer, 2000). Taking the work surrounding this notion as a starting point, this article offers a contribution to the unfolding debate on energy security in an era of climate change.

Accepting that the Anthropocene is not only a geological era, but also a concept that carries an urgent normative connotation, we here explore two of its implications for our understanding of energy security. Firstly, in light of the Anthropocene means we cannot leave the externalities of pursuingenergy security out of the picture. Most attempts to rethink energy security for the 21st century (Yergin, 2006; Bradshaw, 2009; Verrastro & Sarah Ladislaw, 2007) do not live up to this criterion. Because fundamental insecurity persists despite successful attainment of traditional energy security, we reconsider the premises upon which thinking about energy security is based. The first implication then is that under the Anthropocene, the factuality of the 'modern' separation between mankind and nature is breaking down, uncovering a contested web of relations, not reflected in the confident ontology underpinning energy security.

Second and related, we need to take one step beyond discursive understandings of (energy) security. To conceptualise security as discourse and, subsequently, energy security as a discursive political agenda, is to adopt the language of 'radical constructivism' and to treat energy and climate security as 'merely' socially constructed. This comfortably removes from sight the many externalities of their pursuit. The second implication of taking the Anthropocenecondition seriously is then methodical: we must treat security not as merely socially constructed but rather as also built up from—and threatened by—the very material elements that are mobilised and assembled in its pursuit. An adequate conception of energy security needs to incorporate the material processes by which we attain that security, and to conceptualise climate concerns 'as a reality at the intersection of its physical and social history' (Byrne & Glover, 2005). To move beyond the discursive we consider energy security as an *assemblage*, constituted by and dependent on both 'social' and 'material' elements, which in turn directly 'impacts' upon both—rather than being a social construct divorced from 'nature'. Concluding, we argue that by considering the agendas of energy security and climate change as political agencies working on the same elements in different ways, it becomes possible to pin down the shortcomings of energy security. We identify a series of focal points that must be addressed if the debate is to move further and argue that the principles of inclusiveness and symmetry enable us to unsettle our narrow understanding of security and open up space for a broader range of concerns.

Conceptualizations of Security in the Anthropocene Era

Within critical security studies, security is accepted to be an 'essentially contested concept', with 'securitisation' referring to the discursive process by which an issue gets elevated from normal politics and constituted as an issue that warrants extraordinary policies (Huysmans, 2006; Wæver, 1995). In this understanding, security is thus 'more socially constructed than objectively determined' (Barnett, 2001). Whereas this approach sheds important light on the contested and shifting nature of security politics, it also delinks 'discursive' security politics from an 'objectively determined' realm to which nature belongs as we show throughout the following discussion on alternate securitizations of nature.

Securitising National Consumption

Energy security is commonly understood as a political agenda concerned with the governance of energy production and consumption in service of national economies. Securitising an issue like energy provision takes it out of the domain of normal politics to constitute it as an exceptional concern. Yet, importantly, elevating energy consumption to a security issue dwarfs and silences other concerns. Firmly rooted in the realist framework that perceives the world beyond one's national borders as anarchic and relations among states as antagonistic, energy security has been concerned with national referent objects with pre-given interests. Consequently, the imposed relationship between nature and security is quintessentially biased towards concerns stemming from a national interest, conflicting not only with other national interests but also with security conceptions foregrounding subnational or global interests (cf. Lubeck, Watts & Lipschutz, 2007). Additionally, the national energy security paradigm frames the preservation of a fixed supply of natural resources to feed a national economy in a manner that leaves ecology out of the picture. With energy security successfully securitised, only a very limited aspect of the relation between human agency and the natural environment receives political (and analytical) attention.

Environmental and Climate Security

This narrow understanding of energy security—while still in broad use—has come under heavy scrutiny, as is reflected in the broad debate about environmental security. Ironically, energy security's continued and effective purchase has given rise to even bigger threats to national security such as abrupt climate shifts (Barnett, 2001a; Dalby, 2002; Liotta, 2005).

Subsequently, these externalities also became securitised (Floyd, 2008; Trombetta, 2008). Since the mid-90s, climate concerns increasingly appear in national security strategies, framed as threats to national wellbeing (Dalby, 2009). Recent efforts by various international institutions to separate out climate change into different measurable security issues (Brauch, 2009; Brauch & Zundel, 2008) can also be seen as applications of the same principle, in which the relationship between mankind and the environment is again framed through securitisation—environmental security becomes constructed 'in terms of technological and modernist managerial assertions of control within a geopolitical imaginary of states and territorial entities' (Dalby, 2002). The environmental and climate security discourses, while securitizing a widening number of aspects of the relationship between human agency and the natural environment, again constitute the latter as a limited, stable and apprehensible object in service of, or threatening, the former. In this process, the reverse dynamic—by which human agency affects the natural environment—is by and large silenced.

Environmental and climate security are based on the same kind of reductionism as the energy security agenda—a reductionism made evident by the lack of clear evidence, despite almost 30 years of research, for straight forward pathways between environmental change and conflict; between fossil resources and interstate wars; or between climate change and societal collapse (Mcab & Bailey, 2007; Dalby 2009). We thus witness the same principle at work both in energy security and in alternate securitisations that challenge it by incorporating more matters of concern. Both energy security and climate security are thus contested securitisations, each with a limited and conflicting scope of matters of concern. To explore why Anthropogenic insecurity persists despite the efforts mobilised and concerns addressed by these agendas, we need to uncover what these dominant securitisations of energy and climate change share.

Opening the Black-box of Nature

The different agendas—energy security, environmental security and climate security—all present us with a reductionist account of the natural environment and how it is related to human agency. All three agendas are premised upon a modern western, anthropocentric, ontological separation of nature and society, in which nature is a 'black box', a mechanical, factual entity that requires mastery.[1] Society, instead, is

[1] This argument has often been voiced as a (postmodern) analysis or critique against modern social sciences, cf. (Beck, 1995; Latour, 1993, 2004, 2005).

more fluid and determines what counts as a matter of concern that requires us to act upon nature in a certain way. Indeed, it is the concern of a social subject that drives the shifting securitisations of natural objects. Energy security reduces nature to a factual amount of barrels of oil per day, which is of importance to the demands set by a human referent object. While climate security broadens the concern to the social repercussions of this process, it is premised upon the same ontological divide and foregrounds the same, social, concerns. The content of both securitisations is social and disembedded from nature, which merely forms a passive context to be acted upon.

The anthropocentric understanding underpinning the aforementioned securitisations is challenged by insights from climate scientists; foregrounding the notion of the Anthropocene, they emphasise not human control over, but human influence on the environment (Hulme 2010). Recognising the central role of humankind in shaping geological and ecological dynamicssince the Industrial Revolution, Nobel laureate Paul J. Crutzen proposed to call the period characterised by that influence the 'Anthropocene'. Crutzen and others have subsequently advocated a re-embedding of mankind in the environment as the point of departure for feasible social science (Clark & Munn, 1986; Crutzen & Stoermer, 2000). They advocate a shift in focus from concerns such as building pipelines, ever-deeper off shore drilling, the calculation of arable land for food production, and incentivising other nations to reduce emissions, to shifting climate patterns, rapidly decreasing water resources, and the use of the atmosphere as a gigantic emissions dump. In other words, when global economic and consumption dynamics are considered asagencies working upon nature, security becomes linked to different matters of concern.

But ultimately, the challenge goes further: it requires the reinterpretation of what security means in light of a different interpretation of modernity (cf. Litfin, 2003). Starting with the Industrial Revolution, mankind has gained unprecedented control over nature. Yet with increased control came unprecedented influence— 'we', indeed, 'now live on a human-dominated planet' (Lubchenco, 1998). Ironically, due to human agency, nature has come to constitute a severe threat to livelihoods and whole nations, as illustrated by the small island states that are already beginning to move their citizens to secure lands. Furthermore, it is recognised that global and local feedback loops between nature and human interventions therein, as well as non-linear irreversible dynamics, could lead to unforeseen disasters eventually destabilising the global ecosystem (Hansen, 2005; Solomon & IPCC, 2007). As humans are rapidly transforming global ecosystems—often with unpredictable and threatening outcomes—the modernist understanding that a clear and easily defined difference exists between objective factors and dynamics of nature on the one hand, and the contingent processes of society on the other, is giving way to numerous continuing 'border conflicts' (Tsing, 2005). From this perspective a different picture arises, consisting of intricate interwovenness, perpetual feedback loops, and the essential embeddedness of the human enterprise in nature.

Energy Security Assemblages

This section draws upon insights from science and technology studies in general and actor-network theory in particular. ❶It provides an analysis of how securitisations of energy, environmental, and climate can be understood as distinct 'assemblages': associations both of 'social' and 'material' elements, involving political and economic practices, material flows, infrastructures, and ecological environments as well as human resistance and narratives of national security. Assemblages perform and shape the world, and can be defined conceptually as networks of elements linked by actors or programmatic agencies. Rather than solely constructing security discourses *about* some aspect of nature, actors *involve* the aspects of nature concerned

❶ This section draws heavily on the work of actor – network theory (ANT). See: Callon, 1986; Callon & Latour, 1992; Callon & Law, 1982, 1997; DeLanda, 2006; Latour, 1987, 2005; Law, 1992, 2008, 1991; Law & Callon, 1988; Law & Mol, 2008. For a more in – depth discussion and empirical applications of ANT within international security studies, see Schouten, 2010a, 2010b.

by actively transforming them to fit a particular agenda (Latour, 1993). We thus reconceptualise the contested discourses of energy, environmental and climate security as hybrid agencies consisting of a 'complex blending of social and biophysical factors' (Forsyth, 2001) working upon nature in definite—and finite—ways (Latour, 2004, 2005). In order to act upon such vast assemblages, all elements have to be translated into a language that permits intervention, by separating out and translating what matters into economically or politically apprehensible concerns. The notion of 'translation' is pivotal for actor-network theory. It refers to 'all the negotiations, intrigues, calculations, acts of persuasion and violence thanks to which an actor or force takes, or causes to be conferred on itself, authority to speak or act on behalf of another actor or force' (Callon & Latour, 1992). The notion thus literally captures the transformation of elements through the associations made by actors in a securitization.

In line with the rich body of work surrounding such thinkers as Arne Naess and more recently Bruno Latour, who each in their own way argued for a notion of the 'social' that incorporates both nature and mankind as matters of concern (Asdal, 2008; Barad, 2003; Barry, 2001; Bingham & Hinchliffe, 2008; Callon, 1986; Gammon, 2010; Jasanoff, 2005; Mol, 1998; Morin, 2009), we here summarise our analytical lens as based on the criteria of inclusiveness and symmetry. *Inclusiveness* refers to the scope and breadth of a notion of security in terms of the elements assembled as endogenous matters of concern rather than as exogenous matters of fact. ❶

Secondly, *symmetry* is a criterion that implies equal inclusion of both 'social' and 'natural' agencies and concerns. Thus, neither a notion of security focusing primarily on human concerns (as does energy security), nor privileging environmental concerns (as do radical variants of 'deep ecology') will suffice. Being forced to focusinstead to the hybrid agencies that assemble heterogeneous elements, hopefully avoids the kind bias that inevitably results in detached research endeavours and destructive or infeasible policy agendas, which have helped to bring about the Anthropocene era in the first place.

Assembling Energy Security

As discussed before, energy security is commonly understood as 'simply the availability of sufficient supplies at affordable prices', that is, a variable of national economic growth to be secured through markets, political and, if necessary, military action. By extension, political and scholarly concern with energy security is premised on threats to the smooth functioning of national economies arising for instance from sharp increases in prices, instability in oil producing countries or geopolitical tensions. Within this picture, hydrocarbon resources in general, and oil and gas reserves in particular, ❷ are the 'lifeblood of civilization'; for this reason they are a central preoccupation of national security agendas that, accordingly, regularly resurface in global politics as a central concern (Amineh & Houweling, 2007; Marquina Barrio, 2008; Moran & Russell, 2009; Zweig & Bi, 2005).

Specific national energy security strategies may diverge: interests of exporting and importingcan differ, and strategic policies compete with market-based approaches—yet the similarities between national energy security agenda's by far outweigh their differences as the basic assumptions have remained constant over time. The current mainstreamunderstanding of energy security does not deviate from the canonical definition offered by the US Department of Energy in 1985 (Hirsch, 1987), and ever since Winston Churchill made oil-dependence a core concern of British strategy, energy policies have shared an emphasis on securing sustained national energy consumption patterns and a supply-side focus. The core concern is thus 'whether there will be sufficient resources to meet the world's energy requirements in the decades ahead' (Yergin, 2006). Politicians—regardless of their political

---

❶ As with much of the discussion in this section, this distinction between matters of concern and matters of fact derives from Latour (2005); any 'actant' or element can be assembled as a 'black box', that is, a stable building block, or as a capricious concern.

❷ Due to the relative abundance and equal distribution, its material characteristics, and the lack of a global market coal (and biomass) is rarely a concern of energy security.

camp—invoke the 'national' rationale for the inevitable primacy of exploring new oil reserves, as President Obama's (2010) assertion illustrates:

> The bottom line is this: given our energy needs, in order to sustain economic growth, produce jobs, and keep our businesses competitive, we're going to need to harness traditional sources of fuel even as we ramp up production of new sources of renewable, homegrown energy.

Security communitiesand energy companies alike present energy security to their respective audiences neatly cleaned up and seemingly consisting of only market efficiency and strategic concerns—while in fact it incorporates natural elements like the resource endowments of national territories and technical infrastructure like pipelines or oil tankers as much as it does 'social' or 'discursive' ones: a successful securitisation of nature that foregrounds secure access to energy (rather than for instance environmental concerns), needs to assemble 'social' actors consisting of oil companies, US congress men, refineries and platforms, deep sea drilling technologies, but also geothermal tendencies, global consumption habits, and the downsides of alternative technologies.

Numerous studies illustrate the multifaceted and continuous assembling efforts that the pursuit of energy security requires to keep the globe-spanning 'energy security assemblage' in place. Chinese and US oil companies work hand in hand with their respective governments—and, in the case of the US, with the armed forces—in order to explore and extract crude oil (Klare, 2004; Mitchell, 2007). The specific materiality of crude oil shapes not only the territorialisations of global production networks, but also the internal political structures of rentier states (Bridge, 2008; Labban, 2008). The picture of the same assemblage further downstream reveals that 'automobility' at any specific place in the world requires global production, distribution and regulation regimes involving multifarious issues to be enrolled and kept in place (Paterson, 2007; Urry, 2007).

It is equally important for our purpose to note what energy security *doesn't* incorporate as a matter of concern, namely, corrupt regimes financed by fossil revenues; plutocratic dictatorships; and corruption in the global petroleum sector at large (McPherson & MacSearraigh, 2007); the resource curse (Collier, 2007); biodiversity surrounding coal mines and drilling platforms; the military as a major environmental polluter (Deudney, 1999; McNeil, 2009); and the consequences of energy consumption on the environment—all elements impacted by the pursuit of energy security. Conflicts over the redistribution of oil revenues sustain civil wars, and can even threaten the subsistence of states where resource revenues reignite conflicts along ethnic fault lines, sustaining the fragmentation of already weak states (Kaldor, Karl, & Said, 2007; Watts, 2009).

Another example of how specific agencies consciously silence such externalities out of the energy security assemblage, is that in the United States, the Global Climate Coalition organised by the fossil industries successfully undermined a widening of public and scientific concerns on the greenhouse effect throughout the 1990s (Levy & Egan, 1998, p. 343; Antilla, 2005). Similarly, influential International Relations scholars, invoking a supposedly established hierarchy of security issues, actively silence environmental concerns (Lacey, 2005). Through these seemingly disparate assembling agencies, energy security, with its restricted scope of concern, has managed to hold much of such elements stable as 'passive' matters of fact that are merely reacting to interventions stemming from our energy desires and form no cause for controversy. By translating all elements into the economic terms of 'supply' and 'demand', the energy security assemblage produces a parsimonious—social—matter of concern. At the same time, this translation process silences and hides many elements and concerns that respond differently to petro-politics (cf. Çalişkan & Callon, 2010). While these social and material 'effects' are very much linked into the network of elements constituting the energy security assemblage, they are not represented as matters of concern and as such remain largely invisible 'border conflicts' —to be addressed by other actors.

Assembling Environmental Security

Environmental security is qualitatively different from energy security in so far as it does not represent a single parsimonious global assemblage. Instead, it points to the competition between interest groups that are differently affected by energy production processes such as mining, drilling, or energy related development projects (Peluso & Watts, 2001). The many instances of environmental securitisation thus present us with a more diffuse and confused array of matters of concern, ranging from local and transnational competing interest groups to wildlife diversity and the preservation of the 'Gold Coast' of California. They dissolve the rational language of resource supply and demand into a wider array of affected contradicting interests of humans, animals, and whole ecosystems to be protected.

The US reactions to the huge underwater oil spill in the Gulf of Mexico in May 2010 perfectly illustrate how energy security and environmental security are at once linked and at odds. First, in the direct aftermath of the spill, a draft climate bill, which was to encourage oil drilling in US territory, was hastily revised to take the opposing position (Broder, 2010b). Second, Governor Schwarzenegger halted oil exploration projects along the Californian Coast stating his most pressing concerns on television:

> All of you have seen when you turn on the television the devastation in the Gulf. And I'm sure that they also were assured that it is safe to drill. I see on TV the birds drenched in oil, the fishermen out of work, the massive oil spill, oil slick destroying our precious ecosystem. It will not happen here in California. (Rothfeld, 2010)

The sort of environmental security Schwarzenegger evokes here is also about oil, but it assembles it differently and alongside a lot more elements than energy security does—including for instance birds, fisherman, and the Californian ecosystem. Instead of aggregate national concerns, it brings to the fore many of the consequences of oil production that are otherwise silenced. As such, it assembles matters of fact silent in the energy security agenda and translates them into matters of concern. Whereas the environmental security agenda is often treated as a concern utterly separated from the energy security agenda, this example shows how environmental security is literally attached to the same assemblage of drilling platforms and submarine ecologies as energy security—an assemblage that is differently enrolled by invoking environmental concerns. To put it differently, the oilrig off the Gulf Coast, which had previously been a smooth-functioning technical element in an energy security assemblage, was revealed to be itself an unstable network of elements that could not simply be transposed to the Californian coast without possibly unacceptable environmental costs.

Where environmental securitisations gain in inclusiveness and symmetry *vis-à-vis* energy securitisations of related assemblages of elements, they hardly point to straightforward policy agendas. The notion of 'security' underpinning environmental security is much less wedded to the policy-ready state-centrism underpinning energy security. For instance, an environmental securitisation of the Arctic region extends the perspective from that of a single state to that of a hybrid referent object—consisting of biodiversity, indigenous people, and mankind through potentially rising sea levels—threatened by both crude oil production, industrial pollution and rising local temperatures (Kristoffersen & Young, 2010; Martello, 2008).

Importantly, as discussed above, environmental security and climate concerns push and pull the same elements that make up energy security assemblages, albeit in different directions. Each element is part of alternativeand competing assemblages—as shown, an oilrig off the Louisiana coast, while constructed as an element in securing energy supplies, can also be mobilised as part of an environmental security assemblage; and climate concerns can be mobilised to fortify the militarisation of an energy security agenda (Mayer 2012). Whereas climate security foregrounds human and natural concerns more or less on an equal level and includes more elements than either energy or environmental security assemblages do, it has proven more difficult to assemble the political agencies necessary to implement agendas of climate mitigation.

In sum, by symmetrically including the technical and natural elements and the social concerns assembled under the headers of the various agendas in our discussion, this sections makes explicit how each agenda links them differently and to what effect. Beyond mere securitisations, these distinct renderings actively transform the assembled elements to different, and competing, effects—yet the strategic agencies of those spearheading an energy security assemblage always appear dominant.

Conclusion

We urgently need to balance the pursuit of energy security with broader social and ecological concerns. While various studies made important inroads in investigating the conditions enabling such a multidimensional balancing act, this chapter has argued that a tenacious issue remains— existing conceptions of security do not accommodate broader environmental concerns. By revisiting the underpinnings of energy security in light of the*problématique* of the Anthropocene, we argue that it is only by considering both the consumption of hydrocarbon resources and the consequences of their extraction and usage as endogenous matters of concern that redefinitions of energy security will enjoy any success in unsettling unsustainable and treacherous patterns.

The main theoretical contribution of this chapter lies in conceptualising agendas pursuing energy, environmental, and climate security not as social constructs but rather as assemblages. Drawing on insights from actor-network theory, this chapter entails three main points. Firstly, in conceptualising security as assemblages embedded in and linked to the very natural 'objects' they concern, it becomes apparent how competing programmatic efforts working upon nature in fact constitute it as an object amenable to intervention. They are not mere discursive narratives by politically organised groups of humans *about* nature, but rather transformations of nature. As an effect, as Dalby (2002, p. 194) puts it, we have learnt to represent nature 'as an unproblematic object, knowable via classification and experiment, and above all infinitely manipulable in the service of human purpose'.

Secondly, actor-network theory allows us to narrate the effects of competing discourses in a distinct way. The concurrent existence of competing definitions of the relationship between nature and security (that assemble from the same heterogeneous variety of elements but differently), points to the jostling inherent in politics in an inherently unstable world (Callon & Latour, 1992). A move in one node of these vast and complex assemblages reverberates all over because of the different feedback loops and interdependencies between elements: one 'human' intervention mediated by technology impacts on the environment, which in turn 'responds', leading to constrained human acts which modify the assemblages as a whole. By bringing the effects of these assembling efforts into the picture as matters of concern, the condition of the Anthropocene becomes apparent. Rather than critically lamenting capitalist social constructs or abstract but dangerous dominant discourses, we have shown how assemblages of energy, environmental or climate security only persist because of the active assembling efforts of actors and programmatic agencies. Highlighting these efforts is an essential part of actor-network theory and has the advantage of revealing concretely the specific political agencies that, geared at sustaining energy security, impact on nature in complex and varied ways.

Finally, through the notions of inclusiveness and symmetry, our approach uncovers the paradoxes of energy security by bringing the material back into analysis of energy security. Inclusiveness brought to the fore the externalities silenced by energy security, and symmetry showed material and natural elements are as much a part of securitisations of energy as are discursive elements. We were thus able to shed a different light on the question how is it possible that we might successfully attain energy security (e. g. successfully securitize the environment in a particular way) and yet deepen global insecurities.

Energy securityis the most powerful among the securitisation of nature we discussed. It forms an assemblage that holds stable uncountable associations between huge material and financial flows, globally enrolling a wide array of actors and agencies and reaching parsimony ona global scale. Under its header, the use of fossil fuels, national political legitimacy, and the structure of the international system have become deeply intertwined. By analysing how the agencies upholding energy security assemblages neatly separate out its concerns in a language consisting of market efficiency and strategic tools, as well as how material linkages to such externalities as pollution, climate change, and other environmental concerns become silenced, it becomes possible to assess the success of energy security. Energy security, with its restricted scope of concern, is anchored in an anthropocentric myth of limited social concerns prevailing over an extensive natural 'context' that can be filled and drilled with the proper technology.

The downside of this immense power is ironically the paradox of the Anthropocene: whereas human impact on ecological systems is growingquickly, it is at the same time hard to see how 'society' has increased its control over nature, when in fact converging lines and fragile complex interdependencies are laid bare by climate change. It is only by acknowledging this condition, for instance through the methodology of inclusiveness and symmetry, that one could begin to conceive of a notion of security that will not ultimately render us more *insecure*. If the multiple forms of interwoveness of environment (encompassing the climate) and humans became assembled as sharing the status of matter of concern against which to measure interventions, energy security agendas would be less parsimonious, but energy consumption would possibly be better attuned to its consequences for the biosphere.

References

Amineh, M. P., & Houweling, H. (2007). 'Global Energy Security and Its Geopolitical Impediments—The Case of the Caspian Region'. *Perspectives on Global Development and Technology*, 6 (1), 365-388.

Antilla, L. (2005). 'Climate of Scepticism: US Newspaper Coverage of the Science of Climate Change'. *Global Environmental Change Part A*, 15 (4), 338-352.

Asdal, K. (2008). 'Enacting Things Through Numbers: Taking Nature into Account/ing'. *Geoforum*, 39 (1), 123-132.

Barad, K. (2003). 'Posthumanist Performativity: Toward an Understanding of How Matter Comes to Matter'. *Signs: Journal of Women in Culture and Society*, 28 (3), 801-831.

Barnett, J. (2001a). *The Meaning of Environmental Security: Environmental Politics and Policy in the New Security Era.* (New York: Zed Books).

Barnett, J. (2001b). 'Security and Climate Change'. *Tyndall Centre for Climate Change Research Working Paper*, 7.

Barry, A. (2001). *Political Machines: Governing a Technological Society* (London/New York: Athlone Press).

Bingham, N., & Hinchliffe, S. (2008). 'Reconstituting Natures: Articulating other Modes of Living Together'. *Geoforum*, 39 (1), 83-87.

Bradshaw, M. J. (2009). 'The Geopolitics of Global Energy Security'. *Geography Compass*, 3 (5), 1920-1937.

Bridge, G. (2008). 'Global Production Networks and the Extractive Sector: Governing Resource-based Development'. *Journal of Economic Geography*, 8 (3), 389-419.

Broder, J. M. (2010b, May 12). Senate Gets a Climate and Energy Bill, Modified by a Gulf Spill That Still Grows. *New York Times.* Retrieved from http://www.nytimes.com/2010/05/13/science/earth/13climate.html? ref = us.

Byrne, J., & Glover, L. (2005). 'Ellul and the Weather'. *Bulletin of Science, Technology and Society*, 25 (1), 4-16.

ÇaliŞkan, K., & Callon, M. (2009). 'Economization, part 1: Shifting Attention from the Economy Towards Processes of economization'. *Economy and Society*, 38 (3), 369-398.

Callon, M. (1986). 'Some Elements of a Sociology of Translation: Domestication of the Scallops and the Fishermen of St Brieuc Bay'. In J. Law (Ed.), *Power, Action and Belief: A New Sociology of Knowledge*? (pp. 196-223). (London: Routledge).

Callon, M., & Latour, B. (1992). 'Unscrewing the Big Leviathan: How Actors Macro-structure Reality and how Sociologists Help them to do so'. In K. Knorr-Cetina & A. V. Cicourel (Eds.), *Advances in Social Theory and Methodology - Towards an Integration of Micro- and Macro-sociologies* (pp. 277-303). (London/Henley: Routledge / Kegan Paul).

Callon, M., & Law, J. (1982). 'On Interests and Their Transformation: Enrolment and Counter-Enrolment'. *Social Studies of Science*, 12 (4), 615-625.

Clark, W. C., & Munn, R. E. (1986). *Sustainable Development of the Biosphere.* (Cambridge: Cambridge University Press).

Collier, P. (2007). *The Bottom Billion: Why the Poorest Countries are Failing and What Can Be Done About It.* (Oxford; New York: Oxford University Press).

Crutzen, P. J., & Stoermer, E. F. (2000). 'The "Anthropocene"'. *Global Change Newsletter*, 41, 17-18.

Dalby, S. (2002). *Environmental Security.* (Minneapolis: University of Minnesota Press).

Dalby, S. (2009). *Security and Environmental Change.* (Cambridge: Polity).

Deudney, D. (1999). 'Environmental Security. A critique'. In D. Deudney & R. A. Matthew (Eds.), *SUNY Series in International Environmental Policy and Theory* (pp. 187-219). (Albany: State University of New York Press).

Floyd, R. (2008). 'The Environmental Security Debate and its Significance for Climate Change'. *The International Spectator: Italian Journal of International Affairs*, 43 (3), 51-65.

Forsyth, Tim. (2001). "Critical Realism and Political Ecology." In *After Postmodernism: An Introduction to Critical*

Realism, edited by Jose Lopez, and Garry Potter. (London: Athlone Press).

Gammon, E. (2010). 'Nature as Adversary: The Rise of Modern Economic Conceptions of Nature'. *Economy and Society*, 39 (2), 218 - 246.

Hansen, J. E. (2005). 'A slippery slope: How Much Global Warming Constitutes "Dangerous Anthropogenic Interference"?'. *Climatic Change*, 68 (3), 269-279.

Hirsch, R. L. (1987). 'Impending United States Energy Crisis'. *Science*, 235 (4795), 1467-1473.

Hulme, M. (2010). 'Cosmopolitan Climates: Hybridity, Foresight and Meaning'. *Theory, Culture & Society*, 27 (2/3), 277-288.

Huysmans, J. (2006). *The Politics of Insecurity : Fear, Migration, and Asylum in the EU.* (New York: Routledge).

Jasanoff, S. (2005). 'In the Democracies of DNA: Ontological Uncertainty and Political Order in Three States'. *New Genetics and Society*, 24 (2), 139 - 156.

Kaldor, M., Karl, T. L., & Said, Y. (2007). *Oil wars.* (London: Pluto).

Klare, M. T. (2004). *Blood and Oil : the Dangers and Consequences of America's Growing Petroleum Dependency* (1st ed.). (New York: Metropolitan Books/Henry Holt & Co.).

Kristoffersen, B., & Young, S. (2010). 'Geographies of Security and Statehood in Norway's ' Battle of the North". *Geoforum*, 41 (4), 577-584.

Labban, M. (2008). *Space, Oil, and Capital.* (Abingdon England ; New York, NY: Routledge).

Lacey, M. (2005). *Security and Climate Change - International Relations and the limits of Realism.* (London: Routledge).

Latour, B. (1993). *We Have Never Been Modern.* (Cambridge, Mass.: Harvard University Press).

Latour, B. (2004). *Politics of nature : How to Bring the Sciences Into Democracy.* (Cambridge: Harvard University Press).

Latour, B. (2005). *Reassembling the Social : An Introduction to Actor-network-theory.* (Oxford ; New York: Oxford University Press).

Levy, D. L., & Egan, D. (1998). 'Capital Contests: National and Transnational Channels of Corporate Influence on the Climate Change Negotiations'. *Politics and Society*, 26 (3), 337-361.

Liotta, P. H. (2005). 'Through the Looking Glass: Creeping Vulnerabilities and the Reordering of Security'. *Security Dialogue*, 36 (1), 49-70.

Litfin, K. (2003). 'Towards an Integral Perspective on World Politics: Secularism, Sovereignty and the Challenge of Global Ecology'. *Millennium - Journal of International Studies*, 32 (1), 29-56.

Lubchenco, J. (1998). 'Entering the Century of the Environment: A New Social Contract for Science'. *Science*, 279 (5350), 491-497.

Lubeck, P. M., Watts, M. J., & Lipschutz, R. (2007). *International Policy Report - Convergent Interests: US Energy Security and the "Securing" of Nigerian Democracy.* (Washington: Center for International Policy).

Marquina Barrio, A. (2008). *Energy security : Visions from Asia and Europe.* (New York: Palgrave Macmillan).

Martello, M. L. (2008). 'Arctic Indigenous Peoples as Representations and Representatives of Climate Change'. *Social Studies of Science*, 38 (3), 351-376.

Mayer, Maximilian, "Chaotic Climate Change and Security", in: *International Political Sociology* (2012, Forthcoming).

Mcab, R. M., & Bailey, K. S. (2007). 'Latin America and the Debate Over Environmental Protection and National Security'. *DISAM Journal* (December).

McNeil, J. R. (2009). 'The International System, Great Powers, and Environmental Change since 1900'. In H. G. McPherson, C., & MacSearraigh, S. (2007). 'Corruption in the Petroleum Sector'. In J. E. Campos & S. Pradhan (Eds.), *The Many Faces of Corruption : Tracking Vulnerabilities at the Sector Level* (pp. 191-220). (Washington, D. C.: World Bank).

Mitchell, L. (2007). The Black Box: Inside Iraq's Oil Machine. *Harper's Magazine*, 81-83.

Mol, A. (1998). 'Ontological Politics. A Word and Some Questions'. *Sociological Review*, 46 (S), 74-89.

Moran, D., & Russell, J. A. (2009). *Energy Security and Global Politics : The Militarization of Resource Management.* (London ; New York: Routledge).

Morin, M. E. (2009). 'Cohabitating in the Globalised world: Peter Sloterdijk's Global Foams and Bruno Latour's cosmopolitics'. *Environment and Planning D: Society and Space*, 27 (1), 58-72.

Paterson, Matthew. (2007). Automobile Politics: Ecology and Cultural Political Economy. (Cambridge: Cambridge University Press).

Peluso, N. L., & Watts, M. (2001). *Violent environments.* (Ithaca: Cornell University Press).

Rothfeld, M. (2010, May 3). Schwarzenegger Reverses Course on Off-shore Drilling. *Los Angeles Times.* Retrieved from http://latimesblogs.latimes.com/california-politics/2010/05/schwarzenegger-reverses-course-on-off-shore-drilling.html.

Solomon, S., & Intergovernmental Panel on Climate Change. (2007). *Climate change* 2007 *: The Physical Science Basis : Contribution of Working Group I to the Fourth Assessment Report of the Intergovernmental Panel on Climate Change.* (Cambridge / New York: Cambridge University Press).

The White House. (2010, June 15). Remarks by the President to the Nation on the BP Oil Spill, Office of the Press Secretary. Retrieved June 30, 2010, from http://www.whitehouse.gov/the-press-office/remarks-president-nation-bp-oil-spill.

Trombetta, M. J. (2008). 'Environmental Security and Climate Change: Analysing the Discourse'. *Cambridge Review of International Affairs*, 21 (4), 585 - 602.

Tsing, A. L. (2005). *Friction: an ethnography of Global Connection.* (Princeton, N. J.: Princeton University Press).

Turton, H., & Barreto, L. (2006). 'Long-term Security of Energy Supply and Climate Change'. *Energy Policy*, 34 (15), 2232-2250.

Urry, J. (2007). *Mobilities.* (Cambridge: Polity).

Verrastro, F., & Sarah Ladislaw, S. (2007). 'Providing Energy Security in an Interdependent World'. *The Washington Quarterly*, 30 (4), 95-104.

Wæver, O. (1995). 'Securitization and Desecuritization'. In R. D. Lipschutz (Ed.), *On security.* (New York: Columbia University Press).

Watts, M. (2009). 'Crude Politics: Life and Death on the Nigerian Oil Fields'. *University of Berkeley, Department of Geography Working Paper*, 25.

Yergin, D. (2006). 'Ensuring Energy Security'. *Foreign Affairs*, 85 (2), 69-82.

Zweig, D., & Bi, J. (2005). 'China's Global Hunt for Energy'. *Foreign Affairs*, 84 (5), 25-38.

附：中文简介

在“人类世”中转变能源安全思想

梅飞虎　绍腾·皮尔

【摘要】本文希望通过对“人类世”概念的讨论，阐明环境安全的观念对于人类世纪的作用。“人类世”不仅只是一个地理学上的概念，也是一个具有紧急性意味的基准性概念。本文作者尝试用这个概念来重新理解能源安全。一方面我们不能抛开外部因素来谈能源安全，而大部分反思21世纪能源安全的尝试都未能达到这个要求。尽管对传统的能源安全研究来说已经取得很多成绩，但是本质上的不安全仍一直在持续中。因此我们需要重新考虑能源安全的基本前提，也就是说人类与自然之间“现代”分离的真实性正在被打破，从而显现出一张彼此激烈竞争的关系网。然而这并没有反映在以本体论为基础的能源安全思想中。另一方面我们必须超越对于安全概念的话语式理解，即将安全定义为某种话语，随之使其成为一种话语政治议题，这是采用了激进建构主义方法并将能源和气候安全仅仅视为一种超自然的社会建构的做法，同样后结构主义观点也倾向于不再关注众多外部因素。因此，认真考虑“人类世”这一概念有着方法论上的意义：我们不能只将安全视为话语式的社会建构，而要将其视为面临威胁时由物质因素和集体行为动态整合的双重建构。一个完备的能源安全定义需要将安全这个概念的现实的物质过程整合进去。为了超越话语的局限，我们认为能源安全不是独立于自然外的社会建构，而是某种“集成”，它由复合的因素建构，也依赖于这些因素。这些复合因素既是社会的，同时也是物质的。

【关键词】人类世，能源安全，环境安全

非传统安全新议题:安全治理与国际合作

国际非政府组织与非传统安全的治理

李开盛　庞蕾*

【摘要】相对于国家的不足，非政府组织由于其自身的特性，成为了非传统安全的天然促进者。特别是安全治理实践的发展，给予非政府组织发挥作用的舞台，在环境、救灾、减贫、人权等方面有突出的表现。但是，这一舞台本身的“大小”和仍然存在的“设计缺陷”，又成为限制非政府组织作用进一步发挥的阻碍。未来的安全治理框架应该赋予非政府组织以更多的权威，从制度上强化非政府组织在安全治理的地位与作用。

【关键词】国际非政府组织，非传统安全，安全治理，东非大饥荒

在一个仍然以国家为主体的国际社会，国际非政府组织(INGO)的作用越来越难以忽视。尤其是自20世纪80年代以来，一场全球性的社团革命使得非政府组织作为政府和市场之外的第三部门逐渐确立了自己相对独立的地位❶，国际非政府组织也成为国际关系中的一个常用词。研究非政府组织的专家、美国学者萨拉蒙认为，非政府组织“所具有的社会和政治意义堪与19世纪民族国家的崛起相提并论。”❷ 前任联合国秘书长安南在其就任演说中甚至称非政府组织为“新的超级大国”，并预言21世纪将是“非政府组织的时代”。❸ 从当前情况来看，非政府组织还不具备民族国家那样的地位与作用，离安南所说的“新的超级大国”差距更大，但确实“在数量、规模、涉及领域、作用发挥和国际影响上，都呈现出一派兴盛之势”，特别是“在国际公共领域如人权、环境污染、全球变暖、动物保护、艾滋病防治、知识产权保护、人口膨胀、贫困、难民、裁军等非传统安全问题上，发挥出了国家和政府间国际组织都难以企及的作用。”❹ 在这种情况下，探讨国际非政府组织在非传统安全治理中的作用，具有越来越现实的意义。

一、国际非政府组织是非传统安全的天然推动者

传统安全有两个重要特征：一是以国家为指涉对象，即考虑如何维护国家的安全；二是关注

---

* 李开盛：博士，湘潭大学副教授，主要研究领域：非传统安全理论、中国外交战略等；庞蕾：湘潭大学国际关系专业硕士研究生。

❶ 王杰、张海滨、张志洲主编：《全球治理中的国际非政府组织》，北京大学出版社，2004年版，第10~11页。

❷ Lester M. Salamon: “The Rise of the Non-Profit Sector”, Foreign Affairs, July-August, 1994, p. 109.

❸ 金桂华：《欧美同学2006北京论坛实况：海归与中国民间外交（4）》。

❹ 余潇枫、潘一禾、王江丽：《非传统安全概论》，浙江人民出版社，2006年版，第301页。

政治、军事领域。作为相对于传统安全的概念，非传统安全可以包括一切传统安全之外的安全议题，具体来说有如下三类：

第一，以非国家行为体为指涉对象的政治、军事领域安全议题，例如关注战争中的伤员救助、武装冲突中妇女和儿童所受的特别伤害、地雷在战后对平民的威胁，等等。

第二，以国家为指涉对象的非政治、非军事领域安全议题，例如国家的经济安全、文化安全、社会安全等。

第三，以非国家行为体为指涉对象的非政治、非军事领域安全议题，例如贫穷、饥荒和传染性疾病等。

由于安全指涉对象与关注领域的变化，非传统安全对维护安全的主体也提出了新的要求，国家尽管仍是维护非传统安全的重要主体，但其地位与权威受到越来越大的挑战。

（一）国家的消极作用

在传统安全领域，国家是最重要、最有效的安全主体。战争需要国家去组织，谈判需要国家派代表去进行。但在非传统安全领域，由于安全的指涉对象、领域都已发生了变化，国家的地位与作用也发生了变化。拥有强大资源与实力的国家是无可替代的，它仍然是非传统安全的主要提供者。但是，由于以下两方面的原因，国家在维护非传统安全方面的消极作用也越来越突出。

第一，国家的行为受制于国家利益，无法对“非国家”领域的非传统安全问题予以充分关注。在目前的全球事务中，国家利益是一个难以撼动的概念，它在政治关切方面占有压倒性的优势，也是政治领导人做出决定的首要标准。[1] 在一个无政府状态的国际社会中，“主权国家政府的首要职责是保护自己的公民，本国公民的福利比世界上其他地区的人们的福利更加重要。”[2] 或如有的学者所说，“主权国家的行为受自助的国际体系的约束，其行为受追逐国家利益最大化目标的刚性约束，对超出国家利益之外的公共目标天然缺乏动力”[3] 但是，非传统安全问题的一个最重要特征恰在于将指涉对象从国家身上转移，关注个人、民族、地区甚至是整个人类的安全，这种安全与国家利益在范围上是不匹配的，自然也很难得到国家的积极响应。即使是在那些仍以国家为单位的非传统安全问题上，如环境安全、经济安全等，由于利益关系已较传统安全领域发生变化，国家也变得不合时宜。在传统的政治、军事安全领域，国家间的利益区隔十分明显，国家对自身的利益承担完全的责任，因此不太可能有“卸责”行为。而许多非传统安全问题都是跨国界问题，本国利益很难与其他国家的利益区分开来。例如气候变化，它就远非一个国家所能应对，而必须由各国来共同处理，一国对国界以外发生的事情也要承担责任。在这种情况下，就很容易出现“国际公共用地”的悲剧，即谁都不愿意承担过多的责任，从而最终导致共同利益受损。

第二，在非传统安全领域，国家本身是一个重要的不安全来源。许多非传统安全研究已注意

---

[1] Kennedy Graham ed., *The Planetary Interest: A New Concept for the Global Age*, New Jersey: Rutgers University Press, 1999, p. 4.

[2] Mervyn Frost, *Ethics in International Relations: A Constitutive Theory*, Cambridge: Cambridge University Press, 1996, p. 108.

[3] 刘贞晔：《国际政治领域中的非政府组织：一种互动关系的分析》，天津人民出版社，2005年版，第86～87页。

到这一点。如布赞认为，“个人安全与国家安全之间既有联系又存在矛盾。对于个人而言，国家既是威胁的主要来源，又是安全的主要提供者。对于国家寻求安全的行为而言，个人既提供了正当理由，同时也决定了其限度。”❶ 人的安全研究与女性主义安全研究也注意到国家对人的安全的威胁，而批判安全论者则对国家持更加否定的态度。现实证明了理论家的担心，如工业政策对环境的破坏、国家权力对人权的侵犯、在战场上对武器的滥用等。鲁道夫·拉梅尔发现，在20世纪，被自己政府杀死的人数多达1.5亿，与之相比，所有的内战和国际战争中死亡的人数才3500万。❷ 正如大沼保昭所指出的，“保护人权的第一性行为主体当属国家，然而同时，国家尤其拥有警察及军队等强制权力的国家机关，又是人权侵害的第一性主体。”❸ 出现这一矛盾的根本原因有两个：一是由于用于安全方面的资源总是有限的，导致不同安全目标之间常常是一种此消彼长的关系。如果国家不能根据一个国家的实际情况和长远需要来平衡各方面的安全需要，就会导致某些方面的安全受到破坏。例如，中国在改革开放的过程中，把发展经济放在第一位，却忽视了环境方面的安全问题。二是国家出于传统思维和保持自己权力的需要，常常对军事安全、政治安全更为敏感、更为重视，甚至为了军事和政治安全而漠视环境、侵犯人权。“9·11”事件后，美国通过《爱国者法案》，赋予警察监控个人通讯的权利，就是一个典型的例子。

联合国人权事务高级专员办公室2010年10月1日发布了有关1993～2003年刚果（金）境内严重侵犯人权事件的勘察报告。报告记述了在刚果(金)历史上这段充满战乱的时间里，刚果(金）本国和外国的武装团体或军事部队被指对平民大规模实施的摧残、强奸、杀害等严重罪行。

2005年末，联合国刚果(金)特派团在该国东部的北基伍省发现了三个大型无名墓地。此后，联合国人权事务高级专员办公室及其他多个联合国机构在进行磋商之后，提议对1993～2003年刚果(金)境内严重侵犯人权的事件进行勘察，并于2007年5月获得秘书长批准。在这十年期间，刚果(金)曾两次爆发内战，卢旺达、乌干达等多个邻国以及至少20多个武装团体卷入，被称为“非洲的世界大战”，其影响持续至今。联合国人权高专办在2008年7月启动了勘察工作，先后对1200多名证人进行了访谈，收集和分析了1500多份相关文件，并于今年10月1日正式发布了长达500多页的报告。报告记述了1993年3月至2003年6月期间，刚果(金)本国和外国的武装团体或军事部队被指在刚果(金)境内实施的617起大规模洗劫、摧残、强奸、杀害平民等严重罪行，每起事件都有至少两个独立的信息来源来证实。人权高专皮莱表示，这份报告中记录的

---

❶ ［英］巴里·布赞：《人、国家与恐惧——后冷战时代的国际安全议程》，闫键、李剑译，中央编译出版社，2009年版，第36页。

❷ P. Hassner, “From War and Peace to Violence and Intervention”, in Jonathan Moore ed., *Hard Choices: Moral Dilemmas in Humanitarian Intervention*, New York: Rowman & Littlefield Publishers, 1998, p. 19. 转引自：Catherine Lu, *Just and Unjust Intervention in World Politics*, New York: Palgrave Macmillan, 2006, pp. 53 – 54.

❸ ［日］大沼保昭：《人权、国家与文明》，王志安译，三联书店，2003年版，第95页。

侵犯人权事件非常严重。虽然这份报告不是一个裁决，而是证据的集合，但却为司法调查提供了基础，它可能会指向战争罪等罪行，因为战争法禁止杀害平民，它也指向危害人类罪，还有些事件可能构成种族灭绝罪。不过，报告明确指出，只有法庭才能够确定相关方涉嫌犯下了哪些罪行。

——《联合国发布1993~2003年刚果(金)境内严重侵犯人权事件的勘察报告》，引自联合国网站

（二）国际非政府组织的优势

相对而言，非政府组织在维护非传统安全方面有一些国家所没有的优势，主要体现在：

第一，国际非政府组织是不同国家的人跨越国界的自愿组合，对于人的生存与发展的关注是其首要关注点，而这些正是非传统安全的核心内容。这种特点决定了，哪怕是同一个安全问题，国家会更加强调国家，而非政府组织会更加强调人。例如，在战争中，国家的关注点是战争的胜负，而像国际红十字会这样的非政府组织的关注点则是人员的伤亡。事实上，国际红十字会等国际非政府组织一直致力于把国际人道主义法、人权法应用到武装冲突之中，监督政府和武装反对派是否遵守有关人权和人道主义的相关规定。❶

第二，国际非政府组织具有公益性，能够关注到被国家“私利”所掩盖和忽视的领域。除了非政府性和非营利性之外，非政府组织还有一个重要特征，即它“具有公益性目标，或是建立在人道主义的慈善理念之上，其成员是由具有服务于公众利益的共同理想的人所组成的。”❷“主权国家的行为受自助的国际体系的约束，其行为受追逐国家利益最大化目标的刚性约束，对超出国家利益之外的公共目标天然缺乏动力。而非政府组织一般以公益为目标，因而可以出于社会道义去致力于某个特定全球性问题的解决。在政府间国际组织和国际会议上从事倡议和游说的非政府组织有时也被称为‘世界的良知’，它们通过呼吁、演讲、宣传和辩论体现全球各地民众的愿望，反映他们对解决全球公共问题的需要和要求。”❸正是“这种非政治性、非营利性和公益性使之乐于进入政府和企业都不愿、不能从事的‘无利可图’的公共领域，如人权、环保、反战、反核、裁军、慈善等，成为某个具体领域内执著的护卫者。对国家和政府间国际组织起到了拾遗补阙、甚至填补空白的作用。”❹

第三，国际非政府组织由于缺乏国家那样的强制手段，倡导通过软性治理（如倡议、沟通、说服、影响等）方式开展工作，这使得它对以人为主体的非传统安全有益无害。传统的国家之所以常常损害人的安全，在一些情况下倒不是它有意使然，而是因为它所采取的方式所致。国家在内政外交中常因为强调效率而运用警察甚至军事等强制手段，而这些手段极易造成对人的生命财

❶ David Weissbrodt, “Humanitarian Law in Armed Conflict: The Role of International Nongovernmental Organizations,” *Journal of Peace Research*, Vol. 24, No. 3, p. 297, 302.

❷ 王杰、张海滨、张志洲主编：《全球治理中的国际非政府组织》，北京大学出版社，2004年版，第26页。

❸ 刘贞晔：《国际政治领域中的非政府组织：一种互动关系的分析》，天津人民出版社，2005年版，第86~87页。

❹ 余潇枫、潘一禾、王江丽：《非传统安全概论》，浙江人民出版社，2006年版，第302页。

产的损害，从而损及人的安全。相反，“非政府组织的活动方式通常包括如下几类：研究与教育、知识传播；直接提供产品或服务；参与、监督和协调政府或政府间国际组织的决策与行为；信息披露；倡议与游说；抗议与斗争。”❶ 也就是说，在最激烈的情况下，非政府组织所采取的手段也只是示威、抗议而已，这些活动的主要目标也是针对政府，不太可能危及人的安全。

第四，一个特定的非政府组织往往关注某一个特定的领域，有利于聚集问题、解决问题。国家的政局常常变化不定，很难专注于某一个问题。相对而言，“非政府组织能够免受政局变化、经济起伏的干扰，可以长期、始终如一地追求相对单一的宗旨和目标。”❷ 进而言之，哪怕国家的政局稳定，由于它承担了从军事、政治、经济、社会各方面的责任，有时候不免力有未逮，或是在一些领域浅尝辄止，很少集中精力关注一个单一的问题❸。而非政府组织往往都是针对某一特定问题建立起来的，自然也就能集中精力去持续关注并解决之。

第五，非政府组织越来越发达，拥有广泛的资源和专门的技能。❹ 在专门技能上，由于许多国际非政府组织由专业人士所组成，他们在某个问题上往往比国家还要更有发言权，在解决问题方面也更具权威。有的国际非政府组织由于得到广泛的支持，拥有比较雄厚的财政收入，其作用甚至比一些政府间的国际组织还要大（表1）。

表1 “地球之友”2010年财政收入 （单位：欧元）

收入		2010年	2009年
核心收入	会费	337508	330661
	销售	7594	11427
	慈善	26101	8663
	利润和其他	9437	16742
	总和	380640	367493
捐助收入		2371318	2348485
总收入		2751985	2715978

资料来源：Friends of the Earth International, *Financial Report* 2010, p. 5.

第六，相对于政府复杂的决策程序和官僚主义相比，非政府组织能够更加迅速地对紧急需要做出反应，在促进社会创新方面，也比政府要容易得多。❺ 因此，在提供一些紧急、灵活的服务方面，非政府组织反而比国家更有优势。例如，联合国曾试图对1996~1997年刚果（金）难民营发生的屠杀事件进行调查，却受到当时卡比拉政府的阻挠。“人权观察”在当地活动分子的协助下，

❶ 蓝煜昕、荣芳、于绘锦：《全球气候变化应对与NGO参与：国际经验借鉴》，载：《中国非营利评论》，2010年第1期。

❷ 余潇枫、潘一禾、王江丽：《非传统安全概论》，浙江人民出版社，2006年版，第302页。

❸ V. Mathur, *NGO and Global Policy: Current Issue and New Challenges*, New Delhi: Cyber Tech Publications, 2010, pp. 209-210.

❹ 同上书。

❺ Jennifer M. Brinkerhoff, Stephen C. Smith and Hildy Teegen, “Beyond the ‘Non’: The Strategic Space for NGOs in Development”, Jennifer M. Brinkerhoff, Stephen C. Smith and Hildy Teegen eds., *NGOs and the Millennium Development Goals: Citizen Action to Reduce Poverty*, New York: Palgrave Macmillan, 2007, p. 65.

采访证人并拍摄了有关证据，记录了一个沿特定路线屠杀胡图族难民的详细大事记。该资料向国际社会公布后，引发了公众和国际舆论对侵犯人权的关注。

（三）国际非政府组织的作用领域

由于上述原因，在维护非传统安全方面，非政府组织体现出一定的比较优势。在实践中，非政府组织的主要活动领域也正是非传统安全问题的多发地，如环境、救灾、减贫、人权等，下面选择几个主要方面对相关的国际非政府组织及其作用加以简述。

1. 反贫困与促进经济发展

通过促进经济发展而消除贫困、实现人的安全与发展一直是许多国际非政府组织的目标。2000年9月联合国首脑会议上，189个国家签署《联合国千年宣言》，提出旨在将全球贫困水平在2015年之前降低一半（以1990年的水平为标准）的联合国千年发展目标，立即吸引了国际非政府组织的参与。在巴西总统的支持下，超过1000家国际非政府组织在巴西集会，要求坚持联合国千年发展目标，发起了一场要求世界领导人在10年内将贫困减半的全球运动。[1] 2004年9月10日，联合国新闻部与非政府组织举行了第五十七届联席会议，来自全球700多个非政府组织的2700多位代表参加了会议，联合国秘书长安南到会致辞，会议强化了非政府组织在推动联合国千年发展目标方面所扮演的重要角色，从贫困问题、妇女问题、教育问题等多个领域探讨如何推动千年发展目标的实现。[2]

目前在反贫困和促进经济发展方面表现突出的国际非政府组织主要有：

（1）美国普救合作组织（CARE，简称“凯尔国际”）。凯尔国际是一个对抗全球性贫困的救济发展非政府组织，是一个在全球拥有12000个会员的大型国际组织，具有强大的当地性存在：参与地方项目的成员中97%为该国国民。凯尔国际的主要任务是帮助解决贫困的根本原因，使人们能够自给自足，为全世界最贫困社区的个人和家庭服务。该组织主张从全球多样化中吸收力量、资源和经验，提倡创新型解决方案，倡导全球共同责任，推动持续转变。其主要工作目标是：第一，增强自助能力，提供经济机会；第二，提供紧急救助；第三，影响各个层次的政策决定；第四，解决一切形式的歧视。到2010年，凯尔国际已在80个国家开展活动，惠及超过820万人的905个反贫困项目。

（2）国际小母牛项目组织（Heifer Project International，HPI）。总部设在美国阿肯色州小石城，成立于1944年。20世纪30年代西班牙内战爆发，当时一位叫丹·威斯特的美国西部青年农民在为西班牙内战双方的饥饿儿童分发牛奶。他意识到：“这些孩子需要的不是一杯牛奶，而是一头奶牛。”于是威斯特召集朋友返回家中募集小母牛（还没有生小牛的母牛），从而使饥饿的家庭可以自食其力。作为回报，这些受援家庭将所获援助牲畜的后代母畜作为礼品，传递给另一户家庭，帮助他们实现自力更生，从而保证这样的活礼品能够延

---

[1] V. Mathur, *NGO and Global Policy: Current Issue and New Challenges*, New Delhi: Cyber Tech Publications, 2010, p. 293.

[2] 《联合国推进千年发展目标，强化与非政府组织合作》，载：新浪网。

续下去。这种“礼品传递”行动一方面能够使整个项目像滚雪球一样越滚越大，另一方面还能使每一个接受者成了赠予者，从而增加他们的自尊感。自成立后，HPI 已在 115 个国家扶持过数百万个家庭，并向小型农户提供家畜、培训和相关服务。为了表彰 HPI 的贡献，美国总统曾经授予它“志愿者行动奖”和“结束饥饿奖”。

（3）孟加拉乡村银行。是一个发行微型贷款的机构，由孟加拉一所大学的经济学教授葛拉敏·尤纳斯所创立。该乡村银行的贷款原则是：第一，主要面向穷人，特别是妇女，且不用任何抵押。第二，借贷数额小，一般在 100 元左右。农村妇女的贷款动机多是为了从事家庭手工等小事业，所以借贷金额低，而这一点不算大的钱足以改善她们一家人的生活。第三，每周还本付息，还清再借。第四，借款人每五人组成小组，起互助和联保的作用。第五，借款和节约同时进行，每周还款时每人须存 1 ~ 2 元钱。乡村银行自从 1976 年开业以来，已为 200 多万人发放贷款，还款率高达 98% 。这种成功的扶贫模式已被几十个国家采纳，成为发展中国家重要的扶贫渠道。由于在扶贫方面的突出贡献，孟加拉乡村银行及其创始人尤纳斯教授被授予 2006 年的诺贝尔和平奖。

2. 人道主义紧急救援

所谓人道主义救援，通常是指战争、冲突或饥荒、水灾、旱灾、地震等自然灾害原因引发人道主义危机后，以“拯救生命”为由，向难民、灾民等受害者提供的紧急救助，这是非政府组织迄今在国际关系领域最为重要的活动，因为许多国家的政府部门并不愿意从事人道主义救援工作，而倾向于让追求公益性目标的非政府组织去完成。❶ 每当一场国际人道主义危机来临时，许多非政府组织不论其本来的职能领域，都会伸出援手。在人道主义救援领域做出重要的贡献的有：

（1）国际乐施会（Oxfam International，又称“牛津饥荒救济委员会”）。1942 年在英国牛津成立，乐施会的最初目标是供给食物以解决饥荒，曾运送粮食到被同盟国封锁的德国纳粹占领下的希腊。随着经济的发展，简单的慈善救济已经不再是乐施会等非政府组织的主要项目，越来越多的非政府组织意识到“授人以鱼，不若授人以渔”，开始将更多的精力和资金投入到发展援助上面。❷ 所以，除了食物和药物之外，乐施会也向人们提供生活、工作用具，使被救济对象能够自给自足，同时争取开放自由的国际贸易，使贫穷地区生产的货品能以公平的价格出售。目前，国际乐施会总共由 12 个独立自主的乐施会所组成，这些组织分布在大洋洲、亚洲、欧洲和北美洲四大洲，涉及国家和地区包括新西兰、澳大利亚、中国香港、荷兰、比利时、英国、西班牙、美国和加拿大等地，已经在全球 115 个国家与当地 2000 多个社区组织开展工作。它所涉及的议题也越来越广泛，从公平贸易、教育、健康、社会公平、性别平等一直到战争和天灾、民主和人权、气候变化等，都逐渐被纳入乐施会关注的范畴。

（2）天主教救济服务组织（Catholic Relief Services）。该组织成立于 1943 年，最初是美国的

---

❶ 盛红生、贺兵：《当代国际关系中的“第三者”——非政府组织问题研究》，时事出版社，2004 年版，第 305、378 页。

❷ 王杰、张海滨、张志洲主编：《全球治理中的国际非政府组织》，北京大学出版社，2004 年版，第 293 页。

天主教主教团成立的、用于服务于“二战”中幸存者的非政府组织。此后，该组织在规模上不断扩大，已扩大到世界五大洲100多个国家和地区，拥有100多万名会员。这一组织的使命是帮助海外的贫困和弱势群体，努力促进人类生命的神圣和人的尊严。尽管组织的使命根植于天主教的信仰，但是这一组织的业务和服务完全根据人的需要，不论其种族、宗教或种族。该组织的领导机构是由神职人员组成的董事会，其中大部分是主教、宗教徒和天主教教友。天主教救济服务组织拥有严格的效率、问责和透明度标准，其收入的绝大部分被用于资助那些美国之外的穷人。

3. 减少战争损害

在现代战争中，受伤害最大的不仅包括军人，还包括后方的平民。那些致力于减少战争损害的国际非政府组织主要从事反地雷运动、反对小武器贸易、战地救护、制止战争对妇女的损害以及童子军现象等方面的工作，主要有：

（1）国际反地雷组织（International Campaign to Ban Landmines，ICBL）。该组织正式成立于1992年10月，由六个非政府组织所发起，这些组织长期坚持在阿富汗、柬埔寨、库尔德地区、老挝、尼加拉瓜和安哥拉等地进行扫雷。他们之所以反对地雷，不是因为它在战争中的作用，而是因为它在战后对平民的伤害。国际禁雷运动协调官朱蒂·威廉姆斯曾这样说道，地雷之所以和其他武器相异主要在于地雷本身一旦埋设后，无法分辨它要对付的是敌人、士兵或平民，而遭受攻击的平民可能是妇女、孩童，甚至是单纯为了煮晚餐而外出拣拾柴火的老奶奶。那些被杀害的，往往是最无辜、最没有能力保护自己的平民百姓。[1] 在国际反地雷组织的推动下，1997年12月，122个国家于渥太华签署了禁雷公约，全面禁止使用、储存、生产和转让杀伤性地雷。因为这项成就，该组织及其协调官威廉姆斯被授予1997年诺贝尔和平奖。

（2）红十字国际委员会（International Committee of the Red Cross，ICRC）。总部设于瑞士日内瓦，是世界上历史最为悠久且最负盛誉的人道主义机构，也是世界上获得最广泛认可的组织之一。1863年2月9日，震惊于战争惨痛后果的瑞士商人亨利·杜南与日内瓦知名家族中的四位主要人物一起在日内瓦创建了“五人委员会”，为红十字国际委员会的建立打下了基础。根据《日内瓦公约》以及国际法的规定，国际社会赋予红十字国际委员会独一无二的地位，保护国内和国际性武装冲突的受难者，包括战伤者、战俘、难民、平民和其他非战斗员。红十字国际委员会在工作中坚持人道、公正、中立等原则，对减少战争对人类的伤害发挥了重要作用。由于红十字会的杰出贡献，创办人杜南于1901年荣获首届诺贝尔和平奖，红十字组织本身在1917年、1944年和1963年三次荣获诺贝尔和平奖。另外，红十字国际委员会还是联合国大会的观察员。

4. 人权保护

“人权非政府组织可以说是历史悠久。国际舞台上最早的国际非政府组织——反奴隶协会（the

[1] 《Jody Williams 1997获得诺贝尔和平奖之演讲摘要》，转引自刘贞晔：《国际政治领域中的非政府组织：一种互动关系的分析》，天津人民出版社，2005年版，第113～114页。

Anti - Slavery Society）就是1839年在英国成立的。”❶ 在当代国际社会中，人权问题既越来越重要，同时又十分敏感复杂，相关的国际非政府组织也因此成为国际关注和争议的焦点。主要的人权国际非政府组织有：

（1）大赦国际（Amnesty International，AI）。该组织的总部设在伦敦，是全球最大的人权组织，目前在全世界已经有超过300万名会员。❷ 它1961年创立，其发起者是彼得·贝嫩森，他是一位律师，关注良心犯（政治犯）的权利，在《世界人权宣言》签署13周年之际和志同道合者发起了“呼吁大赦，1961”运动。他们在卢森堡的一个旅馆中聚会，标志着这个志愿者组织的诞生。❸ 该组织的主要职能是监察国际上违反人权的事件，其工作目标包括：废除死刑；停止未经合法程式的刑罚与处决；维护囚犯权利，使其符合国际人权标准；保证所有政治犯获得即时及公平的审判；停止招揽未成年军人；释放所有良心犯（政治犯）；为社会边缘群体争取经济、社会和文化上的权利；保护人权捍卫者；禁止酷刑；停止在任何武装冲突中的非法杀害；维护难民、移民与寻求庇护者的人权。该组织于1977年获颁诺贝尔和平奖，1978年获颁联合国人权奖。

（2）人权观察（Human Rights Watch，HRW）。该组织总部设在纽约，以调查、促进人权问题为主旨，于1978年成立。其背景是1975年包括美苏在内的欧安会国家签署包含有人员自由流动和保护人权规定的《赫尔辛基协定》。1976年，罗伯特·伯恩斯坦访问苏联，被苏联著名科学家、持不同政见者萨哈罗夫的精神所感动，遂于两年后创建名为“赫尔辛基观察”的人权组织，其目的是为了监视前苏联对赫尔辛基协定的执行情况。后来，该组织又以“观察委员会”（如1981年设立“美洲观察”）的名义关注世界上其他地区的人权事务，并于1988年联合定名为“人权观察”。人权观察宣称根据《世界人权宣言》中的人权标准，撰写国际人权违反状况的研究报告。他们还通过对可疑的境况进行取证调查，并在本地和国际媒体上刊登报道，促进国际社会对人权暴行的关注。在人权观察的报告中，凸现的问题包括种族歧视、性别歧视、刑讯逼供、童子军、政治腐败，以及司法公正问题。

著名的国际人权非政府组织

非洲民主和人权研究中心（冈比亚班珠尔）
大赦国际（英国伦敦）
安第斯正义委员会（秘鲁利马）
反对奴役国际（英国伦敦）
第19条（英国伦敦）
亚洲人权委员会（中国香港）
防止酷刑协会（瑞士日内瓦）
照料国际（美国亚特兰大）
住房权和驱逐中心（荷兰乌得勒支）
国际刑事法院联合会（美国纽约）
保护儿童国际（瑞士日内瓦）

---

❶ 刘贞晔：《国际政治领域中的非政府组织：一种互动关系的分析》，天津人民出版社，2005年版，第245页。

❷ Salil Shetty，“Activists Use New Tools to Challenge Repression”，*Amnesty International Report* 2011：*The State of The World' s Human Rights*，p. xix.

❸ Tom Buchanan，“'The Truth Will Set You Free'：The Making of Amnesty International”，*Journal of Contemporary History*，Vol. 37，No. 4，2002，pp. 575 - 576.

国际人权联合会（法国巴黎）

粮食第一信息和行动网络（FIAN，德国海德堡）

人权观察（美国纽约）

国际法学家委员会（瑞士日内瓦）

赫尔辛基国际人权联合会（奥地利维也纳）

国际计划生育联合会（美国纽约，英国伦敦）

国际救助儿童联盟（英国伦敦）

国际人权服务（瑞士日内瓦）

土著人事务国际工作组（丹麦哥本哈根）

少数者权利国际组（英国伦敦）

国际乐施会（英国伦敦）

——引自［奥］曼弗雷德·诺瓦克：《国际人权制度导论》，柳华文译，北京大学出版社，2010 年版，第 268 页。

5. 环境保护

环境保护是国际非政府组织的一个重要活动领域。近些年来，气候变化问题日渐突出，国际非政府组织也开始加大了关注力度。许多非政府组织为了加强在气候问题上的信息交换和战略协调，成立了气候行动网络（Climate Action Network，CAN），其成员包括 450 多个非政府组织。在非政府组织数量众多但力量分散的情况下，CAN 在国际谈判中起到了重要的意见综合与力量聚合的作用。主要的环境国际非政府组织包括：

（1）绿色和平组织（Greenpeace）。国际绿色和平组织于 1971 年在加拿大成立，由世界各地的分会组成，总部设在荷兰的阿姆斯特丹，目前有超过 1330 名工作人员，分布在 30 个国家的 43 个分会。绿色和平组织在世界环境保护方面贡献良多，在其中一些环节更是扮演关键角色，如禁止输出有毒物质到发展中国家；阻止商业性捕鲸；制定一项联合国公约，为世界渔业发展提供更好的环境；在南太平洋建立一个禁止捕鲸区；50 年内禁止在南极洲开采矿物；禁止向海洋倾倒放射性物质，工业废物和废弃的采油设备；停止使用大型拖网捕鱼，等等。另外，该组织还把全面禁止核武器试验作为重要目标，努力促进世界和平、全球核武裁减及非暴力。

（2）世界自然基金会（World Wide Fund For Nature，WWF）。该组织成立于 1961 年，总部设在瑞士。它是全球享有盛誉的、最大的独立性非政府环境保护组织之一，在全世界拥有将近 520 万名支持者，拥有一个遍及 100 多个国家的活动网络。WWF 的使命是遏止地球自然环境的恶化，创造人类与自然和谐相处的美好未来，其具体的工作目标包括：保护世界生物多样性；确保可再生自然资源的可持续利用；推动降低污染和减少浪费性消费的行动。自成立以来，世界自然基金会在六大洲的 153 个国家发起或完成了约 12000 个环保项目。目前世界自然基金会通过一个由 27 个国家级会员、21 个项目办公室及五个附属会员组织组成的全球性的网络在北美洲、欧洲、亚太地区及非洲开展工作。WWF 与中国有着良好的合作关系，其标志是中国的大熊猫。自从 1996 年成立北京办事处以来，WWF 共资助开展了 100 多个重大项目，投入总额超过三亿元人民币。

限于篇幅，这里不可能列出所有的国际非政府组织及其作用领域，但以上情况亦足以表明，国际非政府组织的作用领域覆盖面广，而且多在我们通常所界定的非传统安全范畴之内。由此，完全可以说，国际非政府组织是非传统安全的天然促进者，国际非政府组织的地位与作用的提升，必将推动非传统安全得到更好的维护。这种作用也得到了国际社会的普遍肯定，一些非政府组织如国际红十字会、人权联盟、大赦国际、国际禁雷运动、无国界医生组织等非政府组织及其领导人就因在各自领域所做出的贡献而获得过诺贝尔和平奖，有的还得过多次。在过去的一个世纪，国际非政府组织的数量也迅速增加。2004年，世界范围内的国际政府组织是7306个，国际非政府组织的数量则是它的七倍。❶ 这种蓬勃发展的势头，也说明了国际非政府组织越来越有用武之地。正如学者所指出的，“过去20年中非政府组织的影响不断上升，已成为一个显然的事实。”❷

二、安全治理框架下非政府组织的角色

要了解国际非政府组织到底是如何维护非传统安全的，离不开安全治理这一框架。正是这一框架，给予非政府组织发挥作用的舞台。但这一舞台本身的“大小”和仍然存在的“设计缺陷”，又成为限制非政府组织作用进一步发挥的阻碍。

（一）安全治理与非传统安全

安全治理的核心词是治理。它不同于“统治”，统治主要是指政府通过命令、规范来实施的由上到下的权力行为，是权力的单向行使。治理则强调非政府行为体的参与、强调政府与其他行为体之间的协调、强调不同行为体之间的双向互动。正如全球治理委员会的报告中所指出的那样：“治理是个体和制度、政府和私人管理其共同事务过程中所采用的多种方式的总和。它通过一个持续的过程，容纳冲突或多元的利益，并使合作成为可能。它既包括被授权采取强制行动的正式制度，也包括人们或是同意或是认为最有利于他们的非正式安排。”❸

作为一种比较规范的理论范式，“安全治理”最早由埃尔克·克拉曼提出并加以阐述。❹ 她认为，不同行为体之间的安全关系传统上一直以联盟或共同体来界定，但是，那些用来安排越来越多的公共的和私人的安全行为体之间的合作网络既分裂又重叠，更适合用治理概念来描述。❺ 她指出，“自从20世纪90年代以来，全球安全治理概念已成为国际关系分析的新框架。该范式的支持者认为，我们正在见证一场全球政治的转变，即一体化和碎片化的同时推进，其结果是改变了国家作为国际事务首要权威与行为体的角色，因此危及到冷战期间发展起来的国家中心论这一理论视角。全球治理与安全治理方面的文献表明，尽管国家保留了其中心角色，越来越多的私人行为体如跨国公司、

---

❶ 王玲：《国际非政府组织：现状与趋势》，载：李慎明、王逸舟主编《2007年：全球政治与安全报告》，社会科学文献出版社，2007年版。

❷ B. S. Aswal, *NGO in the Human Rights Management*, New Dalhi: Cyber Tech Publications, 2010, p. 70.

❸ Report of Commission on Global Governance, *Our Global Neighbourhood*, Oxford University Press, 1995, http://www.reformwatch.net/fitxers/168.pdf.

❹ 崔顺姬、余潇枫：《安全治理：非传统安全能力建设的新范式》，载：《世界经济与政治》，2010年第1期。

❺ Elke Krahmann, “Conceptualizing Security Governance,” *Cooperation and Conflict*, 2003, Vol. 38, No. 5, p. 10.

非政府组织正在国际政策的制定和实施过程中承担职能。”❶

综上所述，安全治理有以下几个相互关联的主要特征：

第一，维护安全的主体不但包括国家，还包括诸如非政府组织、跨国公司等非国家行为体，而正是由于这些非国家行为体的加入，使得安全维护的方式发生了根本的变化。

第二，正是由于非国家行为体的加入，维护安全的方式不再只是国家的武力和权力、谈判和结盟，还包括非国家行为体所擅长的沟通、倡议甚至是公民直接行动。

第三，由于非国家行为体的加入，国家失去了唯一的发号施令者的地位，整个安全制度不再是由国家从上至下的命令关系，还包括了自下而上的非国家行为体对国家的影响，权力的单向行使变成了各行为体之间的双向互动。

安全治理为传统和非传统的安全问题提供了一个新的处理平台。例如，国家通过和其他行为体（包括其他国家、国际组织、非政府组织和私人公司）的合作，不但为自己及其公民有效地提供安全保障，还降低了国家之间的威胁感以及国家间战争的可能性。❷ 但本报告这里想特别强调的是，由于把非政府组织纳入其中，并采取一种双向互动式的安全维护方式，安全治理成为处理非传统安全问题的一个适宜框架。以国家为中心、以强制为手段的传统安全框架仅仅适用于传统安全问题，无法对非传统安全问题做出有效的反应。新的安全问题需要一种新的安全制度结构。在非传统安全问题日益突出的情况下，安全治理架构的出现可视为一种对新的安全挑战在制度上做出的回应。正如艾莉森·巴勒斯所言，“或许最好将目前情势视为这样一种状态：权力越来越分散，但权威迄今为止并没有出现类似的增殖与强化。导致传统的解决方案与实际中挑战之间的不匹配，从而留给世界一定程度的安全赤字。”❸ 而安全治理通过赋予那些非国家行为体以安全行为主体的权威，把那些国家常常失灵的非传统安全问题纳入治理范围，使作为“解决方案”的安全制度做出适应于实际挑战的调整，从而在一定程度上减少世界所面临的安全赤字。

（二）国际非政府组织与其他安全行为体之间的互动

正是通过安全治理，国际非政府组织有了一个与国家等其他行为体进行互动的合法框架。在目前的安全治理框架下，国际非政府组织没有国家和政府间国际组织那样的决策权，也不能像国家那样通过军队等强制手段保障指涉对象的安全。它主要是通过一些间接的手段如倡议与游说、信息披露和游行示威等来推动、监督国家和政府间国际组织更好地维护非传统安全，必要的时候也会采取一些直接行动。

---

❶ Elke Krahmann, “American Hegemony or Global Governance? Competing Visions of International Security”, *International Studies Review*, Vol. 7, No. 4, 2005, p. 531.

❷ Elke Krahmann, “American Hegemony or Global Governance? Competing Visions of International Security”, *International Studies Review*, Vol. 7, No. 4, 2005, pp. 537 – 538.

❸ Alyson J. K. Bailes, “Global Security Governance: A World of Change and Challenge”, *SIPRI*, *SIPRI Yearbook* 2005: *Armaments, Disarmament and International Security*, Oxford: Oxford University Press, 2005, p. 3.

1. 与国家间的互动

国家仍然是当前国际社会中最主要的行为体，与国家之间的互动是国际非政府组织发挥作用的关键。从近些年的实践看，非政府组织在与国家的互动方面取得了不少进展。特别是在一些与国家利益没有直接冲突的全球性问题上，由于国家对此关注不够，没有兴趣收集和处理这类信息，于是国际非政府组织就能利用自己在这方面的专业知识和技能来说服和促进主权国家参与各种领域的全球治理。[1] 从近些年的实践看，国际非政府组织与国家之间互动比较成功的领域包括：

第一，环境领域。由于环保意识的普遍觉醒，国家与国际非政府组织在这方面开展了比较密集的合作。在国内，绿色运动和环保组织在一些国家发展成绿党，直接影响了这些国家在非传统安全问题上的政策走向。[2] 在国际舞台上，国际非政府组织成为一些在环保问题上起领导作用的国家的坚定同盟军。

第二，减少战争伤害，特别是禁雷运动。政府间的禁雷运动在20世纪80年代就已开始，但效果并不理想。1992年，几家非政府组织发起成立国际禁雷运动，到1999年时参与的非政府组织已经超过1000家。借着这股势头，加拿大政府于1996年10月在渥太华召集会议致力于重启禁雷进程。在非政府组织和加拿大等国的合作下，尽管有一些大国反对，最后仍然通过了禁雷条约。[3]

第三，扶贫与经济发展。1994年，国际非政府组织“福音两千”号召发达国家以及世界银行减免第三世界国家的债务。在该组织的不断努力下，1998年世界银行和国际货币基金组织首先接受了这项计划，随后一系列发达国家都开始采取行动减免发展中国家尤其是最不发达国家的债务。国际非政府组织还与一些国家合作，积极支持联合国提出的千年发展目标。

第四，和一些国家特别是西方国家在人权问题上的合作。大赦国际、人权观察这些人权国际非政府组织所收集的信息往往成为西方国家或联合国人权机构评估有关国家和地区人权状况的主要资料来源。[4] 特别是在向发展中国家推广公民和政治权利方面，那些主要源于西方的人权国际非政府组织是西方国家的得力伙伴。

但两者之间也经常存在摩擦。国际非政府组织与国家之间并不全然是合作关系，相反，在很多场合，非政府组织充当了国家的批评者。鉴于前面指出过国家在不少情况下是制造非传统安全问题的重要来源，这种批评是毫不奇怪的。因此，不少国家对国际非政府组织的活动仍然存在疑虑。例如，国际货币基金和世界银行2006年在新加坡举行年会，新加坡政府以安全为理由禁止一些非政府活动家入境，还禁止举行传统上与官方会议同时进行的公民社会论坛。于是，作为替代，约800名非政府组织活动家在邻近的印尼举行会议，但据说由于来自新加坡的压力，印尼警察命令论坛

---

[1] Keck and Sikkink, *Activists Beyond Borders*, Cornell University Press, 1998, chapter 1.

[2] 余潇枫、潘一禾、王江丽：《非传统安全概论》，浙江人民出版社，2006年版，第304页。

[3] 参见：Jeffrey Atkinson and Martin Scurrah, *Globalizing Social Justice*: *The Role of Non – Government Organization in Bringing about Social Chang*, New York: Palgrave Macmilllan, 2009, pp. 1 – 2.

[4] 孙茹：《人权观察》，载：《国际资料信息》，2003年第2期。

的所有户外活动取消。❶ 即使是西方国家，也经常受到来自国际非政府组织的压力与批评，双方也时有摩擦。例如，“（人权观察的）人权报告几乎囊括当今世界所有国家的政府，对于别人不敢提及的美国政府，‘人权观察’批评得尤其厉害。”❷ 有摩擦是正常的，但是一些国家经常利用自己的地位与权力打压与其不和的国际非政府组织，从而对其形成阻碍，这不利于非传统安全的维护。

2. 与国际组织的互动

在与一些政府间国际组织特别是联合国的互动上，非政府组织也已经取得不少成绩，具体体现在：

第一，在联合国系统中的地位有所提升，主要表现为获得咨商地位的非政府组织数量大幅增长。《联合国宪章》第71条明确规定：“经济与社会理事会得采取恰当办法，并与各种非政府组织会商有关于理事会职权范围内的文件。”1968年，联合国经社理事会通过了第1296号决议，规定：“非政府组织可以在联合国经社理事会以及联合国体系中的其他机构中获得咨询地位”。虽然获得咨商地位并不意味着获得决策权，但非政府组织能够通过参与各委员会的工作、出席各种会议而施加影响，推动国际组织做出自己主张或认同的决策。截至2009年，已有3290个非政府组织获得咨商地位，其中获全面咨商地位的有140个，专门咨询地位的有2170个，注册咨商地位的980个。同时，还有1.2万多个民间社会组织与联合国经济和社会事务部建立了合作关系。这些注册民间组织中大部分都是非政府组织，包括协会、基金、联合会以及近1000个土著人民组织。一些国际非政府组织如国际红十字会还获得了联合国大会观察员的地位，对联合国事务有更大的发言权。

第二，与区域国际政府间组织的互动，其中欧洲社会非政府组织平台与欧洲联盟之间的广泛对话堪称典型。欧洲联盟是迄今为止一体化程度最高的区域国际政府间组织，但是即便如此，欧盟依然因其存在着巨大的民主赤字而在合法性方面颇有欠缺。在很大程度上，欧洲社会组织平台正是通过广泛参与欧盟的活动而帮助提高其合法性，从而促使欧盟在全球治理中扮演更为重要的角色。欧洲社会组织平台成立于1995年，它将欧洲的近40个非政府组织联合在一起，其成员代表着地方、国家和欧洲层面的各种公民社会组织和利益集团。该组织的成员坚持认为，在推进欧洲的社会公平和公民参与方面，非政府组织扮演着关键性角色，因此，非政府组织必须在欧洲社会发展走向的公开讨论中成为欧盟的合法伙伴。❸

第三，出席重大国际会议以及相应的非政府组织论坛。“1992年里约环境与发展大会后，根据会议决议，包括国际金融和发展机构在内的联合国体系各机构，都被责成做出与国际非政府组织合作和联系的有关安排。国际非政府组织更广泛地参与联合国特别会议的准备工作和会议本身，并且争得了最后文件及决议的起草权利。”❹ 另外，在举行一些重大的国际会议时，常常会举行平行的非政府组织论坛，其参与人数之多、议题之广

❶ 参见：V. Mathur, *NGO and Global Policy: Current Issue and New Challenges*, New Delhi: Cyber Tech Publications, 2010, pp. 131 – 132.

❷ 王杰、张海滨、张志洲主编：《全球治理中的国际非政府组织》，北京大学出版社，2004年版，第369页。

❸ 参见欧洲社会组织平台网站。

❹ 王杰、张海滨、张志洲主编：《全球治理中的国际非政府组织》，北京大学出版社，2004年版。

泛甚至要超过正式会议。重大国际会议常常是国际社会做出重大决策的场合，通过参加这些会议，国际非政府组织能够更加直接地对相关决策进程施加影响。以国际气候谈判为例，非政府组织被允许以观察员身份参加《联合国气候变化框架公约》缔约方会议（COP）下的大部分正式、非正式谈判，并可通过在会期发放文件以及与谈判人员面对面交流来影响谈判进程（图 1）。

第四，国际非政府组织中的精英以个人身份直接参与相关国际谈判与决策。许多国际非政府组织的领导和代表人物都是各行业的精英，他们的专业知识常被各方所看重，在一些情况下直接出任一些国际组织或机构的代表，以一种特别的方式发挥了国际非政府组织的作用（表 2）。

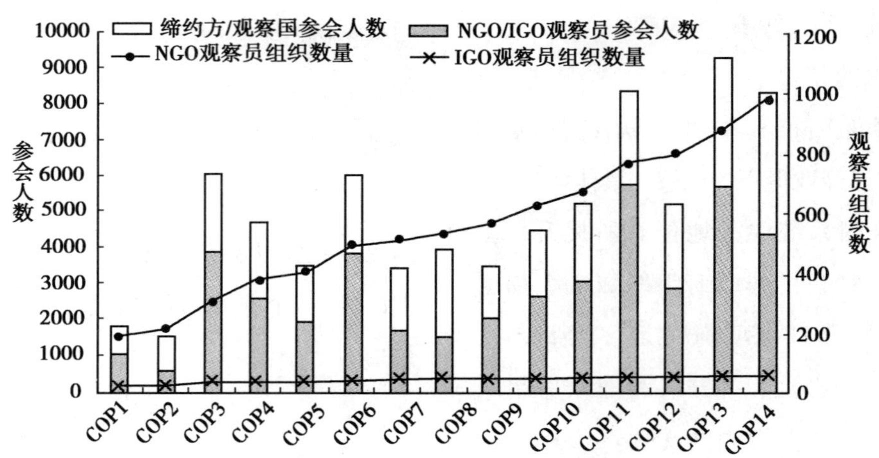

图 1　非政府组织在历届 UNFCCC 缔约方大会中的参与情况❶

表 2　参加 1998 年制定《国际刑事法庭规约》罗马会议的非政府组织代表的多重身份❷

	NGO	政府	IGO
谢里夫·巴西奥尼（Cherif Assiouni）	国际刑法学协会主席	1. 罗马会议筹备委员会主席 2. 罗马规约起草委员会主席 3. 筹备会议和罗马会议埃及官方代表团团长	联合国前南斯拉夫犯罪咨询委员会主席
安德鲁·克莱芬（Andrew Lapham）	大赦国际驻联合国代表	罗马会议所罗门岛官方代表团成员	
埃玛·波尼奥（Emma Bonino）	1. “跨国激进政党”组织领导人 2. “全球议员行动”组织协调官	1. 1994 年联合国大会第六届委员会意大利代表 2. 意大利议会激进政党议员	欧洲委员会人道主义事务委员会委员
阿瑟·罗宾逊（Arthur Obinson）	1. 国际刑事法庭基金会执行官 2. “全球议员行动”组织领导人	特里尼达和多巴哥国家总理、总统	
希尔·范·波温（Theo Van Oven）	国际法学家委员会副主席	罗马会议荷兰官方代表团团长	UN 人权委员会“受害者康复和赔偿”报告人

❶ 蓝煜昕、荣芳、于绘锦：《全球气候变化应对与 NGO 参与：国际经验借鉴》，载：《中国非营利评论》，2010 年第 1 期。

❷ 刘贞晔：《国际政治领域中的非政府组织：一种互动关系的分析》，天津人民出版社，2005 年版，第 165 页。

（三）国际非政府组织的作用评估

从上面的互动中可以看出，国际非政府组织因其志愿性、灵活性和自主性等优势，较好地填补了国家和市场失灵所带来的空白，与政府间国际组织相互补充，在维护非传统安全方面发挥了积极的作用。例如，有学者认为，环境运动在影响国家行为以及国际社会动向方面总体而言是高度成功的。[1] 还有学者曾对国际环境非政府组织的作用进行分析，得出了下表中的结论（表3）。

以上评价并非过誉，但我们也要看到，国际非政府组织在安全治理框架中的作用总体上还是比较有限的。就拿环境领域的气候变化议题来说，在关于温室气体减排第二承诺期的谈判上，非政府组织尽管积极参与了哥本哈根大会等谈判进程，并且付出了很大的努力，希望说服发达国家继续其减排进程，但影响很小。另外，非政府组织在请求政府对人道主义危机做出反应时，其效果也是各各不同。例如，非政府组织在要求干预伊拉克北部以保护库尔德人、或是要求干预索马里局势时，就得到当时美国政府的积极回应；但在卢旺达发生大屠杀时，它们的诉求就成效不彰。[2]

这一结果主要与以下两方面的因素有关：

1. 国际非政府组织自身的问题

第一，缺乏资源，能力不够。一些国际非政府组织，特别是西方的国际非政府组织，拥有丰厚的财源，其实力让一些政府间国际组织都相形见绌。但总体观之，由于非政府组织不像企业那样有自己的财源，也不像国家能够向国民征取税收，其拥有资源主要取决于志愿者的捐助，因此带有相当大的不确定性，整体实力也相当有限。

表3　国际环境非政府组织对三大国际环境谈判的影响程度比较[3]

影响程度指标 \ 三大环境谈判	《北美自由贸易协定》（含环境协定）	《濒危野生动植物国际贸易公约》	《关于环境保护的南极条约议定书》
是否影响谈判的议程	是	是（最明显）	是
是否提供书面和口头意见	是	是（不仅提供意见，而且提供谈判草案）	是
是否参加谈判进程	是	是	是
是否影响谈判进程	是	是	是
协定是否反映国际环境非政府组织的立场和主张	是（部分反映，如签署《北美环境合作协定》，成立北美环境合作委员会）	是（基本反映）	是（部分反映，如“世界公园”的概念被接受，南极环境保护委员会成立）
影响程度	大	很大	大

---

[1] V. Mathur, *NGO and Global Policy: Current Issue and New Challenges*, New Delhi: Cyber Tech Publications, 2010, p. 217.

[2] Francis Kofi Abiew, “Assessing Humanitarian Intervention in the Post - Cold War Period: Sources of Consensus,” International Relations, Vol. 14, No. 2, 1998, p. 75.

[3] 王杰、张海滨、张志洲主编：《全球治理中的国际非政府组织》，北京大学出版社，2004 年版，第 344 页。

如受到金融危机的影响，地球之友2010~2011年的预算不得不减少30%，也就是大约100万欧元。❶ 这种资源的缺乏在很大程度上限制了非政府组织的活动能力。特别是对于那些跨国界活动的国际非政府组织而言，资金与资源的要求更大。一旦缺乏，其活动也就更加受限。由于外来捐助的减少，一些非政府组织甚至在接入支付互联网的费用方面都有困难。❷ 为了弥补资源的不足，“越来越多的非政府组织大量接受了来自政府的捐助，成为政府项目的执行者，从而在一定程度上失去了自身行动的独立性与公正性。”❸ 在地球之友的捐助者名单中，也可以发现荷兰外交部、欧盟等政府和政府间国际组织。❹ 如何保持自身的“非政府性”与维持有效的资源供给，成为许多国际非政府组织面临的两难。

第二，合法性问题。国际非政府组织不同于政府，政府常常是全体选民选举出来的，但非政府组织则是一部分人发起成立的。来自《经济学家》的一篇文章就曾质疑：国际乐施会是谁选出来的?❺ 他们质疑，乐施会宣称代表穷人的利益，但在没有选举机制的情况下，怎么能够保证他们对穷人的利益保持敏感？有人把国际非政府组织称为国际社会的“良心”，这也就是说非政府组织主要是通过自己的“良心”和认识去代表它所服务对象的利益。但是，这跟自己代表自己的利益毕竟不是一回事，“良心”可能沉睡，认识也会出偏差。这个时候，确实有理由问上一句：“非政府组织真正代表了他们尽力所服务人民的利益吗?还是代表了他们自己的观点?”❻ 特别是，在非政府组织的活动极其依赖于外部捐助的时候，它们的所作所为就不一定那么公正与超脱，而是“可能更强调拥有更多资金的利益集团所关注的问题。”❼ 另外，非政府组织内部的治理结构常常也不如民主政府那样民主，有的经过了推举，有的仅仅是协商，有的更是采取公司制的管理方式，这就使得非政府组织更有成为少数管理者实践其信念与认识的可能，而与所被代表群体的利益相去甚远。

第三，代表性问题。作为某一个领域的组织，非政府组织的群体基础常常是相对狭隘的，从而使人怀疑其是否具有足够的代表性。如有学者指出：“非政府组织成立的目的往往是为了满足某些特定人群的利益和需要。这种特定人群的利益和需要，使得大多数非政府组织只能够代表社会中一部分人的社会团体。一些非政府组织在实现这些人群的利益与需求的同时，往往会忽略其他人群的利益与需求。……非政府组织大多是一些专

---

❶ *Friends of The Earth International Financial Report*, 2010, p. 3.

❷ V. Mathur, *NGO and Global Policy: Current Issue and New Challenges*, New Delhi: Cyber Tech Publications, 2010, p. 16.

❸ 盛红生、贺兵:《当代国际关系中的“第三者”——非政府组织问题研究》，时事出版社，2004年版，第384页。

❹ *Friends of The Earth International Financial Report*, 2010, p. 3.

❺ Jeffrey Atkinson and Martin Scurrah, *Globalizing Social Justice: The Role of Non-Government Organization in Bringing about Social Chang*, New York: Palgrave Macmilllan, 2009, p. 30.

❻ B. S. Aswal, *NGO in The Human Rights Management*, New Dalhi: Cyber Tech Publications, 2010, p. 90.

❼ Jennifer M. Brinkerhoff, Stephen C. Smith and Hildy Teegen, “Beyond the ‘Non’: The Strategic Space for NGOs in Development”, Jennifer M. Brinkerhoff, Stephen C. Smith and Hildy Teegen eds., *NGOs and the Millennium Development Goals: Citizen Action to Reduce Poverty*, New York: Palgrave Macmillan, 2007, p. 66.

门性组织，往往集中关注于某一领域的突出问题，其看法上虽然有其独到之处，但是因为其代表性窄、专业性强，观察和考虑问题往往偏重于某一个方面，因而在分析和处理社会问题方面不免失之偏颇，从而不能够从社会的整体角度来考虑问题，甚至不去关心更为广泛的社会问题。”❶ 另外，从地域来看，现在的国际非政府组织多以发达国家为主导。例如，“环境共同体被北方非政府组织所统治，仅仅有 1/4 的环境非政府组织来自南方。”❷ 这种地域的分配不均可能影响到非政府组织在管理决策上的倾向性，使得在制定策略，采取行动，决定组织发展时，不自觉地倾向于发达国家，从而忽视其他地区的正义要求。

2. 治理框架的问题

更重要的是，尽管国际非政府组织的作用越来越重要，但在当前的安全治理框架内，仍然是国家而非国际非政府组织在维护非传统安全方面扮演着主导角色。国际非政府组织发挥作用的程度，在很大程度上取决于与其他行为体特别是国家的互动关系。如果国家认为某个议题不太重要，自然乐得让非政府组织发挥作用。一旦政府觉得某个问题涉及到它的根本利益，如温室气体减排，就会紧紧掌握事件的主导权，国际非政府组织所能发挥的作用就非常有限。这反映出当前安全治理框架在设计和实践运作中的一些缺陷，具体表现如下：

第一，国际非政府组织的地位仍然过低，如在联合国等国际组织中仅仅具有咨商地位，除了那些以个人身份担任相关国际组织或机构职务的非政府组织领导人物外，无法直接对决策施加影响。由于非政府组织仍处于现存国家和国际组织体制的边缘，它们对具有全球影响力的国际组织，特别是政府间的国际组织决策的影响力非常有限。❸

第二，国际非政府组织的作用局限在低阶政治领域。例如，“非政府组织在参与联合国大会和安全理事会工作的努力却从来没有成功过。”❹ 再比如，“非政府组织对政府核军控决策的影响是渐进的，也是有限的；它们也许可以减缓军备竞赛的速度，但很少能完全阻止决策者的一意孤行。”❺ 在传统安全与非传统安全问题日益交织在一起的情况下（如战争引起对平民的伤害），国际非政府组织被排除在国际安全决策机制之外，对非传统安全的维护是一个很大限制。

第三，国家与国际非政府组织之间并没有实现平等的双向互动关系。特别是面对国家的打压，国际非政府组织常常无能为力，双方之间的相互制衡与补充因此打了一个大的折扣。对于那些国家危害非传统安全的行为，国际非政府组织也常常因为缺乏有效手段而无法制止。

---

❶ 盛红生、贺兵：《当代国际关系中的“第三者”——非政府组织问题研究》，时事出版社，2004 年版，第 143 ~ 144 页。

❷ Michele M. Betsill, “Environmental NGOs and the Kyoto Protocol Negotiations: 1995 to 1997”, Michele M. Betsill and Elisabeth Corell eds., *NGO Diplomacy: The Influence of Nongovernmental Organization in International Environmental Negotiations*, Cambridge: The MIT Press, 2008, p. 46.

❸ 盛红生、贺兵：《当代国际关系中的“第三者”——非政府组织问题研究》，时事出版社，2004 年版，第 242 页。

❹ 同上书，第 269 页。

❺ 刘华平：《非政府组织与核军控》，中国社会科学出版社，2008 年版，第 225 页。

总的来看，理想的非传统安全治理框架尚未完全建立，国家、政府间国际组织与国际非政府组织尚未建立一种完全信任与合作的关系，国际非政府组织的地位也有待进一步提升。毫无疑问，由于国家自身所具有的能力、权威以及作为全体国民代表的合法性，使得它在非传统安全维护方面继续扮演着主要主体的角色。但必须指出的是，考虑到国际非政府组织作为非传统安全“天然促进者”的特殊地位，其潜力与作用尚未得到充分发挥，其在安全治理框架中的地位还应进一步提高。这种地位的提高，固然有赖于国际非政府组织自身的进一步完善，更需要从制度上赋予国际非政府组织在安全治理结构中更大的发言权。所以，仅仅强调安全治理框架下国际非政府组织的参与是不够的，“参与不会自动转化成影响”❶。要使国际非政府组织发挥更大、更积极的影响，就必须改进现有安全治理框架的缺陷，特别是赋予非政府组织以更多的权威，如使非政府组织在国际谈判中成为正式的谈判代表，或是增加一些有代表性的非政府组织作为联大的观察员，等等。只有从制度上强化非政府组织在安全治理的地位与作用，才能为其发挥非传统安全“天然促进者”的角色、更好地维护非传统安全提供持续的保障。

三、年度案例：东非饥荒中的非政府组织

2011 年 7 月以来，非洲东北部的“非洲之角”发生 60 年不遇的干旱及连年战争而引起的饥荒，1000 多万人面临严重的生命安全威胁。国际非政府组织和其他国际行为体一起参与救援，发挥了自己应有的作用。

（一）饥荒概况

根据联合国的定义，饥荒状态要达到三个条件：第一，有 30% 以上的儿童处于严重营养不良状态；第二，每天每 1 万人中至少有 2 名成年人或 4 名儿童饿死；第三，在该地区的所有人每天摄入的食物热量远低于 2100 卡路里。❷ 当时，非洲之角的情况有过之而无不及，很多孩子在去往邻国的路上就相继死去，而他们的母亲连掩埋孩子的力气都没有，只能任由自己的孩子曝尸荒野。2011 年 9 月，潘基文在联合国举行的非洲之角问题小型峰会上指出：“非洲之角正在经历危机，而且一天天变得更加严峻。在埃塞俄比亚、肯尼亚、索马里和吉布提，超过 1300 万人需要我们的帮助。”❸

索马里是此次饥荒的重灾区。根据潘基文的上述报告，饥荒已经蔓延到了广大的索马里南部地区，有 75 万人随时可能会饿死，另有 400 万人需要紧急援助。大量的索马里灾民为寻找食物逃往邻国肯尼亚和埃塞俄比亚，导致两国难民营人满为患。根据联合国网站的消息，“2011 年以来，已有大约 17 万索马里人背井离乡，逃往肯尼亚和埃塞俄比亚。现在每天有将近 4000 人逃离索马里来到肯尼亚和埃塞俄比亚的难民营。新抵达的难民的死亡率高达每天 7. 4‰人。大部分死亡的是五

---

❶ Elisabeth Corell and Michele M. Betsill, “Analytical Framework: Assessing the Influence of NGO Diplomats,” Michele M. Betsill and Elisabeth Corell eds., *NGO Diplomacy: The Influence of Nongovernmental Organization in International Environmental Negotiations*, Cambridge: The MIT Press, 2008, p. 26.

❷ 《非洲遭遇 60 年最严重干旱》，载：视觉网。

❸ 《联合国举行非洲之角问题小型峰会关注当地人道主义危机》，载：凤凰网。

岁以下儿童。五岁以下儿童的营养不良率达到26.8%。”❶

这次东非大饥荒是空前的，其原因主要有：

第一，干旱是造成饥荒的直接原因。非洲之角包括吉布提、埃塞俄比亚、厄立特里亚、肯尼亚、索马里、苏丹和乌干达七国，总人口数近两亿，其中逾7000万人长期生活在极易出现粮食短缺问题的地区。近30年来，非洲之角的国家至少每10年就遭遇一次饥荒威胁。去年以来，这一地区持续遭遇60年不遇的大旱，截至2011年5月初雨季过半之时，非洲之角国家降水仅为往年正常值的5%至50%不等。干旱导致粮食减产，加上全球粮价高涨、区域内部分国家冲突不断、自身经济基础脆弱、外部援助不足等因素，非洲之角的粮食安全状况雪上加霜。

第二，粮食价格的上涨加深了危机。非洲之角7国的人均国民生产总值仅为200美元左右，除肯尼亚和乌干达外，其余国家的经济增幅长期落后于人口增幅，而非洲之角国家经济多以农业为主，咖啡、茶叶等主要出口商品高度依赖国际市场价格浮动，这在一定程度上为粮食安全埋下了隐忧。全球粮食价格在历经2008年金融危机后的低潮后，2011年再次攀升。截至4月，索马里市场的红高粱零售价较去年同期上涨150%至200%；肯尼亚内罗毕和蒙巴萨5月玉米批发价格同比上涨60%至85%；埃塞俄比亚玉米价格在3月至5月间上涨60%至120%。高昂的粮食价格使灾民更难获得食物，从而加剧了饥荒。与此同时，非洲之角地区得到的官方发展援助自1990年以来却下降了40%，其中农业领域的援助下降最为明显。❷ 这使得饥荒形势更加恶化。

第三，持续的战乱和动荡的局势使得这里再也经不起任何打击是饥荒严重的深层原因。索马里在过去20年里内战不停，更糟糕的是，因担心国外的援助削弱自己组织的控制权，索马里反政府武装青年党于2009年将大部分的西方援助机构赶出他们的地盘，拒绝联合国世界粮食计划署进入，使得在过去的两年里有22万索马里人离开家乡，到肯尼亚和埃塞俄比亚的难民营里寻找水、粮食和药物。❸ 正是这种战乱加剧了难民现象。根据联合国难民署的统计，在逃离索马里的难民中，有39%的人是由于饥荒，而有几乎同样的比例的人（38%）则是出于不安全因素（图2）。

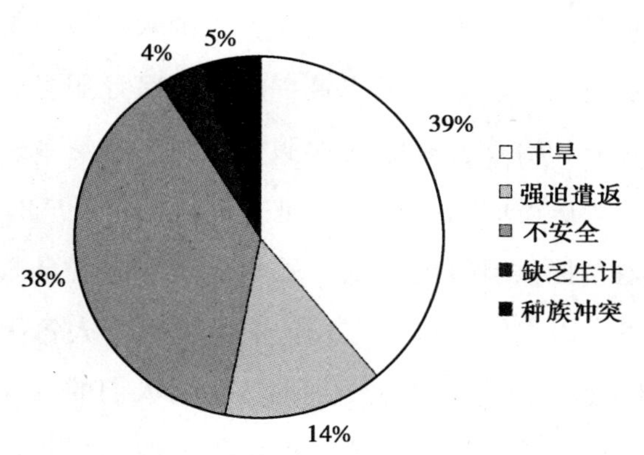

图2　索马里难民迁移原因❹

（二）国际非政府组织的援助行动

面对空前的东非大饥荒，国际非政府组织开展了积极的援助行动。他们的工作主要集中在：

❶ 《关注非洲之角旱灾》，载：《联合国网站》。
❷ 《东非大饥荒》，载：《浙江日报》。
❸ 《干旱和饥荒蔓延 非洲之角在哭泣》，载：《联合早报》。
❹ 《索马里饥荒工作救援报告》，载：《联合国难民署》。

粮食的供给，水资源的不足（饮用水和农业用水缺乏）、儿童或妇女的营养不良、疾病的扩散与防治以及难民问题。现将主要非政府组织的援助工作概述如下：

1. 国际乐施会

为了应对东非粮食危机，乐施会已定下该组织历史上最大规模的非洲援助计划，目标是筹集8000万美元，惠及约350万人。乐施会在其网站中介绍了埃塞俄比亚、索马里和肯尼亚的饥荒情况，呼吁国际社会提供捐助，以帮助东非国家缓解粮食危机。国际乐施会分为两个方面，一是开展紧急救助计划，同时提出长期的发展、保护和支持计划，应对该地区长期干旱的根源。在埃塞俄比亚，乐施会救助的人们已达到70万人。乐施会帮助他们寻找可持续的水资源，改善水灌溉系统，在一些干旱严重的地区，启动紧急水供应，保证每位当地人每天有五立方米的水供应。救助人员还和社区健康工作者一起开展医疗服务，帮助预防和治疗各种疾病如腹泻等。在肯尼亚，乐施会为居民们购买牲畜，向1.8万的养殖户的90万农畜提供料草的补助。乐施会还开展现金救助方案，以提供工作的方式，保证肯尼亚人每天有250～500的肯尼亚先令的收入。男人们的收入主要是通过从事修建厕所、报告牲畜的死亡并在其传播疾病前移走和为新定居的人翻新土地等工作获得的，而妇女主要通过收集和处理新搭起的帐篷和材料的包装丢弃等工作来获得收入。索马里是遭受饥荒最严重的地区，截至2011年8月，乐施会与当地医疗机构联合设立的11个社区治疗护理站已救助了13.6万位营养不良的儿童和妈妈。2011年10月为止，乐施会通过营养方案向索马里东部和南部地区的70万民众提供了饮用和生活用水。❶

2. 红十字会与红新月国际联合会（ICAC）

在此次的东非饥荒中，红十字国际委员会通过当地的红新月会开展活动，进行饥荒救助行动。在索马里的红新月会通过支持治疗给养中心为五岁以下的儿童和一些脆弱人群如孕妇或哺乳期的妇女提供救助服务。目前已有超过一万名的儿童正在接受严重营养不良的治疗，并在原有的18个旧的中心之外，在盖多、巴科勒州、中谢贝利洲、巴纳迪尔建立了九个新的门诊治疗中心，共有超过10万人从红十字会支持的健康中心中获益。今年七八月，红十字会给索马里基萨内和梅迪纳的医院提供了1.2吨的手术和其他药物供给，这些药物救助了650名伤患者，其中有超过2500名妇女和儿童。为了帮助灾民度过危机，在今年的7月和8月，红十字国际委员会和索马里红新月会给在索马里遭受干旱影响最严重的中部和南部地区超过162 000人分发了为期一个月的口粮，同时捐助了134个灌溉用的水泵，帮助人们增加粮食的生产。值得一提的是，国际红十字会在索马里南部反政府武装组织青年党控制区内为4000多个家庭分发了400吨粮食。❷ 在日常生活方面，红新月会致力于防治水源性疾病，迄今已给索马里2.5万人提供了饮用水。另外，红新月会还帮助难民和其他流离失所的人与家人保持联系，通过网上公布名单

❶ 参见国际乐施会网站。

❷ 人民网：《联合国紧急磋商东非饥荒问题》，载：人民网。

等方式，已帮助35位难民与亲人取得了联系。[1]

3. 儿童国际（Children International）

儿童是灾难面前最为脆弱、最需要保护的一部分。在索马里近400万受灾人口中，有一半是儿童。2011年10月27日，联合国儿童基金会驻索马里副代表汉娜·苏丽曼在向有关方面介绍情况时说，索马里南部目前仍有40%以上的儿童患有营养不良，其中一半病情非常严重。[2] 针对此严峻形势，成立于1936年的国际非政府组织儿童国际作出了紧急反应。儿童国际的宗旨是通过赞助帮助世界各地贫困的儿童摆脱贫困，它开展了生命线食品计划（A Lifeline Food Program），以满足急剧增长中的贫困儿童的喂养和营养问题。在非洲之角的饥荒中，儿童国际联合其合作伙伴一起为在索马里和肯尼亚遭受饥饿的孩子提供救济。其中部分援助（2.5万美元）将通过联合国儿童基金会（UNICEF）给肯尼亚最大的难民营的儿童提供紧急援助。每天有超过1500人到达此难民营，正遭受严重营养不良的儿童将收到伴有维他命的营养食物。同时，成千上万的难民还将接收到麻疹和脊髓灰质炎疫苗。[3]

4. 无国界医生组织（Doctors Without Borders / Medecins Sans Frontiers，MSF）

这是一个1971年在巴黎成立、由各国专业医学人员组成的国际性志愿者组织，是全球最大的独立人道医疗救援组织。无国界医生组织的救助行动大多在非洲，主要提供人道主义行动，医疗救助和治疗照顾，给伤患者进行外科手术，防治疾病的扩散以及艾滋病并向儿童提供一些基本的生活食品等。2009年，无国界医生组织在1300名索马里当地员工和100余名内罗毕员工的支持下，对约65万宗病例进行了诊疗。病人中23.8万名为五岁以下儿童，4.9万名孕妇得到产前保健，2.6万名病人在无国界医生的医院或诊所得到收治。外科人员进行了近3000台手术。此外，无国界医生还诊治了200多名患黑热病的病人、2600多名疟疾病人和1300多名结核病人，并为22.4万名儿童注射了疫苗。此外，无国界医生组织还在索马里开展食疗方案，超过3400名儿童参加了此营养方案，并在多个地区进行紧急营养项目。[4]

5. 百事基金会（PepsiCo – Foundation）

成立于1962年的百事基金会是百事公司的慈善部门，主要负责为符合条件的非盈利组织提供慈善捐献。百事基金会致力于在发展水平较低的地区开展可持续的合作关系和项目，并提供改善健康、环境和教育条件的机会。东非饥荒爆发后，该基金会宣布捐资100万美元，用以缓解该地区面临的饥荒。该笔捐款将用于支持百事基金会的三个长期合作伙伴，为非洲受灾地区提供救助。其中包括向国际救援委员会捐款50万美元，用于埃塞俄比亚和肯尼亚的饮水安全和卫生服务项目；向世界粮食计划署捐款25万美元，用于东非粮食分配；救助儿童会捐款25万美元，为索马里、埃塞俄比亚和肯尼亚营养不良儿童提供营养食品。[5]

---

[1] "Somalia: the struggle against food insecurity continues".

[2] 联合国儿童基金会网站。

[3] "Report shows rise in emergency food need among poor children".

[4] "MSF stepping up malnutrition interventions in Horn of Africa".

[5] 国际在线：《百事基金会捐资100万美元以缓解东非饥荒》，载：国际在线。

6. 美慈组织（Mercy Corps）

美慈组织作为拯救难民基金会在 1979 年创立，是由丹·奥尼尔为应对柬埔寨难民逃离饥荒、战争和种族灭绝的“屠戮场”而成立的一个专责小组。它是帮助美国关注人道主义救助的一个重要组织，其主要目标是减轻苦难、贫困和压迫，帮助人们建设安全、高效和公正的社区。饥荒爆发后，该组织在索马里的摩加迪沙给 1500 人临时搭建帐篷，并提供饮用水、开展疾病预防。他们还为 1000 户家庭分发了食物，为 2000 个家庭提供卫生包，并提供家庭现金补助以满足他们的迫切需求。该组织在埃塞俄比亚和索马里边境地区有七个移动的健康小组，为 1100 多个孕妇和低于五岁的儿童提供预防接种、体检和食品。他们所设立的固定诊所治疗儿童的营养不良和严重的疾病，如疟疾或肺炎。该组织还将水运到索马里边境的偏远社区，在肯尼亚的北部区帮助超过 30 个村庄的 20 万人获得生活的水源，并给七个遭受严重旱灾的城镇的 1800 户家庭发放现金券，用以支付粮食和其他急需的项目。❶

（三）行动效果评估

国际非政府组织对东非饥荒的援助是在国际社会“管不了”、部分有能力的大国“懒得管”的局面下进行的。联合国为应对东非饥荒宣布要筹款 25 亿美元，目前仅到位 11 亿美元，仍有 14 亿美元尚无着落。❷ 从目前大国捐款的情况来看，诸大国有所动作但远远满足不了实际需求。中国政府在饥荒暴发后的半个多月时间内，两次宣布向灾区提供紧急粮食援助和粮援现汇，援助总额共计 4.432 亿元人民币，这是新中国成立以来，中国政府对外提供的最大一笔粮食援助。❸ 日本将在已提供的近 1 亿美元援助基础上，追加约 2100 万美元的粮食援助。欧盟宣布提供 567 万欧元援助给数百万灾民。❹ 7 月 16 日，英国政府承诺提供 5225 万英镑的援助。❺ 美国在提供 6300 万美元的援助后，又增加了单独一项 500 万美元援助索马里，❻ 后由于考虑到这笔援助会使青年党受益，美国又撤销了这一计划。❼ 总的来看，对于严重的饥荒形势，大国捐助仍然是杯水车薪。在这种情况下，国际非政府组织的援助起到了一定的补充作用。而且，与国家和联合国等政府间国际组织的救助相比，国际非政府组织还具有如下优势：

第一，国际非政府组织更有热情，更贴近地区的需求，救助活动的成效也更为明显。国家捐助多出于国际形象的考虑，参与的热情不大，往往以提供大批量物资和现金援助为主要方式，不太注重援助的实际效果。而国际非政府组织基于其志愿性，参与热情高，推出的计划往往从实际需求出发，钱少也能办大事。如在解决水资源的问题上，乐施会和美慈队向所在区域的民众提供

❶ “Hunger crisis in the Horn of Africa”.
❷ 刘洋、杨京德：《联合国东非饥荒筹款过半未落实》。
❸ 杨洁篪：《新中国成立以来最大一笔粮援用于非洲之角饥荒》。
❹ “UNHCR chief urges more help for drought－hit Somalis”.
❺ “Andrew Mitchell urges action on Africa drought”.
❻ “US pledges MYM5 Million for Somalia”.
❼ “UN declare first famine in Africa for three decade as US withholds aid”.

水的计划，更能满足人们的生存需求。

第二，非政府组织因其具有更为专业的人员和明确的针对性，所以其开展的活动更能取得良好的效果。如无国界医生组织（MSF）是由各国专业医学人员组成的国际性的志愿者组织，也是全球最大的独立人道医疗救援组织。它在各国的救助工作往往是专业的医疗救助队，在防治疾病上更专业，更迅速。而儿童国际这一专门针对贫困儿童的组织，特别瞄准儿童的发展问题，所采取的措施更加有影响力和深入性。

第三，非政府组织的各种活动交叉进行，更有利于饥荒的缓解。在非政府组织的救助中，将水资源问题与满足和提高灌溉条件相连，在解决饮用水问题的同时注意防止水源性疾病，在提供粮食供应时将营养问题相提并论。对这些问题的交叉考虑，不仅可以解决眼前的饥荒问题，同时也有效地预防可能因饥荒而产生的一系列中、长期问题。另外，非政府组织开展的活动如开展现金换工作的计划，能够充分调动人们的积极性，在保证当地就业率的同时，又可满足人们的基本收入，从而使灾民走出伸手要援助的被动接受状态。

与此同时，国际非政府组织的援助也存在着一些问题：

第一，与政府间组织的协调不够。在 2011 年 9 月召开的非洲之角饥荒问题峰会上，各个国家和地区性的政府间组织相继发言，但其中并未出现非政府组织的身影，非政府组织的活动和取得的成效也未被提及。这说明在现今仍是以主权国家为主导的国际关系中，非政府组织的作用受到国际社会的忽视。联合国的世界粮食计划署、联合国儿童基金、联合国救济委员会在开展活动时，往往通过联合国自己的组织机构，而没有与在当地的非政府组织的活动相协调。这样，非政府组织的活动可能与联合国等政府间组织的活动造成一定的重复，不利于提高有限资源的利用效率。

第二，非政府组织在援助过程中还面临一个如何与当地政权的协调问题。在索马里的西部和南部地区主要是由青年党所盘踞着。它因担心西方的援助削弱自己的控制力，一度将西方的各种援助机构（自然也包括国际非政府组织在内）都赶出此地区。国际非政府组织常常在战乱、冲突等陷入无政府状态的地区开展工作，与地方势力的关系一直是决定着非政府组织工作成效的关键。由于青年党的抵制，国际非政府组织在索马里大部分的活动只能集中在青年党撤出的一些南部地区，从而大大影响了援助行动的效果。

截至今日，东非大饥荒仍然没有结束，国际非政府组织挽救当地人民生命安全的努力也仍然在进行之中。他们所取得的成就反映出在一个仍以国家为主导的国际社会中，国际非政府组织可以与国家、政府间国际组织相互补充，在非传统安全领域扮演相当重要的角色。他们所面对的问题则表明，当前国际安全治理的框架仍然是不健全的，国际非政府组织的地位尚未得到应有的承认，与国家等其他国际行为体的关系尚未完全理顺，其在一个仍然动乱不定的国际社会中开展工作的能力也仍然有待提高。东非大饥荒的惨痛现实是对国际社会的一个残酷提醒：必须立即行动起来解决这些问题，否则等到下一次危机到来时，我们所能做的仍然是杯水车薪。

东亚非传统安全问题新趋势与治理新思路

崔顺姬 *

【摘要】2011 年对东亚来说是充满危机和挑战的一年。日本发生的复合型灾害、泰国等东南亚地区发生的特大洪水、以湄公河事件为代表的跨国犯罪问题等都凸显了东亚非传统安全问题的复杂性、综合性以及对人的安全危害性等特征。其影响力直接波及能源、环境、粮食、食品等领域。为应对日益复杂和紧迫的非传统安全威胁，东亚应努力探索建构综合性、可持续性和以人为本的安全治理新路径。

【关键词】非传统安全问题，东亚区域合作，安全治理路径

本文首先回顾了 2011 年东亚非传统安全问题现状，重点分析了体现非传统安全问题复杂性、综合性以及对人的安全危害性三大特征的典型案例——日本遭遇的复合型灾害、东南亚遭遇的特大洪灾、中国的旱涝灾害以及湄公河事件。其次探讨了这些非传统安全问题带来的对能源与环境安全、粮食与食品安全的影响。这些影响切实反映了非传统安全威胁对人的安全所带来的挑战。在此基础上，本文探讨了未来东亚非传统安全合作的新思路，提出东亚非传统安全治理应进一步探索综合性、可持续性和以人为本的新路径。

一、东亚非传统安全问题新趋势

1. 自然灾害与非传统安全威胁的综合性影响

2011 年东亚非传统安全问题首先集中体现在自然灾害，且突出体现了非传统安全威胁的互系性及综合性特征，其最为突出的例子是日本的三重复合型灾害和东南亚遭遇的特大洪灾。

2. 日本“3·11”复合型灾害及其影响

3 月 11 日在日本东北部近海发生的大地震是由 3 个 8 级以上地震同时发生所造成的，其最大威力达到了里氏 9.0 级。之后日本接连遭受海啸、余震与福岛核泄漏等重重考验。对日本而言，这是自 1923 年关东大地震以来最严重的一次自然灾害。据日本警察厅 3 月 28 日公布的消息，此次复合型灾难造成的死亡人数达 10 901 人，失踪人数 17 649 人，另有 2776 人受伤，同时灾难造成成千上万的日本人无家可归。❷此外，大地震和海啸造成的经济损失达 3500 亿美元，到 2011 年年底日本已有

* 崔顺姬：浙江大学公共管理学院政治学系副教授，浙江大学非传统安全与和平发展研究中心研究员。本文系浙江省哲学社会科学规划课题一般项目《非传统安全治理——东北亚区域合作前景与我国的对策》（项目编号：11JCZZ03YB）、首批浙江大学研究生全英文课程建设项目《国际关系全英文课程建设》（项目编号：188310＊193226101_ 4）的研究成果之一。

❷ 《日本大地震死亡和失踪人数已超 28000》，载：中新网，2011 年 3 月 29 日。

500多家私人企业破产，其债务总额超过95亿美元，主要集中在建筑、机械制造和宾馆服务领域。[1]日本发生的复合型灾害再次让人们切身感受到地震等自然灾害能对人类生命财产和安全造成巨大威胁与破坏，也促使我们进一步关注如何建立更加完善的抗震救灾机制，并再次敲响了人们对灾害危机管理及非传统安全危机管理的警钟。

日本作为自然灾害多发国，其灾害预防体系、国民防灾意识、公共设施建设等经验等都值得很多国家借鉴。“3·11”地震中，日本的很多房屋不是被震塌而是被大地震后的大海啸给直接卷走。尤其是日本公共场所，特别是学校能抵御如此强震，还成为灾民的避难之所。[2]日本校舍的安全指标也是在历经大地震中不断吸取教训和改善的结果，在每次大地震中政府吸取经验教训，逐年加固校舍，最终将学校，尤其是中小学校建成最坚固的应急避难堡垒。加固校舍，最早可追溯到1923年的关东大地震。当时日本学校的建筑大多是木结构或砖瓦结构，关东大地震导致不少学校教学楼倒塌，学生集体遇难，这让日本政府深受刺激，决定以“学生的生命维系着国家的未来”为最高原则，提高校舍抗震性。1995年阪神大地震之后，日本文部省在抗震检查中发现，私立学校教学楼几乎都超过了文部省规定的抗震基准，而公立学校由于经费不足，在抗震设计和施工上，有一半未符合规定。日本政府因而加大对校舍抗震改造的资金投入。2008年中国汶川地震发生后，日本更加反思自己的校舍建筑问题，开始加大对校舍抗震加固排查并投巨资开启抗震加固项目。据媒体报道，仅2008财年，日本政府就已拨付专款1150亿日元用于校舍的抗震加固。[3]

然而，被认为世界抗震减灾榜样的日本，在面对“3·11”复合型灾害时也显得束手无策，日本政府的领导能力也令不少人质疑。但正如日本问题专家刘江永教授所指出的，虽然当时的日本政府上台不到两年，存在缺乏执政经验等问题，但是问题的核心还在于本次灾害是一种前所未有的复合性的灾难。日本在地震的预测、民间防震意识训练、建筑的抗震程度方面都是世界领先的。“3·11”发生的是特大地震和海啸，是日本历史上第一次，加上发生福岛核电站的核泄露事件，这种情况都是前所未有的。[4]也正是此次灾害的多重性、复合性和超常规性，激起了全球性的对非传统安全威胁尤其是对核能源安全的重新审视与思考。

3月11日发生的9级强烈地震，引发了约10米高海啸。3月12日日本政府确认受地震影响，日本福岛第一核电站发生核泄漏——海啸冲进福岛第一核电站，摧毁了作为备用电源的柴油发电机。地震后立即自动关闭的核反应堆因没有电力供应而无法冷却，温度和压力不断升高。此后，这座核电站6座反应堆中的3座相继发生问题：氢

---

[1] 《日本大地震和海啸造成经济损失达3500亿美元》，载：商务部网，2012年1月9日。

[2] 回想2008年我国汶川地震，学校成为重灾区而学生成为罹难人数最多的群体，这也成为我国对校舍安全格外关注的契机。汶川地震后中国政府启动全国中小学校舍安全工程，提出3年内完成对现有校舍的安全排查、抗震鉴定与抗震加固工作；因此从2009年开始校舍的抗震加固成为各地政府及相关部门的重要工作。

[3] 《日本震策：震不乱的秩序》，载：《南方新闻》，2011年03月17日。

[4] 《专家：日本政府面对地震灾害的表现可圈可点》载：人民网，2011年03月18日。

气爆炸、放射性物质外泄、乏燃料池缺水、核燃料棒堆芯熔毁，等等。日本文部科学省16日宣布，在距离福岛第一核电站约21公里处的福岛县浪江町附近检测到每小时330微希伏的辐射量，这相当于正常情况下的约6600倍。后来，在群马县的空中飞尘中检测到放射性碘和铯，在东京的自来水中检测出放射性元素，福岛的牛奶和菠菜放射性元素超标，等等，虽然这些放射性元素剂量尚不足以对人的生理产生危害，却对人的心理产生了巨大冲击。核辐射问题迅速引发了敏感性效应且波及的领域也不断扩大，从最开始的食品领域蔓延至体育、旅游等诸多完全出乎预料的领域。譬如，在灾害发生后不到一星期内就有1000多名在日中国公民搭乘国内各航空公司增派的商业航班回国；在主客场回合制的比赛中，有中韩的体育俱乐部拒绝到日本比赛；中国还专门召见了日本驻华大使丹羽宇一郎。这是中国政府第一次为一个纯粹的、极其典型的非传统安全问题专门召见对方国的大使。同时，日本复合型灾害也引起了他国民众的恐慌，表现在美国西海岸的碘片、海藻片抢购事件，俄罗斯的口罩等卫生用品与酒的抢购事件，韩国的海带及饼干的抢购事件，中国内陆的食盐抢购事件，以及亚太各国股市齐跌等，这足以说明日本核泄漏事件的外溢效应被放大。更重要的是此次复合型灾害不仅导致日本以及周边多国民众的恐慌，还为全球核安全管理敲响了沉重的警钟，如欧洲掀起反核热浪，德国、法国、意大利等国爆发反核示威游行；多个国家核电发展计划紧急刹车等。

3. 东南亚历史罕见洪灾

除日本发生的特大复合型自然灾害之外，2011年下半年几乎整个东南亚地区遭遇了历史罕见的洪灾。7月下旬开始的强降雨持续了约4个月，泰国、柬埔寨、越南和老挝相继发生严重水灾。这场特大洪灾不仅给当地人民生命财产造成了重大损失，还重挫了灾区工业生产，吞噬了大片农田，延缓了政府经济改革，拖累了国民经济增长。据柬埔寨国家救灾委员会2011年10月份公布的数字，仅两个多月，柬埔寨的洪水灾害就使全国18个省市的150万人口受到影响，247人死亡，近60万公顷农田被淹，1000多所学校被迫停课，约2500公里道路不同程度受损。在同一时期，菲律宾全国减灾管理委员会也公布，洪灾已造成102人死亡，39人失踪，数万人因洪水还未消退无法返回家园。由于台风横扫吕宋岛北部的多个农业大省，造成农业和财产损失高达150亿比索（约合3.44亿美元）。此外，洪水造成老挝至少23人丧生，6万多公顷农田被毁。同时，暴雨引发湄公河水位上涨，越南南部湄公河三角洲地区也发生数年来最为严重的水灾。水灾冲毁6000多公顷稻田，造成越南湄公河三角洲地区18人死亡。❶

此次东南亚地区受水灾影响最严重的国家当属泰国。据泰国内政部防灾减灾署12月16日提供的信息，洪涝灾害持续4个多月，到年底尚有包括曼谷、巴吞他尼、暖武里在内的中部地区9个府80个县的3652个村庄或社区仍受洪水困扰；并确认有740人在洪涝灾害中丧生。❷此次洪灾首先对

❶ 《罕见洪灾重创东南亚 多国下调经济指标》，载：国际在线，2011年10月25日。

❷ 《最新灾情》，载：宁夏新闻网，2011年12月19日。

泰国的农业造成了巨大损失。罕见的大范围水灾吞噬了大片农田。据泰国防灾减灾厅公布，被淹没的农田面积大约为155万公顷（约占全国稻田总面积的1/10）。洪水泛滥后，泰国政府已经把预计主要稻谷产量从2500万吨降至2100万吨，并制定政策大幅提高农产品收购价格。作为全球最大稻米出口国的泰国，这种损失必将导致全球米价上升。分析人士指出，稻田遭遇洪灾减产，引发亚洲、中东和非洲发生食品通胀的担忧。❶ 其实联合国粮农组织已经发表说，截至2011年年底洪灾已经给东南亚国家农业造成了严重损失，包括大米在内的大片农作物遭到毁灭性打击，其中泰国约为12.5%、菲律宾约6%、柬埔寨约12%、老挝约7.5%、越南约0.4%的稻田均遭到破坏，洪水还冲走或毁掉了大量仓储粮。❷

更为严重的是洪水首次冲入了曼谷以北多个重要工业区，致使泰国几处大型工业园区纷纷停产。作为全球生产链上重要的一环，泰国受灾已影响到一些国际产业链。泰国工业联合会主席帕永萨·差素提蓬说："影响已波及国外企业，因为许多泰国工厂是国外企业的供应商。"比如，日本汽车制造商本田汽车公司已经关闭位于大城府的工厂并宣布暂停生产直至10月21日。此外，10月以来，丰田、福特、五十铃等国外汽车制造商相继宣布停止在泰国工厂的生产，预计重创数千辆汽车出口。据泰国相关研究机构的初步调查显示，持续3个多月的洪灾给泰国造成的经济损失超过了600亿泰铢（约合19.4亿美元），相当于其国内生产总值的0.6%。❸

此外，大量文化古迹也被水浸泡。洪灾致使大城府的许多古迹和寺庙也都被水浸泡，对于历史文化古城大城府的影响极大。联合国教育、科学及文化组织将派遣一支专家组前往大城府，评估当地世界文化遗产受损状况。大城府距离曼谷大约80公里，历史上是泰国阿瑜陀耶王国国都，历史遗迹众多，其中阿瑜陀耶历史公园被列入教科文组织世界文化遗产名录。❹

4. 自然灾害在中国

2011年我国也呈现出灾害多发频发、水旱灾害并重、旱涝交织影响、灾贫效应叠加以及城市灾害突出等特征。❺尤其是在各类自然灾害中水旱灾害尤为严重，譬如2011年全国年平均降水量较常年少8.8%，为1961年以来最少；然而进入6月以来长江中下游地区和西南地区则连续出现多次强降雨过程，给人民生活造成巨大影响。据国家减灾委办公室统计，仅6月份全国受灾人口就达6753.1万人，因灾死亡279人，失踪93人，紧急转移安置202.9万人；农作物受灾面积6732.8千公顷，其中绝收832.9千公顷；倒塌房屋13.2万间，损坏45.2万间；直接经济损失达571亿元。❻造成这种损失的更多原因是我国南方地区出现旱涝急转和旱涝并重现象。如南方有些冬麦区冬春

---

❶ 《泰国特大洪灾致工业园区被淹 全球米价可能上涨》，载：《北京日报》2011年10月18日。

❷ 《东南亚遇罕见洪灾 工业农业遭受重创》，载：中国经济网，2011年12月02日。

❸ 《泰国特大洪灾致工业园区被淹 全球米价可能上涨》，载：《北京日报》，2011年10月18日。

❹ 《泰国特大洪灾》，载：《北京日报》2011年10月18日。

❺ 民政部国家灭灾委：《2011年全国自然灾害基本情况》，载：民政部网站。

❻ 国家减灾委：《6月自然灾害造成279人死亡93人失踪》，载：民政部网站，2011年07月01日。

连旱、长江中下游和西北地区春夏连旱、西南地区夏秋连旱均给人民生活造成较大影响。旱灾造成的直接经济损失占自然灾害总损失的比例达30%。然而进入6月，长江中下游地区先后遭受4次强降雨过程，区域平均降水量达227.8毫米，创50年来历史同期最大值；约2周时间累计降下近1500亿吨雨水，相当于3.7个三峡水库总库容；6月6日，贵州省望谟县出现短时强降雨，降雨量最大达310毫米，山洪灾害造成52人死亡和失踪。❶值得注意的是灾害与贫困叠加，在全国受灾县总数中7成以上（1900多个县）属于“老、少、边、穷”地区，这些地区自救能力较弱，灾害与贫困叠加效应明显，因而也加大了应急救助及后续恢复重建工作的难度；全国因灾造成的死亡或含失踪人口、紧急转移安置人口、倒塌房屋数量中，超过80%分布于上述地区。

总之，2011年东亚面临的各种自然灾害警示人们，自然灾害愈加呈现严重性、复合性、国际性的特征；对人的生存与环境造成了巨大危害。如何同心协力应对重大自然灾害的侵扰和加强灾害治理能力，是东亚各国必须共同面对的严肃而紧迫课题。

4. 非传统安全与跨国犯罪

随着经济全球化的加深，国际跨国犯罪日益增多。2011年，走私毒品、武器等跨国犯罪对东亚地区的经济和社会发展造成了极大影响，日益成为东亚各国所面临的共同挑战。据联合国毒品和犯罪问题办公室9月13日发布的《2011全球苯丙胺类合成毒品评估报告》，东亚和东南亚地区已经成为包括冰毒、摇头丸在内的新型毒品“重灾区”。此前6月份中国国家禁毒委员会也发布《2011中国禁毒报告》，称“金三角”是对中国危害最大的毒源地。❷在2008～2010年期间，老挝、缅甸、泰国和中国缉获的苯丙胺类兴奋剂数量增加了4倍。与海洛因等传统毒品相比，这种毒品加工更便利，成本也低，成为毒贩的新选择。新型毒品的生产又带动了传统毒品生意，“金三角”的罂粟种植又出现回升势头。随着“金三角”地区合成毒品贸易额出现上升趋势，周边国家面临的威胁不断加深。泰国2010年毒品犯罪案件为8年来之最，在老挝发生的同毒品走私有关的暴力案件已达历史最高水平，缅甸截获的冰毒与前一年相比也成倍增加，同时大量毒品通过中缅边境进入中国。❸2010年，云南冰毒缴获量超过海洛因缴获量，是同期缴获冰毒最多的一年。由于湄公河连接缅甸、老挝、泰国等多个国家，也被一些贩毒分子和组织看作可利用的渠道。

在这种背景下，近年来湄公河水域走私毒品、武器弹药等犯罪活动日益突出，船舶遇袭事件频发。湄公河航线一直被认为是促进东亚地区经济繁荣和旅游的“黄金水道”，是我国全面加强与大湄公河次区域国家经济合作的重要纽带，也是中国－东盟自由贸易区重要的运输通道之一，自2001年通航以来，为加强中国与沿岸国家经贸往来、保障周边稳定发挥了重要作用。但是近年来，湄公河流域的安全形势趋于严峻，过往商船遭遇

---

❶ 《长江流域两周降水量相当于3.7个三峡》，载：《北京日报》，2011年6月17日。

❷ 《湄公河“金三角”新毒王很嚣张》，载：《世界新闻报》，2011年10月14日。

❸ 《“金三角”毒品走私更隐秘 流入中国数量巨大》，载：《人民日报》，2011年10月17日。

非法武装人员抢劫、敲诈、枪击等事件时有发生，已严重威胁沿岸国家人民群众的生命财产安全，影响本地区的和平稳定。2011 年 10 月发生的“湄公河事件”再次证明了该地区跨国犯罪作为非传统安全威胁的严峻性和紧迫性。10 月 5 日，中国籍船舶“华平号”和缅甸籍船舶“玉兴号”在泰国湄公河金三角流域遭武装人员袭击，造成 13 名中国船员在内的两艘船上的船员被杀害。

湄公河事件发生在以威胁澜沧江 - 湄公河国际航线而著称的“金三角”地区，虽然事件本身是跨国贸易中的个体安全受到暴力威胁并死亡的刑事犯罪案件，但关涉到东亚国家在跨国犯罪等非传统安全治理上的合作问题。澜沧江 - 湄公河发源于中国青藏高原唐古拉山脉，流经缅甸、老挝、泰国、柬埔寨和越南等国，干流全长约 4880 公里，是亚洲唯一的一江连六国的国际河流。澜沧江的河床落差达 4600 米，平均比降为 2.2‰，是我国云南和东南亚的能源宝库，其水资源是大湄公河流域最丰富、最具开发价值的战略性资源。加之近年来围绕澜沧江 - 湄公河的水资源开发利用问题次区域相关国家已经发生矛盾和争议，❶因此有必要以综合性和复杂性视角看待湄公河事件。同时作为非传统安全问题，湄公河事件也体现了国家安全与人的安全的不可分割性以及国际合作应对危机的必要性。事件发生后中国政府高度重视，强调要保护我国人民生命财产安全以及要建立完善安全相关机制的必要性。于是在事发后不久（10 月底和 11 月底）先后在北京召开中老缅泰四国湄公河流域执法安全合作会议和四国联合巡逻执法部长级会议。会议通过了《湄公河流域执法安全合作会议纪要》，发表了《关于湄公河流域执法安全合作的联合声明》，并于 12 月 10 日正式启动四国联合巡逻执法以共同维护和保障湄公河航运安全，促进湄公河流域经济社会发展和人员与船舶安全往来。

二、东亚非传统安全：全方位影响

1. 对能源与环境安全的影响

进入 21 世纪，随着能源危机和气候变暖问题进一步凸显，核能重新受到青睐。如随着世界能源供应压力日趋增大，国际化石能源的价格长期高位运行，东亚各国和世界很多国家开始重新考虑发展核能，掀起了近年来核能复兴的浪潮。日本、俄罗斯、印度、韩国、中国、印度尼西亚、马来西亚、泰国、越南甚至新加坡等国都制定了不同程度的核能发展规划或新建核电站计划，使亚洲成为世界上在建核电站规模最大的地区。然而日本福岛核事故为这种核能源发展趋势敲响了安全警钟，世界多个国家核电发展计划紧急刹车，如德国宣布关闭七座 1980 年以前投入运营的核电站，并暂停延长核电站运营期限计划，瑞士、韩国、印度和中国等都决定重审本国的核电发展计划。就日本国内而言，核泄漏事故使核电的“安

❶ 围绕湄公河水资源的非传统安全问题研究，请参见：Evelyn Goh，‘China in the Mekong River Basier：the Regional Security Implications of Resouce Development on the Langcang Jiang”，in Mely Caballero - Anthony et al.，eds，Non - Traditional Security in Asia：Dilemmas of Securitization，Aldershot：Ashgate，2006，pp. 225 - 245；郭延军：《大美工和水资源安全：多层次治理及中国的政策选择》，载：《外交评论》，2011 年第 2 期，第 84 ~ 97 页；李志斐：《澜沧江—湄公河水域争端对中国周边安全环境的影响》，载：张洁、杨丹志主编：《中国周边安全形势评估（2011）》，香港社会科学出版社，2011 年版。

全神话”破灭，日本国内反对核电的呼声越发高涨。日本于2006年5月制定《新国家能源战略》，力求在2030年以后将核电发电量比例提高到总发电量的30%～40%。该战略还提出，日本“要发挥迄今为止积蓄起来的技术优势等，为推进世界的原子能发电发挥先导作用”。❶可以说核泄漏事故对日本的能源战略几乎是毁灭性的打击。

那么日本等东亚国家能否因此停止核能源发展而继续依赖化石燃料呢？化石燃料包括天然资源，如煤炭、石油和天然气等。人类社会从运用水车到蒸汽机的发明，以及煤炭等化石燃料的大量使用引发了工业革命，英国借助工业革命的先发优势建立其世界帝国地位。然而随着工业化的发展化石燃料远不能满足全球不断增长的能源需求，更重要的是化石燃料存在着环境污染的威胁，人类不断地燃烧化石燃料而排放二氧化碳是加快全球变暖的因素之一。核能的发展可以说弥补了这些不足，正如有些学者和专家们所承认，“核能作为新能源的代表，具有清洁、发电效率高、占地少、容量大、不受气候干扰等优点”，“在21世纪，世界不可能离开核能”。❷ 目前全球范围内电力供应的13%～15%来自核电。世界主要能源消费大国对核能依赖程度则更高，各国核电占本国总电力的比例分别为：法国77%、韩国38%、德国32%、日本30%、美国20%、英国20%、俄罗斯16%。相比而言，中国核电在电力结构中比重小很多，约占1.8%。❸

发达国家的核电站大多数建成于20世纪60和70年代，但在此后的发展历程中也经历了几次波及全球的安全事故。首先是1979年美国三哩岛核事故，由此全球核能的发展经历了一段停滞期；1986年苏联切尔诺贝利核电站发生爆炸，造成前后近10万人丧生，数百万人因辐射影响健康，6万多平方公里的土地被污染，恢复生机需待800年以后。这致使核电发展又一次陷入低谷。2011年日本福岛核事故，作为50年来仅次于切尔诺贝利核事故的严重灾难，使全球核能工业发展再次蒙上了阴影，也不禁让人思索：未来的新能源之路究竟该如何走下去？在这种能源、环境、安全等问题的困境中，人类正在寻求可再生的清洁能源。

可再生能源的发展与局限性：根据联合国环境规划署发布的《2010全球可持续能源投资趋势》，2009年可再生能源发电约占全球发电总量18%，其中水电占了15%，风能、太阳能、生物质能等发电量加起来仅占全球总发电量的3%。在中国，2009年煤电占电力总装机容量的75%，水电装机约占22.5%，风电、太阳能、生物质能等发电所占比例不足1%。可见，各种可再生能源的发展也都有局限性。水力发电，是目前最成熟的可再生能源，发电技术在世界各地得到广泛应用，但是要求水电弥补核电的缺口，难度很大。目前，发达国家的水能资源已基本开发完毕，不具备实现水电大规模增长的可能，未来的发展潜力主要集中在发展中国家。但从长远看，发展中国家的水力发电也同样面临着水资源开发殆尽的问题，水电开发造成的环境污染和生态破坏也在不断引

---

❶ 《日本〈新国家能源战略〉出台》，载：中国国家能源局，2006年7月28日。

❷ 《日本大地震劫难警示录：科学而安全地利用核能》，载：新华网，2011年03月23日。

❸ 陈晓进：《全球核能何处去?》载：《世界知识》，2011年4月25日。

起争议。

在一些能源需求较小、地理和气候条件都适宜的国家，风电和太阳能或许能成为其主要能源。但是风电和太阳能利用都易受地理条件和气候状况的限制，对于能源消费大国，它更适合作为在地理和气候条件适宜的局部地区进行分散利用，即形成分布式能源供应。此外，风电和太阳能发电都具有不稳定性、不连续性特点，容易对电网造成冲击，影响安全、稳定供电。在储能技术成熟之前，风电、太阳能发电的并网问题很难得到解决，无法作为主要的发电能源。生物质发电虽可以避免地理和气候条件限制，但也存在着生物质资源不足、品质不佳、收集困难等问题；而且生物质发电也适合进行分散式布局，很难形成大规模的电力供应。此外，可再生能源发电成本相对高昂。目前生物质发电（沼气发电）的成本为煤电的1.5倍，风力发电成本为煤电的1.7倍，光伏发电成本为煤电的11~18倍。

此外，近年来页岩气（Shale Gas）作为能源发展领域的新趋势得到越来越多的关注甚至被称为是页岩革命。页岩气，特指赋存于页岩中的非常规天然气，是一种极具开发价值的新能源，通过水力压裂技术开采。这种一度被认为开采成本过高的能源，近年已开始在美国开采。而且据美国能源情报署（EIA）发布的调查报告，目前32个国家技术上可开采页岩气。在全球范围内页岩气总储量高达6600万亿立方英尺，中国、阿根廷、墨西哥和北欧的储量都相当丰富。这种潜在的供应量已得到很多国家的关注。但是，关于页岩气同样存在争议，如开采页岩气的碳排放量要高于开采常规天然气，欧洲数个小规模页岩气项目都因存在环境隐患而被叫停。因此，页岩气的开发还有待观望。

总之，鉴于以上种种考虑，福岛核事故将难以改变今后的核能发展大趋势，但的确凸显了人类面临的如何平衡能源、环保、安全等问题的困境。在尚未找出最佳突破口之前，人们将更注重核能源及核电安全。福岛核事故将促使各国加快淘汰服役超期的老旧核电站，采用更先进和更安全的第三代核电技术；在规划设计中，也会将核安全置于最为重要的目标。同时东亚各国也将和全球共同合作以应对气候变暖和致力于寻求节能环保的可再生新能源。

2. 对食品卫生安全与粮食安全的影响

食品卫生安全：日本福岛核事故对东亚及全球所造成的影响还在于食品卫生安全领域。福岛核事故中，由于核燃料棒没有得到冷却而发生熔解，造成大量放射性物质外逸到环境中，如放射性物质铯-137、碘-131和锶等。这些放射性物质降落在核电站周围的土地上，或随蒸汽聚集在云层中，通过降雨落到地面，污染了土壤、牧场、水源以及庄稼。放射性物质更随风飘散，影响到范围更广的地域，污染了当地的水源及食物。事故后，日本政府要求47个省的相关部门监测其所属地的食品安全，包括蔬菜、水果、肉类、水源、海鲜等。经过检测，日本政府发现核电站周围省份出产的牛奶和菠菜中放射性碘和铯超标。按照正常水平，碘-131在蔬菜中的含量不能高于2000贝克/千克，而铯的含量不能超过500贝克/千克，而在距离福岛核电站97公里的日立市，食品部门检测出菠菜中的放射性碘和铯都超过正常水平的27倍。另外，日本福岛、茨城、栃木和群马县出产的牛奶放射性物质也超出正常水平。

许多国家担心日本的放射性物质会漂洋过海影响本国的食品安全，加之因缺乏必要的专业知识而引发恐慌，造成了不少国家发生如“抢盐”“抢海带”等事件。食品安全问题关系到民众身心健康，极易引发公众恐慌。据统计，日本每年食品出口占全世界食品出口总量的5%，大部分是加工食品和海鲜类。尽管这个比例不算大，但如果这些食物中的一部分受到污染，也将不可避免地带来世界性的食品安全问题。出于这种考量，很多国家都实施了对日本蔬菜食品的进口限制。除了因日本核辐射引发的食品安全问题，2011年世界其他地区也发生了诸多食品安全问题。如在中国，双汇瘦肉精事件、馒头添加防腐剂事件、地沟油制售食用油事件，等等。食品卫生安全问题已严重影响着人们的日常生活。

粮食安全：粮食安全问题成为2011年东亚乃至国际社会最关注的安全议题之一。据联合国粮农组织发布的数据显示，2011年2月食品价格指数达到历史新高，为238点。接下来的几个月虽有小幅下降，但仍维持高位。❶据中研网“2011年全球粮食供应形势预计”：受到美国就业数据表现强劲、美元走强以及投资者及基金逢低买入的综合影响，芝加哥期货交易所农产品期价5日全线反弹。虽然之后农产品期价有所调整，但对于2011年的世界粮食供给形势和粮价走势，权威机构多次发出担忧的声音。❷

东亚因面临严重的人口压力，粮食价格容易走高，加之持续数月的东南亚洪灾对地区粮食生产造成的巨大冲击，使得粮食安全问题成为东亚地区的重点议题。据2011年10月份的报道，这场洪灾已使泰国大约100万公顷稻田受洪水侵蚀，受灾面积约占全国稻田总面积的1/10；柬埔寨有近60万公顷农田被淹；菲律宾由于台风横扫吕宋岛北部的多个农业大省，造成农业和财产损失高达150亿比索（约合3.44亿美元）；此外，持续强降雨还导致老挝6万多公顷农田被毁；水灾使越南冲毁6000多公顷稻田。❸ 洪水还冲走或毁掉了大量仓储粮。综合各国官方公布的数据，水灾已导致这些国家总共约150万公顷水稻被毁或处于被淹没的威胁之中。致使联合国预计整个地区将不可避免地受到粮食价格上涨的冲击。正是对这种粮食安全的担忧，早在10月7日，东盟与中日韩三国农林部长第33次会议签署了《紧急大米储备协定》（APTERR），旨在发生天灾造成供应与生产失衡时应急，这标志着“10+3”粮食安全合作机制化建设取得重大进展。在11月召开的东盟与东亚系列会议中，地区粮食安全问题和灾害救援机制等议题被置于重要位置。在“10+3”机制下建立了被称之为“血库”的外汇储备库和“粮库”的紧急大米储备库，成为维护东亚地区稳定与发展的重要部分。加强合作确保粮食储藏安全，避免因自然灾害侵袭造成粮食损失已经成为东亚安全共识。

---

❶ 《联合国粮农组织：粮农组织食品价格指数和农产品价格指数》。

❷ 《2011年全球粮食供应形势预计》。

❸ 《罕见洪灾重创东南亚 多国下调经济指标》，载：国际在线，2011年10月25日。

三、东亚非传统安全治理新思路

2011年东亚非传统安全威胁呈现前所未有的复杂性、紧迫性、综合性以及对人的安全的极大威胁性特征。应对此类非传统安全威胁，合作是必不可少的途径，但以何种方式进行合作、治理应达到怎样的目的仍值得深思。本文据此展望东亚非传统安全治理新思路，提出综合性、可持续性和以人为本的安全治理新路径。

1. 非传统安全治理：综合性路径

首先，综合性治理强调不同领域、不同层次之间的相互关联性和互系性，认为非传统安全治理不可能只针对某个问题的个体治理，即只见单个问题的表象而不见问题之间的相互联系和影响。比如，湄公河事件看起来是一起跨国刑事犯罪案件，但事件直接关涉到跨国贩毒问题和国际航运的安全问题，同时因澜沧江－湄公河是中国与大湄公河次区域国家全面加强经济合作的重要纽带，又直接涉及中国与东盟国家的自由贸易问题，作为跨多国的国际河流，它又牵涉到围绕水资源的错综复杂的利益关系以及对环境和粮食等问题的影响。同样，日本的特大地震和海啸以及东南亚的洪灾，其影响也远远超出了自然灾害的范围，而是波及核能源安全以及粮食安全、食品安全等领域。这种综合性特征正是非传统安全问题的主要特征之一，因此综合性治理理应注重不同领域间（如环境、经济、社会等领域）和不同层次间（如个体、社群、国家、区域、全球）的合作。

传统的安全往往把国家作为安全的唯一提供者，但随着愈加复杂、隐蔽、棘手的非传统安全威胁的凸显，即便是世界上最强大的国家，单靠一国力量也无法有效应对。因此，不同行为体的跨层次、跨区域合作是综合治理的必然路径，在治理进程中重要的是要有整体的、统观大局的视野以充分调动包括国家、区域组织、NGO、相关企业、市民社会在内的一切可利用资源，提高治理的综合能力。2002年11月，中国与东盟发表的《关于非传统安全领域合作联合宣言》标志着双方在非传统安全领域全面合作的开始。该宣言明确强调了非传统安全问题的复杂性以及综合运用政治、经济、外交、法律、科技等综合手段加以应对的必要性。从这个意义上，温家宝总理在11月召开的东亚领导人系列会议上强调，在当前复杂严峻的国际政治经济形势下“调动一切积极因素”加强“团结、发展、合作”的东亚发展方向有其重要意义。[1]调动一切积极因素，甚至也包括媒体的作用。近年来，在促进东亚区域合作方面，媒体承担的功能在提升，媒体的作用也越来越得到重视。韩国驻华大使馆政务公使赵镛天强调说，东亚区域合作，如果想要获得进一步的深入和发展，我们必须要深入思考舆论媒体的作用，因为多样化的信息让人们更好地理解整个事件的来龙去脉并帮助人们作具体的判断和行动。[2]在这种大背景下“10＋3媒体合作研讨会”在中国国务院总理温家宝的倡议下于2007年首次召开，迄今已举办四届。东亚各国的媒体合作已经成为“10＋3”合作的重要组成部分。

---

[1] 温家宝：《中国坚持由东盟主导东亚合作进程》载：新华网，2011年11月20日。

[2] 赵镛天：《东亚区域合作：挑战与机会》载：《大众日报》，2011年11月9日。

此外，从实际操作层面，非传统安全治理从个体治理走向综合治理，有利于准确把握安全威胁引发危机的触发点和临界点，尽可能将安全维护控制在社会解组、民族分裂、政权倒台、战争爆发等非常态危机的临界点之前。而最为理想的状态则是提高安全的指数以确保良好的安全环境，从这个意义上讲安全治理的综合性路径和可持续路径相互联系且互为补充。

2. 非传统安全治理：可持续性路径

非传统安全治理的持续性路径要区分短期应急性应对和长期可持续性建构、治标与治本之间的差异，强调安全治理的环境性和整体性效果。从20世纪60年代就致力于和平研究的和平学权威约翰·加尔通常常将和平研究比作医学和健康学。加尔通在区分“积极和平”与“消极和平”的概念时提出，和平可以被定义为暴力的不存在，但只是暴力的不存在未免也太消极了。借助于医学和健康研究，他强调真正的健康不单单是没有疾病，而是锻炼出有抵抗力的健壮身体。从此引申出，“积极和平”就是一种对终止暴力行为的“条件”进行的建构。❶其实这和中国的传统思想很相似。中医和西医的最大区别就在于西医更直接，常常直接采取对有病毒或感染的部位进行手术等治疗方式；而中医则擅长调节体内的平衡。中医强调的“治未病”和养生调理的道理就在于通过调节和提高身体的抵抗能力来防止被疾病感染。因此中国文化中隐含着很多对安全和治理的独特理念，那就是更注重寻找问题发生的根源（root causes）和改善大的环境。秦亚青在探讨中国文化对中国外交政策的影响时也强调了中国文化对“环境性”的重视（以区别于西方强调的个体主义），以及中国文化对当今外交政策的影响。❷同样这种文化特征也可以或应该影响东亚非传统安全的治理模式。

从这个意义上，非传统安全治理应避免停留在“漏一块补一块”的被动局面，并注意偶发性、零散性安全事件向密集型、连带性危机事件的转变。地震、洪水、海啸等自然灾害的发生往往不可控，因此灾害发生后的应对、救济、保障和重建体系和机制的建构极为重要。因此，安全维护的短期应对与长期建构的结合是非传统安全能力建设的着眼点所在，也是建构“积极安全（positive security）”的关键。同时各国应充分认识到本国安全与区域安全乃至全人类安全的相互依赖性，力求摆脱狭隘的国家利益观，以合作求和平、求发展、求安全。

3. 非传统安全治理：以人为本的路径

安全治理注重安全威胁的来源和安全维护的途径与方法，同时更注重安全维护的目的和对象，即安全的指涉对象（referent object of security）。在传统的以国家为中心的、以权力为导向的安全研究中，国家作为安全的指涉对象几乎没有受到任何质疑，安全即意味着国家主权不被干涉或领土不被侵犯。但是始于20世纪70年代的对安全内涵

---

❶ Galtung, Johan, “Twenty – five years of peace research: ten challenges and some responses”, Journal of Peace Research, Vol. 22, No. 2, 1985, p. 145; Galtung, Johan, “On the effect of international economic sanctions: with examples from the case of Rhodesia”, World Politics, 1967, Vol. 29, No. 3, pp. 378 – 416.

❷ 秦亚青：《中国文化及其对外交决策的影响》，载：《国际问题研究》，2011年第5期，第21～33页。

的“扩展”和“深化”，不仅将安全研究的领域从军事领域扩展到包括经济、社会、环境等诸多非传统安全领域，更重要的是安全的指涉对象和关注点从国家安全深化到将社会、人（作为个体或集体）甚至将某种价值也列为安全维护的对象。而联合国提出的“人的安全（human security）”概念在更大程度上走向了“以人为本”的“非传统”的安全研究。尤其是人的安全常常把关注点聚焦于贫困、疾病、性别公平等安全议题当中。

亚洲诸多非传统安全问题在多方面体现了对弱势群体的威胁。自然灾害、粮食安全、食品安全等对贫困和老弱病残幼群体带来了愈加严重的影响。如果忽视了对这些群体的关注，以人为本的安全治理路径将成为空头支票。我国近年来无论是在“十二五”规划中还是在政府工作报告中强调的改善民生谋发展和“让人民生活得更加幸福、更有尊严”的目标，就体现了对人的安全的高度重视。因此，安全治理的综合性和可持续性路径必须围绕着以人为本的路径展开，三者相辅相成。综合性路径、可持续性路径和以人文本的路径的综合是进一步探索和实践东亚非传统安全治理的新思路。

中国的非传统安全合作与外交能力建设

甘均先　毛艳 *

【摘要】最近一年以来，中国在国际非传统安全合作上主要取得了三大进展。一是开展了关于核能利用的国际合作，二是与东盟的反恐合作得到深入发展，三是在国际气候谈判中的话语权逐渐得到提升。三大进展体现出中国在非传统安全外交中更加重视议题、重视合作机制的倾向，但中国在今后的非传统安全合作中还应该加强议题创造、议程控制、沟通谈判、信息传播等方面的外交能力。

【关键词】核安全，气候变暖，湄公河，议题，传媒

一、中国与国际社会非传统安全合作的新进展

近年来，非传统安全问题在国际社会中的重要性略有减弱，传统的安全焦点问题有些失焦，比如，随着本·拉登被击毙，全球反恐问题在最近两年有所降温，亚丁湾反海盗问题也不再像2010年那样吸引眼球，曾经肆虐全球的禽流感在最近几年没有爆发出预想的威力。相对于前些年的非传统安全危机，近年来非传统安全问题没有爆发性的表现，显得较为平静。对于中国而言，今年呈现出的非传统安全新热点主要是日本的核泄漏危机、湄公河联合执法以及中国在气候大会上的新姿态。前一个问题反映了非传统安全的问题领域在扩展，第二个问题反映了中国与东盟非传统安全合作的深化，第三个问题则反映了中国在一些非传统安全问题解决办法上的新态度和新思路。

1. 新问题：日本核泄漏引发的非传统安全危机

过去一年非传统安全领域的一个新问题由日本的核泄漏引发。在2010年之前，国际社会关心的非传统安全威胁主要是公共卫生、恐怖主义、能源安全等。2011年以后，日本核泄漏引发的核能利用安全则成为一个新的非传统安全威胁源。日本核泄漏引发了国际社会的巨大担忧，法国对本国的核电站进行了重新评估，德国6万人游行示威要求政府取消核电站❶。日本核危机的一个积极影响是刺激了中日之间就核能源的安全使用进行

* 甘均先：浙江大学国际政治所讲师，主要研究非传统安全问题与中国外交；毛艳：华中师范大学政治学研究院2009级博士，主要研究中俄关系等。

❶ 《数万德国人游行要求终结核电，遭总理默克尔拒绝》，载：《新民晚报》，2011年3月13日。

国家间合作，同时也刺激了中日在核危机下的人道主义救援，比如中国派出国际救援队奔赴日本灾区，三一重工援助一辆62米长泵车支持日本的救援行动。❶

核能利用在苏联切尔诺贝利核泄漏事件之后就曾经成为一个重大安全问题，在当时的国际社会中造成恐慌。但是随着第三代民用核能的开发，核能利用的安全性得到了较大保障。全球核能开发在20世纪90年代得到迅速发展，其原因在于核能相对其他清洁能源具有无可比拟的优势。在其他清洁能源中，水电开发基本已经达到极限值，太阳能在经过最近几年的迅猛发展后也产生了较多负面影响，风能经过爆发式增长之后也没有较多的发展空间。相对这些清洁能源而言，核能除了技术瓶颈之外，其他限制则少很多，尤其可以摆脱太阳能和风能利用的自然条件限制。但是，核能的不利之处在于其安全性是一个极具争议性的话题。随着全球能源需求的巨大增长，能源紧缺常态化，国际社会很多国家包括法国、美国在内都主张加大开发核能，中国也提出了加快核能建设的国家规划。但是日本地震造成的核泄漏事件为国际民用核能带来持久的阴影，如何避免核泄漏造成的安全问题，成为国际社会关注的焦点。同时，如何通过国际合作来促进核能的安全使用也成为国际社会的一个重要议题，比如中国核工业集团与比尔·盖茨计划在核能利用上展开合作。❷

2. 新方式：中国与东盟的合作继续深化

从区域合作的角度来看，中国与东盟的非传统安全合作是过去一年里一个较大的亮点。一般而言，国际非传统安全合作基本由重要的事件驱动。中国与东盟在湄公河的联合护航也是因为偶发事件而触发。2011年10月5日，中国两艘商船“华平号”和“玉兴8号”在湄公河金三角区域遭到袭击。袭击事件发生以后，中国与泰国展开了联合调查，并藉此促进了中国与泰国、缅甸等国家在湄公河流域的联合巡航行动。❸ 作为事故多发区的湄公河金三角地区，巡航活动其实早就应该开展。这次袭击事件促使相关国家采取联合巡航，不仅增加了湄公河流域国家机制性合作的内容，而且加强了相关各方的政治友谊。

在联合巡航之前，湄公河流域国家主要针对水资源的分配和周边地区的生态保护进行了富有成效的合作，联合巡航是中国与东盟国家合作的新领域。联合巡航不仅使湄公河流域地区的合作增加了新的平台，而且也使打击毒品走私的合作得到了深化。随着中国与东盟一体化趋势不断加强，昆明—新加坡高铁正逐渐从筹划走向实施的阶段，中国与东盟交通的升级将增大湄公河流域国家进行非传统安全合作的必要性，如何打击跨国交通干道的犯罪活动将成为中国与东盟国家非传统安全合作的重要议题。

3. 新态度：中国在气候问题上的话语权逐渐增大

中国在应对非传统安全问题上的态度转变最为明显地反映在德班气候大会上。中国在大会召开前夕向国际社会宣布，中国可以就“实质性减

---

❶ 《三一重工重型泵车驰援日本核泄漏灾区》。

❷ 《比尔·盖茨与中核联合开发核能》，载：《成都晚报》，2011年12月4日。

❸ 王梦婕：《湄公河流域各国共建快速反应部队联合巡航》，载：《中国青年报》，2011年10月15日。

排”与国际社会进行谈判。此举表明，中国改变了以前在国际气候谈判中所固守的“不接受强制性减排份额”的安排。中国的谈判态度完全突破了先前的框架，开始朝向更加灵活的谈判策略转变。

中国的转变一举扭转了曾经的“强硬者”形象，为中国在气候谈判中赢得了话语优势。加拿大媒体《环球邮报》认为中国为气候谈判带来了希望之光，德新社认为中国的声明使沉闷的谈判恢复了生机与活力，英国《金融时报》认为中国的立场可能使美国陷入孤立，日本《读卖新闻》认为中国的灵活立场使中国在气候谈判中逐渐获得主导权。❶ 在德班气候大会以前，中国的气候形象总体来说呈现为负面。造成这种状态的原因一方面是因为中国对自身的减排努力宣传得不够；另一方面是因为中国在气候谈判中一直不愿意就“强制性减排”进行谈判。中国的态度促使西方一些国家指责中国“不负责任”，指责中国是气候谈判的“阻碍者”。中国的态度也直接造成美国以此为借口，逃避承担减排的国际责任。德班大会上，当中国宣布可以谈判减排份额时，国际谈判的压力就部分地转移到西方国家如何实现自己多年来许下的资金和技术承诺上了。

4. 中国在非传统安全国际合作中存在的问题

（1）制度化程度依然不高

相对于传统安全问题如军控等，非传统安全问题更容易获得制度化的解决。尽管如此，当前中国与国际社会在非传统安全领域的制度解决方案仍然不够。中国与中亚、俄罗斯以及东南亚的制度化合作相对来说取得了较大的进展，但中国与其他地区和国家的非传统安全制度解决方案仍显不足。中美虽然已经在太阳能等领域展开了合作，但大规模的制度性合作基本没有。中欧虽然就恐怖主义等问题开展过合作，但并没有就重要的非传统安全问题展开制度性合作。中国与非洲在非传统安全领域也没有制度化的合作机制。

（2）临时应对型方案仍然占据主流地位

中日之间、中国与东盟之间的非传统安全合作很大程度上由偶然事件驱动，并不是因为事先规划的国际合作。这种应急式思维表明中国仍然没有将国际非传统安全合作上升到国家战略的高度来重视，而是被动地处理即时发生的非传统安全问题。当然这种思维也在发生缓慢的变化，比如，中国应对气候谈判的态度转变就是经过深思熟虑的结果，而不是临时之举。但总体来而言，中国在应对跨国性非传统安全问题上有方案、无战略。

（3）非传统安全合作的范围仍然需要拓展

与中国进行非传统安全合作最为密切的地区是东盟，其次是中亚和东北亚。除此之外，中国与世界其他地区的非传统安全合作还有很大的扩展空间。中国与欧洲、非洲、拉美的合作相对比较狭窄。一方面，中国与这些地区的外交关系并不如与中国与周边国家的关系这样密切，中国与它们在非传统安全威胁上的跨国联系并不强。另一方面，中国在这些地区的战略利益没有在周边的战略利益这样坚实，因此中国与这些地区的非传统安全合作并不广泛。如若中国迅速成长为一

---

❶ 《中国成德班气候大会明星》，载：北方网。

个世界性的大国，在世界范围内的利益分布更加宽广，那么中国与国际社会的非传统安全合作就会得到加强。

二、国际非传统安全合作对中国外交的启示

1. 中国非传统安全外交的现实意义

自2000年以来，中国在非传统安全领域积极开展外交行动，并取得了丰硕的成果。首先，中国在诸多非传统安全领域与国际社会展开了合作。在反海盗方面，中国与法国、英国和美国展开合作，积极保卫国际航道的安全，为包括中国在内的国际贸易作出了积极贡献。在反恐领域，中国与上合组织成员国签订打击恐怖主义的协定，维护中亚地区的安全环境。其次，中国在非传统安全领域签订了一些协定。比如，2000年，中国与东盟签署了《东盟与中国禁毒行动计划》；2002年，朱镕基总理与东盟国家签订了《中国与东盟关于非传统安全领域合作联合宣言》，藉以加强中国与东盟国家在贩卖妇女儿童、海盗、恐怖主义、武器走私、洗钱、国际经济犯罪和网络犯罪等方面的合作。2004年1月，中国与东盟签署了《中华人民共和国政府和东南亚国家联盟成员国政府非传统安全领域合作谅解备忘录》，将反恐、禁毒和打击国际经济犯罪定为双方的重点合作领域。在新能源开发领域，中国与美国在2011年11月签订了备忘录，联合开发清洁能源协定并展开了合作。[1]

总体而言，中国在非传统安全领域的外交取得了较大成绩。相比以前的非传统安全外交，近年来中国在非传统安全领域的外交行动具有一定的突破。

首先是思维上的突破，这种突破突出反映在德班会议上。当中国提出可以进行责任承担方面的谈判时，西方国家就无法再利用这一借口来指责中国。在西方国家兑现自己的承诺之前，中国始终占据着气候谈判领域的道德高地。在较长的一段时期内，中国不会因为气候问题而备受西方纠缠。这一态度的转变为中国在国际气候谈判带来了全面的转机，从而为中国带来了话语权。可以确信，中国在未来的国际气候谈判中将会处在一个比较有利的谈判地位。

其次，中国在湄公河流域的护航显示了中国外交的主动性，这种主动性在以往的非传统安全外交中并不多见。中国在湄公河惨案发生之后，主动提出在湄公河联合护航。在外界看来，湄公河惨案可能导致中国与泰国等国家产生外交冲突，但中国却将危机变成合作的契机。从危机到契机，中国在外交上逐步摆脱了以往刺激—反应式外交，不仅变得越来越主动，而且也激发出中国在外交领域的创造力和智慧。

再次，突发性事件对于刺激非传统安全合作具有重要意义。最近几年中国的非传统安全外交表明，突发性事件既可以为中国外交带来挑战，也可以带来契机。如何抓住突发性事件，变危机为契机，是中国外交面临的一项重要课题。突发性事件往往为外交机构和国际关系带来重大压力，处理不好，有可能成为国家之间的冲突因素，处理得好则可能为国家之间的合作注入新的活力。

---

[1] 赵建华：《中美签署谅解备忘录，合作开发清洁能源》，载：中国新闻网。

突发性事件驱动的国际合作常常具有持久性，国家为了避免重复先前的破坏，更愿意达成长久合作的平台。

总结最近几年的非传统安全外交，中国逐渐摆脱了以往的被动外交思路，更加侧重于主动创造解决的方案。这是近年来中国非传统安全外交中富有意义的两个外交突破。

2. 中国非传统安全合作的未来拓展

（1）区域拓展

目前与中国非传统安全合作最多的区域主要为东盟、中亚和东北亚，但中国与南亚、西亚、非洲以及拉美的非传统安全合作则较为稀缺，中国与欧洲、美国的合作介于前两者之间。

中国与印度等南亚国家具有很大的非传统安全合作潜力，但由于地理位置的特殊性，以及中印关系无法获得实质性改善，导致两者之间的非传统安全合作比较滞后。但是随着中印缅孟区域合作的加快，中印之间面临的非传统安全问题也将迅速增加，尤其是全球变暖导致的冰川融化对于中印两国都有较大影响，因此两国在气候暖化领域的安全合作存在巨大空间。

相对于印度，中欧之间的非传统安全合作虽然开始较早，但是两者之间的合作提升较为缓慢。中欧在环保领域、外层空间探索等领域存在时断时续的合作，但是这些合作强度不大，完全与两者之间的经济实力不对称。中欧之间存在巨大的非传统安全合作潜力，但由于意识形态方面的原因，中欧非传统安全合作受到了很大阻碍。美国对于与中国开展非传统安全合作较为积极，合作领域也较广泛。中美已经在新能源开发、核能利用等领域展开了积极合作，但是由于美国对中国崛起的忧虑和防范，导致两国之间的合作无法在其他领域展开。比如在航道护航、反海盗、救灾、渔业等领域，两国无法展开实质的制度性合作。在非洲和拉美两个区域，中国与之进行非传统安全合作的领域更加稀少。

合作的稀缺意味着未来提升的潜力很大。中国应该顺应安全全球化的思路，与世界其他地区积极展开非传统安全合作。

（2）领域扩展

中国当前的国际非传统安全合作领域主要集中在新能源、环保、反海盗、反毒品等。合作领域相对狭窄，且很长时间没有在其他领域取得进步。领域的扩展很大深度上意味着非传统安全合作的深化。深化非传统安全合作的思路应该首先在周边区域展开。虽然中国与东盟、东北亚、中亚等区域的非传统安全合作已经制度化，但继续深化的空间仍然很大。中国与东北亚国家以及东盟国家在渔业上存在着诸多的摩擦和纠纷，如若能在这个领域展开合作，形成一个解决渔业纠纷的多边机制，那么多年来困扰中国渔民的安全问题就可以得到有效解决。其次，中欧、中美之间也可在一些新领域如太空探索等方面展开合作。空间安全是一个全新的领域，它需要高技术门槛，因此中美、中欧之间存在广阔的合作空间。

（3）思维拓展

中国在非传统安全合作上的思维拓展是非常必要的。首先，安全合作总是涉及到国际责任的分担，中国应该在国际责任的承担上做出更加灵活的处理。一方面，国际责任承担太多，会对中国经济发展造成负面的影响，不利于国内人民的生活改善；另一方面，拒绝国际责任，会导致国家形象受到损害，受到国际社会的攻击，影响到中国外交的话语权。也就是说，国际责任这块道德高地要尝试着占领，但不能以重大的代价去换取。完全的承担国际责任和拒绝承担都不利于中国发展和中国外交，必须采取中间路线——按照自身能力逐步地承担责任。[1] 其次，在非传统安全合作上，中国外交需要创造性的思路，化危机为转机、化冲突为合作、化零和为双赢。在处理非传统安全问题上，既将相关国家联合起来合作，同时还要促使安全合作孵化出经济收益。这样的合作可持续性较强，也会得到相关国家国内社会的认可。

三、中国应对非传统安全国际合作的三大外交能力建设

随着全球化的加速，以及非传统安全问题越来越进入到国际社会的视野，应对非传统安全威胁的外交活动将愈加丰富，在一个国家中的地位也将越来越高。外交手段之所以在应对非传统安全危机中显得重要，原因在于国际社会发生的显著变化导致武力在国际社会中的作用逐渐变小。武力曾经在国际冲突中扮演着主要解决工具的角色，但是在全球共同命运感增加的背景下，武力逐渐将为绝大多数国家最后使用的工具。尤其是，大规模杀伤性武器的开发，导致了大国之间的战争代价太大，从而使大国逐渐将武力作为一种基本的威慑，而不是行动工具。在武力作用逐渐减弱的情况下，外交就成为国家之间解决非传统安全威胁的主要手段。反映在非传统安全危机中，外交的作用尤为明显。

对于非传统安全问题来说，外交突出的原因还在于非传统安全事件为本身的性质和特点。从宽泛的意义看，传统安全事件大多属于社会性事件，即反映人与人之间的冲突关系，而非传统安全事件则大多属于非社会性事件，即反映人与自然或者人与技术之间的关系。最为典型地如全球变暖，它主要反映为人与自然的关系；造成公共卫生事件的病毒则反映了人与反病毒技术之间的关系。它们都是社会外部性事件，而不是人类社会对自身的困扰。人类社会之间矛盾冲突的缓解是武力作用降低的重要因素，同时也促成了外交作用的显著上升。

从中国非传统安全外交的过程结合 2011 年的外交活动，中国外交还需要在以下三个领域提升外交能力。

1. 议程塑造能力

中国虽然取得了相当大的外交成绩，但在外交议程的塑造上仍存不足。当代外交谈判其实就是讨论各国提出的议题并确定合理的解决方案，因此，议题在各种国际谈判中都是核心。什么是议题呢？议题首先必然是一个问题，否则就没有国际讨论的必要性。实际上，国际社会中的议题基本都是国际社会面临的棘手难题，需要国际社会共同解决。既然议题是问题，那么就需要解决方案，需要国际社会各方就这些问题进行沟通，以共同寻求各国都能接受的解决方案。在当今国际社会，大多数的国家间关系发生在谈判桌上，而不是战场上。因此，武器很大程度上仅仅作为

[1] 甘均先：《中国责任论评析》，载：《国际展望》，2010 年第 4 期。

防卫和威慑来发挥作用。谈判桌上，国家间关系主要体现为就不同议题或者同一议题的不同看法进行交锋，或者说，议题就是一国外交的武器。国家应该像开发武器一样，开发外交议题。

议题的重要性还在于，议题的获得意味着外交话语权的获得。那么一个国家的话语权从何处而来呢？一般认为话语权来自国家实力如经济、军事实力等，但是这种认识并不完整，因为一个有实力的国家并不一定就意味着拥有外交话语权。话语权，从其字面意义来看，就是说话的权利，就是让自己的声音被他人听见，并重视。这就意味着，自己要“说什么、怎么说”，是极其重要的。这个“说”其实就代表着议题的创造与阐述，“说”的内容就形成国际议题。如前所述，议题是外交话语权的核心。当一个国家拥有了自身的议题，并能对国际社会产生相应影响力，就表示该国拥有了国际话语权。由此可见，议题能力建设是国家外交能力建设的重中之重。

一个成功议题必须具备三项主要条件。

首先，一个议题要想获得成功，必须具有前瞻性。只有在其他国家没有发现之前提出该议题，才有可能获得人们的认可。因此，要创造一个成功的议题，就必须在问题产生之前便挖掘出该问题，然后在合适的时机提出来。如何才能创造出前瞻性的议题呢？一般来说，前瞻性议题主要来源于前瞻性的问题，而前瞻性问题的获得与发现则主要依靠研究者和行业相关者从日常工作中去发现，前瞻性议题要求研究者必须先人一步发现该问题。这就需要外交研究者把研究思维放在未来3～5年内可能发生的问题上，甚至是10～20年可能发生的问题上，而不是仅从当前的政治事件中去寻找线索。

其次，一个成功的议题还必须具备道德性，也就是说该议题必须符合国际规范，而不是建立在某个或某些特定国家的利益基础之上。任何一个创造国际机制或者提供解决方案的国家，其提供的议题都无可置疑地会首先服务于本国的利益，但是如果仅仅是出于本国利益的考虑而提出的议题是不可能长久存在的。因此，一个成功的议题必须具备相应的道德性。当然，在国际议题中，纯粹讲道德是不可行的，但是完全不讲道德也必然会失败。

再次，外交议题能力还与如何运用外交议题的策略有关。提出适合自身的新议题是获得话语权的基础，但是议题提出之后还涉及到另一个重要步骤，即如何利用好手中的议题。从议题本身的操作来看，抛出议题的时间、议题排列的顺序以及议题如何得到宣传都将影响到议题的效果；[1] 有效的议题宣传将带来主动权；媒体对某一个议题曝光度的增加可以影响到该议题在国际社会中的凸显度。[2] 就抛出议题的合理时间而言，若能早于其他国家并充分引起国际社会的关注，那么就将获得“先发优势”；若在其他国家抛出议题之后，能够及时跟上并参与其中，也能享有一定程度的优势；但若在其他国家抛出议题相当一段时期后介入，则可能会在议题参与上较为被动。从

---

[1] 毛艳：《中国气候外交议题策略探析》，载：《国际展望》，2011年第1期，第56页。

[2] 布里古特·斯塔奇、马克·波义耳、乔纳森·维尔肯菲尔德：《外交谈判导论》，陈志敏、陈玉聃、董晓同等译，北京大学出版社，2005年版，第93页。

议题顺序的角度看，国家应该首先考虑那些具有“优先性”的议题，也就是那些国际社会需要急迫解决的议题，比如，“国际金融秩序”问题优先于“北极领土争端”问题，“气候变化”问题优先于“反恐”问题。一般来说，人们较为关注优先的议题，而对那些若干年后才可能发生的问题，则不会太过重视。“议题联系”主要是针对国家之间的外交博弈而言的。一个国家要想获得自身的国家利益，就会很自然地在议题博弈中将相关议题联系起来。因为任何一个国家都会同时拥有一些对自己有利的议题和一些对自身不利的议题，那么在这种议题组合中，如何处理好不同议题之间的关系就显得十分重要。精致的“议题联系策略”或“议题包裹策略”可以为国家带来一定的主导权。“议题联系策略”将导致议题数量的增加，使谈判复杂化，但同时议题的增加也使每一个谈判方所考虑的有利结果的组合增多，因而也会使谈判获得成功的可能性增大。❶“议题包裹策略”是指某些国家将一个难以解决的议题内置于一个更大更容易获得解决可能性的议题中。在创造出议题之后，还必须将议题向国际社会宣传，以引起国际社会的重视。议题宣传主要和国家传媒的影响有关，传媒的作用主要在于可以影响到议题的突显度。新闻报道可以通过各种不同的媒介向人们传播，起着为高级政府官员设定议程和提供国际事件的信息及相关分析的关键作用，也经常会塑造世界各国精英与公众的看法。❷ 对于美国和西欧国家而言，它们拥有世界性的传媒，可以迅速地将其要宣传的议题传播出去。但对于发展中国家而言，不仅没有具备国际影响力的传媒工具，也存在着语言上的障碍，因此打造强大的媒体传播平台对于中国在非传统安全领域的外交非常重要。

2. 言说沟通能力

外交的主要形式在于谈判和沟通，外交的成功与否主要取决于沟通的有效性。对于中国非传统安全外交而言亦是如此。一般而言，沟通可以分为三种主要类型。

首先是直白型的讲述方式，即直接将需要表达的东西不带任何修饰地告诉公众。这种风格不拐弯抹角，不隐含保留，可以让对方迅速地了解自身，比如将中国外交的气候政策通过新闻发布会等方式直接陈述出来，就属于这种方式。这种方式的优点在于直接，国外媒体直接就能捕捉到中国需要传达的信息，缺点在于对方也会仅仅从政策的角度来观察中国，而很难从中国自身的角度来理解中国。

其次是情感温馨型，中国外交基本属于这种类型。中国外交官吴建民曾经谈到，中国在对外交流时应该采取温馨的对话，情感真诚，以“诚”和“情”动人。巧妙的公共外交应该达到“随风潜入夜，润物细无声”的效果。❸ 这种讲述方式显然很适合中国。中国是一个在传统文化上比较重视道德礼仪的国家，中国重视跟其他国家之间的

---

❶ 布里古特·斯塔奇、马克·波义耳、乔纳森·维尔肯菲尔德：《外交谈判导论》，陈志敏、陈玉聃、董晓同等译，北京大学出版社，2005 年版，第 47 页。

❷ 同上书，第 93 页。

❸ 王娟：《浅谈新闻传播中的公共外交策略》，载：《当代传播》，2010 年第 4 期，第 112 页。

友谊，而不完全是经济利益的关系。中国文化所特有的谦逊、平和的风格使中国公共外交的基本理念是寻求理解，不强加于人。[1] 根据德里达的友谊政治学，随着国家长时间的相处，国家之间必然发展出友谊，而不是仅仅在经济层面的利益关系。这种类型需要国际社会各国具有同样的友谊情结。中国文化比较适合这种交流类型，但是现实却有点背离，因为西方社会比较重视气候问题上的经济利益交换，而不是"同乘一舟"的共同命运感和友谊感，因此中国的温馨讲述可能不一定会得到对方的积极响应，反而招来的是对方不停地苛求，这种结果最终会挫伤中国对于发展友谊的积极性。

第三种是议论探讨型，它是典型西方式的话语讲述方式。西方传媒比较喜欢使用对立的两派进行争论，来揭示出问题的内在矛盾。这种方式的好处就在于，它可以让人看到问题的不同角度，更加全面地认识问题的本质。

以上的话语交流方式各有利弊。因此对于中国非传统安全外交来说，这些方式只能作为一个组合来使用，而不是单单使用某一种方式来讲述中国的非传统安全问题。严肃的政策分析、热烈的矛盾讨论与温馨的对话都需要在非传统安全外交中存在。但有一点是必不可少的，那就是中国在阐述安全问题上的真诚性。哈贝马斯的"话语伦理"中十分重要的一条，就是话语交流中内容的真实性与态度的真诚性。[2] 他认为，真诚是话语交流成功的基本条件。在中国非传统安全外交中，不管是任何影像资料还是新闻发布会，或者是相关的讨论，都应该真诚地讨论中国面临的实际问题和未来可能的政策选择方案。任何不真诚的外交，都无法得到国外民众的理解，也不可能获得外交话语权。

3. 信息传播能力建设

中国外交需要借用传播平台迅速传播非传统安全领域的合作形势和政策。当今大众传媒具备快捷、迅速的特点，要想让国际社会了解中国，就必须利用这些媒体。

中国与国际社会可以通过以下手段进行有效地沟通。新闻发布会制度是政府与国内外公众传递和沟通信息的重要手段，也是协调政府与新闻媒介关系的重要工具。[3] 新闻发布会的好处在于，可以通过外国媒体记者的现场提问解答，当场释疑，并迅速通过国外媒体即时传播到国际社会，使部分国际压力得到瞬时的解答和释放。另外一种传播方式就是由外交官亲自在国外报刊发表文章影响国外公众的看法。外交官在国外媒体发表文章是一种非常好的外交手段，比如中国外交部副部长、前驻英国大使王莹在2008年法国等国家抵制中国奥运会的事件发生之后，就专门在《金融时报》上刊文发表自己对相关事件的看法，并希望国外媒体给予中国更多地理解。该文刊出后引起了很大反响。还有中国驻英国使馆在《经济学家》上发文反驳英国媒体对于"艾未未事件"的论述，由于国外人士不了解这个事件的真相，完全从人权的角度来评述。鉴于此，中国驻英国

---

[1] 吴白乙：《公共外交——中国外交变革的重要一环》，载：《国际政治研究》，2010年第3期，第119页。

[2] 陈学明、吴松、远东编：《通向理解之路：哈贝马斯论交往》，云南人民出版社，1998年版，第200页。

[3] 詹文都主编：《政府公共关系》（第二版），华南理工大学出版社，2009年版，第194页。

使馆将事实和真相讲述出来，这样有利于国外公众了解整个过程，消除误解。此外，通过发布研究报告或白皮书也是一种比较有效的传播渠道。白皮书是一国政府对相关领域活动的规范报告，白皮书的关键在于它的正式性。任何一国发布白皮书都表明它对该问题的重视和真诚度。白皮书可以发挥两种功能：一是监督功能，帮助监督国内机构对于非传统安全问题的关注；二是宣传功能，可以改变中国在安全问题上的国际形象。如果中国发布食品安全方面的年度白皮书或研究报告，那么中国以前在食品安全上的负面形象则很容易得到消除。

中国媒体可以积极主动地“走出去，请进来”，开展与国外电视媒体之间的交流，从而加强媒体间相互了解，纠正国外媒体的片面和误导宣传，消除民众间的疑虑和误解，促进应对气候变化危机的国际合作。❶ 外交学院教授曲星认为中国媒体应该从“搭台唱戏”（本国媒体直接向外国播出）向“借台唱戏”（在外国的传媒上播出我们的节目）进展，进而达到“让别人唱我们的戏”（通过投资控股等方式让外国媒体自发制作对中国客观友善的节目）❷ 的境界。

中国还可以创造性地运用新传媒来推进非传统安全外交。当前最时兴的国际交流工具则为youtube、facebook、twitter 等。这些媒体被称为新媒体，它们是一种流动的、个体互动的、能够散布控制和自由的媒体，尽管这些新媒体高度依赖于计算机，但它并不仅仅是数字媒体，在更大程度上，新媒体是一种互动性的媒体。❸ 奥巴马就曾经利用这些传媒获得了总统选举的胜利，他“充分利用了网络工具，视频、播客（ 视频分享）、博客和网页广告等多管齐下，最大限度地争取到了网民的支持，最终赢得了竞选”❹。这类交流工具的好处在于其便捷性、即时性，可以迅速而方便地与其他国家公众进行交流。但更为关键的是，这种交流工具的沟通无障碍性，它可以使政府官员直接与其他国家的公众直接进行交流，对诸多问题展开讨论，是一种极为“草根”的交流方式。这种方式可以增加“我在现场”的感觉，增强了新闻的冲击力。❺ 此外，它的好处还在于其双向互动特征❻和亲民性，它可以大幅度地拉近官员与民众的心理距离，创造出亲近感，从而获得支持。它们还可以提供多次传播的机会，形成传播累积效应。一般传媒如电视或者报纸无法在速度上跟它们相比，facebook、twitter 等工具可以将信息迅速地传播给其他国家的民众，传播扩张效应非常明显。

小　结

总体说来，近年来中国在非传统安全国际合

❶ 王颖春、张守营：《气候谈判应有更多中国声音》，载：《中国经济导报》2009 年 7 月 25 日，B06 版。

❷ 曲星：《公共外交的经典含义与中国特色》，载：《国际问题研究》，2010 年第 6 期，第 9 页。

❸ Wendy Hui Kyong Chun, Did Somebody Say New Media, New Media, Old Media : A History and Theory Reader , New York: Routledge, 2006, p. 1.

❹ 赵可金：《美国大选与美国政治的走向》，载：《国际政治研究》，2009 年第 1 期，第 67 页。

❺ 赵凯：《我国媒体公共外交战略应有的特色》，载：《新闻记者》，2010 年第 3 期。

❻ 李忠斌：《新媒体与奥巴马政府的公共外交》，载：《美国研究》，2011 年第 1 期，第 113 页。

作上取得了一定的进步。这些进步表明中国在应对非传统安全问题上的外交能力得到了提升，比如德班气候谈判中对议题的掌控、使用新的传播手段（召开新闻发布会）等。但随着非传统安全问题逐渐在全球形成网络化的交织状态，中国仍然需要继续提高谈判中的议题控制能力、沟通能力和信息传播能力。

中国与非传统安全

中国政府非传统安全应对能力评估与实证分析

胡税根　徐元帅*

【摘要】本文在对非传统安全政府应对能力评估的理论分析基础之上，借鉴企业管理中平衡计分卡的评估思想，运用层次分析法，建立了评估指标体系，提出了我国政府非传统安全应对能力的评估模型。在实证分析中，本文选取“5·12”大地震的应对作为分析对象，对我政府非传统安全应对能力进行了评估，并根据评估中发现的问题，对中国政府非传统安全应对能力建设提出了相应的对策建议。

【关键词】中国政府，非传统安全，应对能力，绩效评估

一、绪论

1. 研究的背景

改革开放以来，中国经济持续快速增长，但政治、经济和社会之间的矛盾日益突出，目前正处于经济社会转型和体制转轨的关键时期。从发达国家经济社会发展的时间序列来看，这一时期正好对应着非传统安全事件的频发阶段。这一阶段往往是人口、资源、生态、经济、社会分配等社会矛盾瓶颈约束最严重的时期，也往往是“经济失调、社会失序、心理失衡、社会伦理需要调整重建”的关键时期。❶ 中国目前所面对的非传统安全状态也印证了这样的境况。中国的非传统安全威胁已经从偶发性转向密集型，典型的如公共危机事件呈现出高频次、大规模的特征和常态化趋势。非传统安全威胁之所以被关注，不仅仅是由于它的强敏感性、高连带性和明显的聚集效应，更是因为重大的非传统安全问题往往以突发危机的形式爆发，其产生的影响会“内传”和“外溢”，造成大范围的连锁反应直至危害普遍安全。同时，伴随着全球化的进程，全球已经形成一个十分敏感的共振系统，国际国内的非传统安全威胁相互交织，国际因素可能影响国内的安全形态，国内安全问题的处理失当也将带来国际共振，这已是不争的事实。

第一，从国际环境来看，“三股恶势力”和跨国犯罪活动对我国造成了越来越严重的直接危害。近年来，藏独、疆独以及台独势力的分裂活动越来越猖獗和频繁，并不断与外国敌对势力结合，

* 胡税根：浙江大学公共管理学院，教授；徐元帅：浙江大学公共管理学院行政管理专业研究生。

❶ 朱德武：《危机管理——面对突发事件的抉择》，广东经济出版社，2002 年版。

给中国的发展带来了巨大的不利影响。同时，跨国走私、国际洗钱、跨国毒品贩运等跨国犯罪活动对我国经济持续发展和社会政治稳定造成了越来越严重的冲击。第二，从社会环境来看，中国在当前环境下所遇到的非传统安全问题往往受到多元和复合交叉因素的影响。“全球性的问题、地区性的问题、国家层次问题、次国家层次问题和公民个体安全问题”都需要中国政府从立体综合的角度作出正确的应对。❶ 第三，从生态环境来看，不合理的能源结构和落后的能源利用方式所造成的生态环境的破坏和污染问题，越来越明显地成为经济快速发展的同时，我国政府不得不面对的非传统安全问题。此外，水灾、雪灾、旱灾、地震等频繁发生的自然灾害，时时威胁着人民的生命财产安全。第四，从人口环境来看，中国目前面临着五大人口安全隐患，一是人口基数庞大而且持续增长；二是男女比例失衡（见图1）；三是人口老龄化现象显现；四是人口城市化对战略性稀缺资源压力加大；五是人口流动冲击固有体制，改变人力资源分布格局。❷ 由于这些隐患所引发的公共健康问题、公共卫生问题、失业问题、犯罪问题、教育问题等处理不当都会引发社会的不稳定。第五，从经济环境来看，中国面对的很多经济安全问题都是转轨性安全问题。随着全球经济一体化，一国的经济安全不在是独立的经济发展问题，势必受到全球经济蝴蝶效应的影响。金融安全、资金外逃、贸易争端、人民币升值风险以及经济震荡等经济安全问题涉及诸多的体制问题。❸

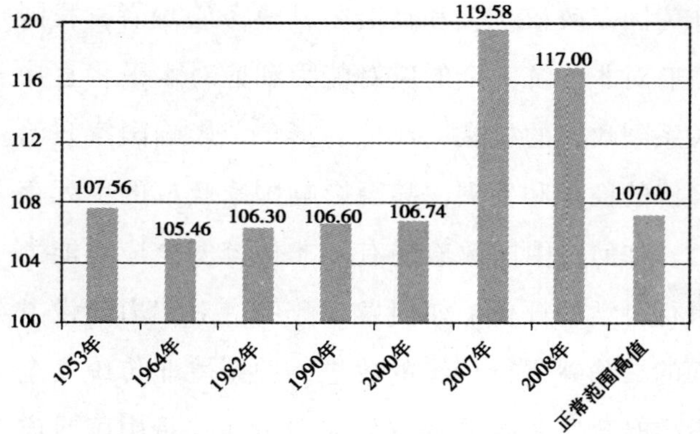

图1　全国人口性别比发展趋势（女性=100）❹

全球化进程的加速以及冷战的终结使传统意义上的军事斗争手段和胜负不再具有确保国家、社会和公民的安全权益的绝对意义。世纪之交，特别是“9·11”恐怖袭击、SARS爆发、“5·12”大地震以及2008年下半年以来美国次贷危机引发的全球性金融危机，使得中国政府和学界已经开始对“非传统安全”有了全新的理解和诠释，而对非传统安全管理和应对问题的研究也越来越凸显其价值、意义和迫切性。

政府作为公共利益的代表者、公共权力的行使者和公共服务的提供者，在非传统安全的应对中处于举足轻重的特殊地位。当社会因非传统安全事件而危及公共安全、破坏公共秩序、损害公

---

❶ 余潇枫、潘一禾、王丽江：《非传统安全概论》，浙江人民出版社，2006年版，第60页。

❷ 方向新等，中国人口安全报告：《预警与风险化解》，红旗出版社，2005年版，第2页。

❸ 余潇枫、潘一禾、王丽江：《非传统安全概论》，浙江人民出版社，2006年版，第59页。

❹ 中华人民共和国国家统计局编：《中国统计年鉴2009》，中国统计出版社。

共利益时，政府应责无旁贷地履行实施法律、采取紧急措施应对这些事件的法定职责。非传统安全的应对能力已成为政府执政能力的重要方面。作为国家政权机关和社会公共事务管理者，我国政府对非传统安全的应对能力和应对水平将直接关系到政府的权威、地位和形象，影响国家政治经济的稳定和发展，甚至影响国家政权的生死存亡。如何对中国政府现有的非传统安全应对能力进行科学的评价，如何发现政府应对能力建设方面的缺陷并进行持续的改进，关系着非传统安全发生时政府是否能够有效应对危机，是中国政府需要面对的共同的、紧迫的现实生存问题。

2. 研究的目的与意义

政府作为公共利益的代表者、公共权力的行使者和公共服务的提供者，在非传统安全的应对中处于举足轻重的特殊地位。当社会因非传统安全事件而危及公共安全、破坏公共秩序、损害公共利益时，政府应责无旁贷地履行实施法律、采取紧急措施应对这些事件的法定职责。作为公共利益的代表者的政府，其应对能力和应对行为将直接关系到公众对政府的信任，也直接影响着政治经济的稳定和发展，进而关系到国家政权的稳定与存亡。本文的研究目的就是以非传统安全理论研究为起点，展开对非传统安全政府应对能力的评价指标体系及其评估应用的研究，提出中国非传统安全应对能力建设的政策建议。

具体而言，本文的研究价值和意义在于：第一，本研究旨在梳理中国面对的各个领域的非传统安全风险以及政府的应对状况。随着全球一体化和信息多元化的发展，日益突出的非传统安全威胁已经成为任何国家或政府都必须认真对待的重大问题。如 SARS 事件不仅是一次严重的疫情，更是开放的信息多元化背景下全球性公共危机。“5·12”大地震的应对不仅直接提升了中国政府的形象，也暴露了政府在非传统安全应对能力建设中的一些经验和不足。因此，根据非传统安全的应对环境、应对程序及应对效果等而寻求建立非传统安全应对能力的评估体系，有助于评估和了解中国政府现有的非传统安全应对能力。第二，非传统安全应对能力评估对于改进政府应对突发事件的政策系统和提高应对能力具有十分重要的意义。在全球化的时代，国际问题不断涌现，非传统安全频繁发生，任何政府都不可避免的要面对突发公共事件。作为国家政权机关和社会公共事务管理者，政府应对非传统安全的能力将直接关系到政府的权威、地位和形象，影响国家政治经济的稳定和发展，甚至影响国家政权的生死存亡。非传统安全固然具有不确定性，但是也是可以预防的。通过评估和了解中国政府现有的非传统安全应对能力，将有助于发现政府和相关部门现有应对状况的不足，完善相关的应对框架和具体措施，为决策提供科学的参照。第三，通过跨学科的交叉研究，有助于推动非传统安全学科发展。通过非传统安全与政府能力建设和绩效评估相结合，国际关系的理论研究与国内公共治理、社会管理相结合，全局性的、普遍性的现实问题研究与前瞻性的、战略性的未来趋势研究相结合，从而推动多学科、跨学科、综合的安全学科的发展。本研究将运用定量化研究，构建非传统安全政府应对能力评估的指标体系并计算各个指标的权重值，从而为未来政府应对非传统安全能力的科学评估提供一种可操作性较强的计算方法。第四，非传统安全应对能力评估研究有助于中国争取和平、发展与合作的国际战略环境。20 世纪中下叶开始，联合国越来越多关注生态环境、能源资源、贫困、经济危机、人的安全等低政治安全领域。本文认为，非传统安全管理和应对是安全思想的革命，也是中国和谐发展的重大国家战略领域。中国政府应对非传统安全的能力评估研究有利于对未来可预见的非传统安全威胁进行有效的预警、防范和应对，有利于国家发展的增长方式与社会和谐的保障方式在长远战略思考与阶段性实施中得以相互协调，也有利于中国在世界范围内更好地争取和平、发展与合作的国际战略环境，促进“和谐世界”战略目标的实现。

3. 相关概念的界定

非传统安全问题由来已久，只是这类问题在开始时并没有带来普遍的威胁，且往往与传统安全相缠绕并附属于传统安全问题。随着“冷战”的结束以及全球问题的普遍化，在新的安全威胁条件下，安全问题的研究开始有了新的“分界”。军事安全与政治外交安全被称为“传统安全”；而直接造成人类生存威胁或国家安全威胁的其他安全问题开始被划入“非传统安全”（non - traditional security）。作为一个概念，它是冷战后被提出来的，西方学者也有用“非常规威胁”（unconventional threats）、“非传统威胁”（non - traditional threats）、“非传统问题”（non - traditional issues）、“新威胁”（new security）来指称非传统安全。非传统安全区别于传统安全“研究的主要焦点是战争现象”，❶ 对非传统安全来说，安全研究的主要特点是“非战争现象”。熊光楷认为“非传统安全威胁是相对于军事、政治和外交等传统安全威胁而言的，指出此之外的其他对主权国家及人类生存与发展构成威胁的因素，主要包括恐怖主义、贩毒走私、严重传染性疾病、海盗活动、非法移民、环境安全、经济金融安全和信息安全等方面。”❷ 王逸舟认为，非传统安全指的是人类社会过去没有遇到或很少见过的安全威胁，具体地说，是指近些年逐渐突出的、发生在战场之外的安全威胁。非传统安全问题的重点在于安全威胁的“非传统性”，即现有安全认知的不确定性和国家安全对策的不适应性。❸ 余潇枫认为，非传统安全是一切免于由非军事武力所造成的生存性威胁的自由，其价值目标是人的安全和社会的安全。❹

总体来看，理论界目前还没有给非传统安全作一全面而完整的定义。非传统安全与传统安全的界线在很多情况下是模糊的，如非传统安全因素和传统安全因素交织的政治安全问题，非传统安全问题的跨国蔓延所带来的军事安全问题等。正因为非传统安全界定的无定论，造成了近年来越来越多的将发展中出现的曲折和困难全部划归为非传统安全的状况，如资源保护、经济短期波动、互联网管理等。

安全的概念正如幸福和健康的概念一样都是

❶ Stephen M. Walt，“The Renaissance of Security Studies”，*International Studies*，Quarterly 35，No. 2

❷ 熊光楷：《协力应对非传统威胁挑战》，载：《世界知识》，2005 年 8 月 8 日。

❸ 王逸舟：《重视非传统安全研究》，载：人民网。

❹ 余潇枫、潘一禾、王丽江：《非传统安全概论》，浙江人民出版社，2006 年版，第 52 页。

没有任何精确意义的“模糊的符号”。[1] 但是笔者认为，安全问题作为政治研究的特定概念，其含义是特殊的，一旦问题上升到安全研究的领域，便立即具有了“政治色彩”，是作为安全这一纯公共物品提供者的政府不得不介入的领域。因为，安全事务永远指涉人的安危和社稷民生。同时，安全作为纯公共物品，与国家的治理过程密不可分，完全需要政府来提供，并且只有政府提供才能以最小的投入获得最大的产出。在给定的资源条件和客观环境下，“好”的治理可能使风险处于可控状态下，从而使安全保持在比较理想的状态；而“坏”的治理则有可能使安全风险突破临界点从而导致安全状况的恶化直至失控。[2]

理论界对政府能力概念的界定大致分为以下三种，一是从政府职能的角度认为政府能力“就是承担或实现其职能的主观条件和能量”；[3] 二是从社会发展角度将政府能力界定为“政府为实现自己的职能，推动和促进社会经济、政治、文化的发展而进行各种政治活动所需要的行政本领”；[4] 三是引入环境的因素，认为政府能力“指政府能否成功地适应环境挑战的程度”。[5]

目前，对非传统安全政府应对能力的概念尚没有完整和清晰的界定。综合上述非传统安全和政府能力的内涵分析，我们认为：非传统安全政府应对能力是为保障公民和社会所应享有的免于由非军事武力造成的生存威胁的自由，政府预防、控制、消弭非传统安全威胁和危机，维护社会正常秩序所具有的条件和能量。因此，非传统安全政府应对能力是政府综合治理能力在非传统安全领域的重要组成部分，它反应了政府非传统安全应对的状态和效果。

二、国内外研究现状

1. 国外研究现状

国外的非传统安全研究主要集中在欧美西方发达国家。发达国家对非传统安全问题的研究起步于 20 世纪 70 年代。1972 年罗马俱乐部发表《增长的极限》使非传统安全进入人类视野。

从学术渊源上来说，在非传统安全领域，国际政治经济学理论、环境政治学理论、批判理论、构建主义等理论流派对其研究作出了重要贡献并构成了主要的学术渊源。[6] 在国际政治经济学领域，以罗伯特 · 吉尔平为代表的新现实主义将国际政治与国际经济关系相结合，事实上将“经济安全”这一“非传统安全”的范畴纳入国际安全的视野，其次，相对于传统现实主义，其更注重国际合作的研究，重视东西南北关系的改善。[7] 新自由主义对非传统安全研究意义更加显著，基欧汉和奈的关于“复合相互依赖”特征以及复合相互依赖条件下政治过程的分析事实上研究明确昭

---

[1] See Terry Terriff. Security Studies Today ［J］. Cambridge：Polity Press，1999，p. 1 –3.

[2] 王逸舟：《中国与非传统安全》，载：《 国际经济评论》，2004 年 11 月。

[3] 姚悦龙：《提高政府能力 促进市场经济发展》，载：《华东经济管理》，2001 年第 3 期。

[4] 陈炳水：《政府能力初论》，载：《浙江社会科学》，1998 年第 3 期。

[5] Almond，G. A. ，Powell，G. B. Comparative Politics：A Developmental Approach ［M］. Boston：Little Brown and Company，Inc. ，1966.

[6] 刘中民、桑红：《西方国际关系理论视野中的非传统安全研究》，载：《世界经济与政治》，2004 年第 4 期。

[7] ［美］罗伯特 · 吉尔平：《国际关系政治经济学》，杨宇光等译，经济科学出版社，1988 年版，第 6 页。

示出非传统安全研究的基础和方向所在。❶ 环境政治理论对于非传统安全研究的理论贡献在于，它将环境安全引入了安全研究，并使环境安全成为非传统安全研究的一个重要领域。1988 年世界环境与发展委员会发表题为《我们共同的未来》的报告，专门阐述了安全与环境的关系。批判理论认为提倡新型的世界安全应逐渐取代传统的国家观念。其代表人物沃克指出：真正的安全主体只能是民众，不是国家，国家安全定位的安全意识和政治认同是以其他实体和集团的不安全为代价的。批判理论所设计的个体安全和全球安全也正是非传统安全问题的探讨主体。❷ 以巴里·布赞、奥利·维夫为代表的哥本哈根学派运用构建主义方法进行安全研究，其基本论点是在安全事物中，无论是安全的指涉对象和行为主体都远非传统安全的行为主体——国家所能承载，而是一个多元化的复杂网络，为非传统安全提供了不同层次的安全主体在安全的社会构建中如何发挥作用的参考。❸ 从非传统安全的行为主体来说。Muthiah Alagappa 把非传统安全所涉及的行为主体分为五个层次，即个人、社会、国家、国际、全球。❹ 在非传统安全研究的视野中，个体安全、团体安全与全球安全因生态安全、信息安全等问题的凸显而被重新提出和重视；同时，国家安全也因恐怖主义、分离主义、极端主义等问题的突显而被重新考察和定位。

从非传统安全的研究对象几乎拓展到涉及人类生存的一切方面，即经济、文化、社会、生态等安全，其中经济安全包括国际贸易、国际金融、国际市场等安全内容；社会安全包括人权安全、跨国犯罪、移民难民、洗钱贩毒、走私偷渡等安全问题；文化安全包括信仰安全等内容；生态安全包括太空安全、全球生态、环境安全等；从非传统安全研究的政策指向来说。安全研究的成果最终要转化为国家安全战略和安全决策才能体现价值，并且安全研究的成果对国家安全战略与决策的指向起着直接的影响。

从非传统安全政府应对能力评估来看，西方发达国家历来重视非传统安全政府应对能力评估的研究。国外学者对政府能力的研究也往往从政府决策战略的角度进行分析和探讨。Nelissen（2002）在其研究中运用 JEP 三角分析框架评估各种新型治理模式中的政府能力，并将政府能力区分为潜在能力和有效能力。Polidano（2000）从政府的政策能力、实施权威和运作效率三个方面建立数据支持的指标体系和评估方法，用定量化的方法展开对政府能力的评估比较研究。Coggburn 和 Schneider（2003）认为政府的管理能力直接影响政府的政策绩效，政府的行政安排和管理行为对政府政策的计划、行动和结果都会产生影响。Robert Heath（2004）认为对非传统安全事件及处理办法进行评价是非传统安全应对的重要方面，并且

---

❶ 罗伯特·基欧汉、约瑟夫·奈：《权力与相互依附》，门洪华译，北京大学出版社，2002 年版，第 30 页。

❷ R. B. J. Walker. One World, Many Worlds: Struggles for a Just World Peace. Lynne Rienner Publishers, Boulder, CO and Zed Books, London, 1988: 119 – 128.

❸ Barry Buzan. People, States and Fear: An Agenda for International Security Studies in the Post – Cold War Era [J]. Hemel Hempstead, Havwster Wheatsheaf, Boulder CO.: Lynne Riener, 1991.

❹ Muthiah Alagappa (ed.). Asian Security Order: Instrumental and Normative Features. Palo Alto: Stanford Unibersity Press, 2003: 536.

他提出了一个简便又综合的评价方法，即把非传统安全的危机情境分为事前、初始、冲击和恢复阶段，每个部分都从结构、系统、过程和人四个方面加以检查，由此得出按顺序排列的具体的分析。Boseetal 和 Luetal（2003）等人认为在政府应对能力评估的评估主体的选择上需要群体决策（group decision making），即需要一群评估者而不是一个评估者，来实施非传统安全应对的评估工作，原因是对非传统安全事件及其应对能力的评估需要不同的人来提供多种观点，而单一的评估者可能不具备足够的知识。Ross P. Buckley 和 Sarala M. Fitzgerald（2004）对马来西亚政府应对金融危机的能力进行了评估研究，以说明马来西亚政府的政策是否有效。文章通过对其应对政策的评估表明，马来西亚政府的做法显示了其对金融危机的应对能力。事实表明 IMF 计划并不适合它传统的文化环境，马来西亚在处理金融危机的过程中采取的政策是正确的，适合它特殊的国情，对穷人更为有利。Gilbert Burnham（2006）对发展中国家非传统安全政府应对能力的情况进行了研究，认为发展中国家需要更为有效的评估工具。尽管一些评估工具已在发达国家使用了很多年，但是对于发展中国家而言，还需要有新的方法。此外，在评估的指标体系上，不少学者认为应根据模糊理论，采用 MCDM（多准则决策）的方法。由于非传统安全应对能力的评估包含了多个层面，每个层面都有各自的多重准则和次准则，因此首先要确认评估准则以及他们的重要性，并赋予这些准则相应的权重，用主观或客观的数据去评估（Bouyssou 2000；Kara - apilidis and Pappis 2000；Yoon and Hwang 1995）。

除了理论上的探讨，西方国家在实践中也形成了比较成熟的评估体系，如美国的 EMAP 项目。此项目开始于 1997 年，作为一项评估非传统安全事件应急管理的体系，EMAP 的标准建立在 NFPA1600 的标准之上，并用合适的语言进一步阐述了这些标准的内涵。EMAP 由 10 人委员会管理，其评估是一个自发的过程。2003 年 1 月到 2004 年 12 月间，EMAP 对美国的国家和地区非传统安全应对状况开展了评估，实践表明 EMAP 项目更多是关注非传统安全事件回应阶段的评估，对恢复重建阶段的评估关注的较少。

2. 国内研究现状

我国对非传统安全的研究起步较晚，但近年来，随着非传统安全对中国的威胁不断扩大，国内学术界对非传统安全的研究得到显著加强，进行了富有成果的理论探索。从阶段性来看，中国现代国际关系研究所翟坤认为中国在非传统安全的研究和实践上可分为三个阶段。第一阶段是冷战结束到 1997 年，学术界和政界开始反思安全概念，提出包括军事、科技、环境、资源、文化、经济等内容的综合安全观。体现在外交政策上，“新安全观”开始在官方文件中出现。第二阶段从 1999 年到 2001 年“9·11”事件，非传统安全问题研究逐渐展开，由于 1997 年爆发的东南亚金融危机，从而使中国高度关注经济安全和金融安全。另一方面，上海合作组织的成立和发展，逐渐完善处理传统和非传统安全威胁的机制。第三，“反恐”成了中美战略合作的粘合剂。第三阶段是从“9·11”事件到现在，我国政府明确了非传统安全问题的重要性，并颁布了相应的文件，将非传统安全提到国家战略安全的角度，并在各种国际场合强调非传统安全威胁因素的上升。如我国在2002年7月31日的东盟地区论坛外长会议上提交《中方关于新安全观点的立场文件》；2002年11月4日我国与东盟发表《关于非传统安全领域合作联合宣言》；中国政府工作报告及党的十六大、十七大报告中正式将非传统安全提到国家安全战略的高度，明确提出“传统安全威胁和非传统安全威胁的因素相互交织”，强调保障非传统安全是我国国防的任务。❶

从非传统安全在中国的研究进展来看，中国学者对非传统安全的真正关注始于1997年东南亚金融危机。一些学者开始探讨经济和金融危机对国家安全的影响，在如何防范金融危机和经济犯罪方面出版和发表了许多文章和著作。这些研究侧重分析了经济全球化对中国经济的影响，如何减少全球化的负面影响，以及中国加入世界贸易组织后的经济安全和产业安全。2003年5月21日，《人民日报》第7版发表王逸舟的“重视非传统安全研究”文章，标志着非传统安全防范进入学者的论述范围。同年，王逸舟出版了《全球政治和中国外交》一书，对非传统安全的全球化背景作了专门阐述。❷ 2005年，中国社会科学院亚太研究所举办“东亚非传统安全研究”，来自日本、韩国、新加坡等20多位专家出席词汇，并就安全挑战——转型与多元化、移民与跨国界问题、公民社会与国家关系、东亚协作与纷争等问题进行探讨。❸ 2007年，由浙江大学“非传统安全与研究发展中心”编写了一套“非传统安全与现实中国”丛书，包括对非传统安全与公共危机治理、粮食安全、信息安全、公共卫生安全、文化安全、食品安全、产业安全、能源安全、人口安全、金融安全的分类研究与探讨。2003年“非典”危机的发生，加速了我国对非传统安全政府应对能力的关注和研究，不仅研究国际上成熟的非传统安全政府应对能力评估框架体系，还深入调研我国当前政府应对能力的实际状况，出版了大量符合我国实际情况的著作和论文。

第一，关于危机管理的探讨。这一方面的研究主要包括危机管理的内涵、分类、特征等方面，主要有许文惠、张成福主编的《危机状态下的政府管理》（中国人民大学出版社，2003）、薛澜等撰写的《危机管理——转型期中国面临的挑战》（清华大学出版社，2003）、秦启文等著的《突发事件的管理与应对》（新华出版社，2004）等。同时，不同的学者从不同的角度对危机管理展开论述，如张成福、薛澜、韩小明等从公共管理角度的论述；代鹏等从经济学角度对于国家援助体制的论述；薛金明等从法制建设的角度展开的研究等。闪淳昌认为政府面对的突发公共事件，通常是指突然发生，造成或者可能造成重大人员伤亡、财产损失、生态环境破坏和严重社会危害等重大社会影响的关系公共安全的紧急事件。❹ 张成福将危机事件划分为自然危机和人为危机两类，区分的标准在于某种灾难或者危机的直接原因是否可

❶ 翟坤：《关于非传统安全问题》，载：《党建研究》，2003年第9期。

❷ 王逸舟：《全球政治和中国外交》，北京世界知识出版社，2003年版。

❸ 余潇枫、潘一禾、王丽江：《非传统安全概论》，浙江人民出版社，2006年版。

❹ 闪淳昌：《建立突发公共事件应急机制的探讨》，载：《中国安全生产科学技术》，2005年第1期。

以确认为人的行为。[1] 薛澜将危机的成因归结为两种情形，即由自然灾害和人为因素引起的突发性事件和由社会中对抗的统一体引发社会冲突行为而导致的社会失衡和混乱。[2] 龚卫国（2007）从应急预案评估的角度对政府危机管理的能力进行了论述。其引入模糊综合评价方法对预案进行评估，为科学定量评价应急预案提供了一个新思路。总体来看，在危机管理的基本理论方面我国学术界已经作了比较全面的研究。

第二，关于非传统安全研究。中国学者主要围绕非传统安全的产生根源、非传统安全与传统安全的区别与联系、非传统安全与新安全观等问题，提出了自己的观点。其中的代表著述有：王逸舟发表于《人民日报》的“重视非传统安全问题研究”（2003）和《国际经济评论》的“中国与非传统安全”（2004），俞晓秋等在《现代国际关系》发表的“非传统安全论析”（2003）等文章，陆忠伟主编《非传统安全论》（2003），余潇枫等著《非传统安全概论》（2006），于俊平等著《非传统安全问题与重大突发公共安全事件应急对策》（2006），查道炯主编《中国学者看世界——非传统安全卷》（2007），傅勇著《非传统安全与中国》，张曦主编、余潇枫执行主编“非传统安全与现实中国”丛书（2007、2008）等。这些著述比较全面地探讨了非传统安全的起源、概念等理论问题，就多领域的非传统安全问题做了多维分析，并在非传统安全的对象、主体、领域、手段等问题上达成基本共识，政府也积极地进行非传统安全应对能力建设，初步形成了一些值得重视的经验与做法，对综合理解非传统安全问题具有极为重要的意义。

第三，关于评估问题的研究。张成福教授指出政府应对非传统安全事件的评估指标除了必须具有可持续性、可衡量性、能够实现、具有相关性和及时性外，还必须明确、具有弹性、有机地与政府管理工作相整合、能够被政府部门和社会接受、能够反映国际社会的经验等。[3] 吴江教授认为对非传统安全应对评估应当涉及非传统安全的全部内容，应当从政府管理基础工作和事件影响两大方面进行评价。李经中在提出用特定年份的危机指数来评判政府提供公共安全的能力。何海燕等提出从以下方面对非传统安全的政府应对能力进行评价：一是对非传统安全事件发生过程中各项实施对策的评价；二是对政府应急计划的评价；三是对事件发生中传播工作的评价；四是对政府应对绩效的评价；五是对非传统安全预警的评价。王耀刚等人在《广义公共卫生管理体系及其层次分析法评价》一文中运用层次分析法建立了广义公共卫生管理体系层次结构模型。

第四，关于评估指标研究。周庆行、唐峰（2005）基于层次分析法对非传统安全状态下公共府门危机决策能力的评估指标权重展开研究。主要研究了层次分析法在公共危机决策绩效评估中的具体应用。张小明（2006）认为非传统安全政府应对能力的评估机制设计，指向的是非传统安全事件中实时评估和事后评估，主要包括评估的价值

---

[1] 张成福：《公共危机管理：全面整合的模式与中国的战略选择》，《中国行政管理》，2003 年第 7 期。

[2] 薛澜：《危机管理——转型期中国面临的挑战》，清华大学出版社，2003 年版。

[3] 张成福：《公共危机管理：全面整合的模式与中国的战略选择》，《中国行政管理》，2003 年第 7 期。

导向、评估主体、评估内容（客体、对象）、评估方法、评估结果的运用以及公共危机管理绩效评估的元评估等主要内容，并详尽阐述了评估指标设立的维度。吴建勋（2008）直接对地方政府应对非传统安全的能力评估展开研究。他认为非传统安全事件处理的绩效评估是非传统安全应对的最后一个环节，并对地方政府应对非传统安全的能力评估展开了探索性的论述，建构了由过程指标、结果指标和地方政府特色指标集成的一个指标体系。

从国内外的相关研究来看，对非传统安全政府应对能力评估的研究，不仅需要掌握各相关学科的知识与手段，还需要展开诸多学科的综合性研究。总的来说，学术界相关研究理论发展的主要趋势如下：

首先，研究方法日趋多样。对非传统安全政府应对能力评估的研究由过去主要侧重于定性研究转向对确定危机临界指标、构建非传统安全事件管理预警以及重大非传统安全事件管理的数学模型等定量化问题的研究。从单一学科研究转向多学科研究。学术界相关研究逐渐由过去的主要采用政治学的研究方法发展为政治学、管理学、社会学、统计学以及数学等多种学科研究方法的综合运用。同时，引入非传统安全分析假设模型研究，并将社会经济发展、政治发展的不平衡，传统文化等一系列变量因素引入非传统安全政府应对能力评估的理论研究中，丰富了当代非传统安全政府应对能力评估的理论研究方法和思路。

其次，研究领域逐步扩大。学术界在对不同政府应对非传统安全状况进行充分理性分析的基础上，试图解决一系列重要的理论与实践问题，研究领域由过去的重大自然灾害应对扩展到非传统安全的成因、政府应对风险、政府应对能力评估指标体系以及政府应对与危机发展的关系等研究层面。在操作层面上，国外非传统安全政府应对能力评估研究开始关注非传统安全事件预警、防范的可行性，政府应急管理决策的选择与危机控制的途径和方法；后危机管理的评价和改进；社会危机应对评估体制等。

再次，研究认识不断深入。随着理论深化和实践发展，在政府应对能力评估研究中对非传统安全事件的认识由最初的单一、偶发事件上升到循环发生、具有生命周期的事件。除了周期划分等细节外，在对政府应对能力的评估研究上也基本上对此达成共识，认为非传统安全事件像疾病一样，有一个特定的进程或发展周期，危机状态不是一下子形成的，政府也不可能将危机状态一下子拉回正常秩序。在不同的时期，政府发挥的作用以及政府应对的效果是不同的，相应的政府能力评估指标也会有变化。

最后，研究倾向于应对能力提升。除继续开展传统的非传统安全政府应对能力评估的基础理论研究外，更侧重于政府应对的体制与机制建设，非传统安全事件控制的途径和方法等涉及管理学科操作与技术层面研究，在评估政府应对能力的过程中研究提升政府能力的可行路径。非传统安全政府应对能力评估本身不再作为研究的最终目的，通过对危机的分析，归纳出解决危机的方法，才是相关研究的学术着眼点。通过对政府应对能力的科学评估，找出政府在非传统安全领域管理机制的缺失，进而分析提升政府应对非传统安全事件的可行途径。

但综观以上理论成果，我们可以发现，我国学术界对非传统安全政府应对能力评估这一课题的研究仍然还处在初级阶段，与国外相比尚显稚嫩。尤其要指出的是，在目前国内公共管理领域的著述中，关于非传统安全的应对能力评估如何在政府中运用，继而完善政府的相关能力研究少之又少，而且有不少研究成果局限于国外经验的介绍和关于我国政府危机管理绩效评估的初步探索，缺乏科学的评估标准和完整的评估框架。由此可见，尽管我国学术界开始重视对非传统安全政府应对能力评估，但是无论是政界还是学术界，对这一问题的研究深入程度还是远远不够的。

三、中国非传统安全环境与应对能力发展分析

1. 中国非传统安全环境分析

在非传统安全越来越受到政府重视的同时，中国所面临的非传统安全威胁也在不断地持续和加深。中国面对的非传统安全已从低风险进入多元风险加速集聚和陆续爆发的重要转型阶段，非传统安全威胁及其带来的安全事件已经从偶发性转向密集型、从零散性转向连带性、从小幅度转向大面积，典型的如公共危机事件呈现出高频次、大规模特征和常态化趋势。非传统安全威胁及其应对之所以被关注，不仅仅是由于它的强敏感性、高连带性和明显的聚集效应，更是因为其往往以危机突发的形式爆发，产生的影响会“内传”和“外溢”，造成大范围的连锁反应直至危害普遍安全。同时，伴随着全球化的进程，全球已经形成一个十分敏感的共振系统，国际国内的非传统安全威胁相互交织，国际因素可能影响国内的安全形态，国内安全问题的处理失当也将带来国际共振。这已是不争的事实，对非传统安全的关注及其应对迫在眉睫。这些都从不同侧面考验着政府的治理能力，政府必须“建立健全合理的长效机制以适应社会发展的需要，满足公众不断增长的公共需求”。[1] 中国非传统安全应对局势的严峻性，从近年来非传统安全发生的频率可见一斑(表1)。

环境恶化、资源危机、疾病流行、跨国犯罪、恐怖威胁，一些不发达地区的贫困、社会秩序不稳定，以及人权保障、主权让渡与干涉等问题困扰着中国。现实迫使中国政府反思确立以人为本的新的安全观以及加强非传统安全应对能力建设这一现实课题的紧迫性。中国政府在非传统安全应对的新历史阶段，提出了新的安全理念，即建设“和谐社会”。建设一个持久稳定、持续繁荣的和谐社会是人民和政府的共同愿望，也是中国发展的必然要求。这就要求政府从非传统安全应对的视野出发，秉持一种开放的态度来重视“人的安全”这一新安全理念的确立，重视灵活多样应对机制的构建，重视国际合作领域的开拓，重视政府自身应对能力的提高。结合中国当前面临的非传统安全环境，本文对中国面对的主要非传统安全因素进行识别和分类（表2）。

---

[1] 胡税根，徐元帅：《中国政府公共服务标准化建设的价值研究》，《肃行政学院学报》，2009 年第 5 期，第 47 ~ 48 页。

表1　近年中国非传统安全大事件

时间	事件回放
2003 年 12 月 23 日	重庆开县井喷事故。该事件是建国以来重庆历史上死亡人数最多、损失最重的一次特大安全事故
2004 年 2 月 15 日	吉林省吉林市中百商厦发生特大火灾，造成 54 人死亡，70 人受伤，直接经济损失 426 万元
2005 年 11 月	松花江水体污染。中国石油吉林化学工业公司双苯厂爆炸事故对松花江水体污染，威胁下游群众安全并造成国际影响
2005 年 6 月	四川发生“猪链球菌”感染事件
2007 年 3 月	山西汾阳“1·21”矿难，由于地方政府不作为，事故被瞒报
2007 年 7 月	山西省洪洞县“黑砖窑”虐待工人事件，惊动中央、轰动全国
2008 年 1 月以后	南方部分地区出现低温雨雪灾害，3287 万人受灾，倒塌房屋 3.1 万间；因灾直接经济损失 62.3 亿元
2008 年 3 月 14 日	西藏自治区拉萨 3·14 打砸抢烧事件
2008 年 4 月 28 日	胶济铁路火车相撞事故，事故造成死亡 72 人，受伤 416 人
2008 年 5 月 12 日	“5·12”大地震是中华人民共和国自建国以来有记录的最大地震，直接严重受灾地区达 10 万平方公里
2008 年 6 月 28 日	贵州瓮安“6·28”打砸抢烧事件
2008 年下半年	“三鹿”有毒奶粉事件、“毒鸡蛋”事件
2008 年 11 月 15 日	杭州地铁塌陷事故，致 21 人死亡
2008 年 11 月	重庆等地连续出现出租司机罢运事件
2008 年下半年起	美国次贷危机引发的全球金融危机，危机对我国经济造成重创……
2009 年 4 月份后	甲型 H1N1 流感（猪流感）疫情全球蔓延，至 2010 年 2 月 28 日，中国报告确诊病例 12.7 万例，死亡病例 793 例
2009 年 7 月 5 日	新疆乌鲁木齐“7·5”打砸抢烧严重暴力犯罪事件
2010 年年初	西南五省遭遇持续干旱天气，受灾群众达 6000 多万余人，200 多万人因旱返贫，当年经济损失超 350 亿元
2010 年 1 月 16 日	南宁至广州高速铁路广东云安县境内一隧道因塌方、泥石流冲击，造成 5 人死亡、4 人受伤、1 人失踪
2010 年 3 月 28 日	山西华晋焦煤有限责任公司王家岭煤矿发生特大透水事故，事故造成 153 人被困，38 人死亡
2010 年 4 月 14 日	青海省玉树藏族自治州玉树县发生 7.1 级地震，共造成 2220 人死亡，70 人失踪
2010 年 5 月 13 日	南方多个省市出现特大暴雨天气，造成浙江、江西、湖北、湖南、福建、广东等省局地发生洪涝灾害
2010 年 8 月 8 日	舟曲遭遇特大泥石流，造成 1463 人遇难，失踪 302 人，累计门诊治疗 2244 人
2010 年 9 月 20 日	受台风“凡亚比”影响，福建、广东、广西三省共 222.49 万人受灾，129 人因灾死亡，造成直接经济损失 60.90 亿元
2011 年 3 月 11 日	受日本福岛核危机影响，我国多个城市出现恐慌性抢购“碘盐”事件
2011 年 6 月 4 日	康菲公司 19－3 号油田发生石油泄漏事故，造成渤海 5500 平方公里受到污染
2011 年 7 月 23 日	两列高速列车在浙江温州附近追尾，致使 40 人死亡，近 200 人受伤
2011 年 11 月 16 日	甘肃省正宁县发生校车相撞事故，共造成 21 人死亡（其中包括 19 名儿童），43 人受伤

表 2　中国非传统安全分类及威胁表现

序号	非传统安全分类	威胁表现
1	社会安全	“疆独”和“藏独”分裂势力；宗教极端势力；暴力恐怖势力；境外国际敌对势力；邪教势力；国际公共安全问题等
2	环境安全	气候变化造成的干旱与洪涝灾害，土地荒漠化和沙尘暴，地震、酸雨、泥石流，以及冰雪灾害等
3	公共卫生安全	重大传染病、群体性疾病、食品药品安全、职业性疾病、自然与事故灾难引发的公共卫生安全等
4	经济安全	金融体系不稳定、产业结构不合理、城乡二元结构矛盾、区域经济失衡、外汇储备利用结构、国际经济动荡等
5	能源安全	能源种类不足、战略能源依赖进口、能源储备不足、缺少能源定价话语权、能源利用结构问题等
6	人口安全	人口老龄化、人口素质提高、男女比例失调、人口流动问题、人口素质提高等
7	文化安全	意识形态挑战、传统文化价值缺失、文化市场发展混乱等
8	信息安全	核心技术缺乏、网络舆论争夺、互联网文化渗透、网络防御能力建设、信息泄密隐患加重等

2. 中国非传统安全应对认知发展分析

改革开放以来，发展作为国家战略的最高目标一直未变，与之相适应，为发展提供安全保障的国家安全战略的主要目标也没有变。但是，在不同的时期和不同的发展阶段，中国应对非传统安全所面对的安全场域的重要性程度是不一样的。根据中国面对的实际情况以及安全观发展的不同阶段，可以将非传统安全的认知和应对划分为三个阶段：

一是中国初步应对非传统安全威胁挑战的时期。这一时期虽然冷战的思维和阴影依旧存在，但中国在对国际形势的判断和意识心理的认同上已经逐步开始发生转变。十一届三中全会确立了以经济发展为中心的国家战略和在和平的国际环境下一心搞经济建设的安全战略，改变了过去“战争与革命”的时代观和随时准备“早打、大打、打核战争”的安全战略。同时，探索“一国两制”的方式解决中国的统一问题，找到了一条通过和平方式完成统一大业的新途径。这一时期，军事和政治安全已不再是国家安全战略的唯一命题，中国政府开始逐步探索应对非传统安全的思路和方式，开始了彻底改变战略安全设定的历史转型。

二是中国多方面应对非传统安全挑战与“新安全观”形成的历史时期。苏联解体标志着长达近半个世纪的冷战彻底终结，中国面对的国际国内安全环境以及与之相适应的安全思维发生了急剧的变化。大国的国家安全战略不再以军事安全为重心，一些非军事威胁开始越来越多地危及国家的利益、社会的稳定以及人的安全。这一时期，中国明确了“和平与发展”作为时代主题的安全思维，开始逐步拓展安全的内涵，越来越重视军事和政治威胁之外的国家安全问题，对非传统安全的研究和应对探索逐步规范化、体系化，为新安全观的确立提供了重要的思路和构想。

三是中国全面应对非传统安全挑战与国家安全战略再定位时期。进入21世纪，传统安全没有弱化，非传统安全却更加凸显，中国国家安全环境比冷战时代更为复杂和严峻、更为不确定和复合化。中国开始全面应对非传统安全问题，正式将非传统安全纳入政府的执政议程和执政能力建设的范畴。面对越来越明显的非传统安全威胁，中国逐渐更新安全观念、调整安全战略，不断提高自己的应对能力，以“和谐世界”和“和谐社会”的安全立意及发展目标，越来越多地赢得国际社会的认可，为发展中国家和世界各国人民做出了贡献。❶改革开放30年来，中国在非传统安全威胁的应对中完成了从不自觉到自觉、从非战略高度到战略高度、从零散到系统、从被动到主动的发展过程。伴随这一过程的是，非传统安全问题从非战略高度进入到国家安全战略的高度；非传统安全引申的新安全观，从不被关注进入到国家安全战略理论体系；非传统安全能力建设越来越显得迫切并受到重视，党的十六大报告、十七大报告已经明确将非传统安全应对纳入其执政议程。

3. 中国政府非传统安全应对能力发展分析

从上一节的分析可以发现，近年来非传统安全在中国发生的频率呈明显上升的趋势，非典爆发、禽流感、2008年冰雪灾害、“5·12”大地震以及2010年上半年西南地区的特大旱情，都在考验着中国政府应对非传统安全的能力。在一次又一次的非传统安全应对中，SARS爆发和“5·12”大地震抗震救灾是全面展示当时中国政府应对非传统安全的典型案例。

在SARS应对初期，中国政府应对非传统安全的能力存在严重的不足和漏洞，不仅未能及时扭转危机局势，而且也受到了公众的广泛质疑。“2002年年底，中国广东佛山爆发SARS。2003年2月，广东当地卫生部门并未引起重视，导致该病毒由佛山市蔓延至广州市；4月初，SARS迅速传播到中国各地，造成349人死亡。一时间，全国上下人心惶惶，每个人都在买口罩、量体温、喝中药。”❷ 面对SARS的爆发，中国政府表现出的非传统安全应对能力低下，说明在此之前应对能力建设的缺失。首先在SARS爆发之初，政府部门缺乏足够的重视，也毫无处理大范围非传统安全威胁的经验，导致病毒迅速蔓延；其次在危机公关方面，政府进行了信息封锁，犯下了隐瞒和歪曲疫情的错误。虽然政府的出发点是平息公众恐慌，维持社会稳定。但当疫情失控而在全国范围内爆发时，则引起了更大的恐慌和对政府的不信任，使得中国政府形象严重受损。直到SARS疫情在北京再度爆发，政府才意识到事情的严重性，临时组建了吴仪总理领导的组织体系，采取措施动员社会配合应对，并正确引导舆论，但那时已经失去了非传统安全应对的最佳时期。在“5·12”抗震救灾中，中国政府的非传统安全应对得到了锻炼，具备了一定的非传统安全整体应对能力。首先在应对意识上，中国政府不仅给予了足够的重视，而且还表现出了战胜危机的坚定信心；其次在应对效率上，中国政府在这次抗震救灾过程中

---

❶ 余潇枫、李佳：《非传统安全中国的认知与应对（1978～2008年）》，载：《世界经济与政治》，2008年第8期。

❷ 薛澜：《危机管理——转型期中国面临的挑战》，清华大学出版社，2003年版。

也表现出了非常高的效率。快速应急反应使救援队伍抓住了最有力的时机，从而保证了整个救灾工作的效率；三是在社会动员方面，完全透明、及时的信息传递，极大地调动了公众参与和配合的积极性。在一些危机应对过程中，以温家宝总理为代表的高级官员亲赴灾区第一线，做出了许多令人感动的行为，带动了中国传统文化中的“清官崇拜”的情节，极大地感染了普通民众。❶

经过历次非传统安全应对的考验，中国政府的应对能力建设已经具备了可持续发展的基础条件。具体表现在：一是“以人为本”安全观的确立。长期以来，在中国政府意识中“国家安全”往往比人的生命更重要。但是在最近历次非传统安全应对中，可以看到政府始终将人民的生命安全放在第一位；二是应对体系初步建立。政府已经逐渐掌握了非传统安全发生和发展的过程阶段，并通过专门理论和专业技术的应用，在每一个阶段建立相应的应对机制，从而改变了过去临时应对的局面；三是信息披露机制建设得到了重视。政府反思和总结了SARS应对的教训，在应对能力建设中重视信息的准确披露和舆论的引导，树立了政府权威；四是政府敢于面对和承担责任。在2008年冰冻灾害的应对中，CNN在报道《中国总理为雪灾造成的交通混乱道歉》时说道：“中国总理温家宝向由于恶劣天气和电能危机被困在全国各火车站的成千上万名旅客道歉。对于中国政治家来说，这是一个罕见的举动。”政府的正面应对和抚慰民心的行为反映出政府应对非传统安全时敢于直面公众，正视失误与困境的态度。

综合来看，虽然中国政府应对非传统安全的能力不断改善，也经受了数次重大危机的考验，但是非传统安全应对形式日益严峻和政府应对能力相对不足之间的矛盾仍然显得十分突出。在政府应对能力建设进行反思和总结的基础上，仍然需要通过合适的理论框架来对中国政府应对非传统安全的能力进行科学的评估。

四、政府非传统安全应对能力评估指标体系的构建

1. 指标体系构建的概念模型

目前，政府绩效评估方法主要有“4E”标准、标杆管理法和平衡记分卡法。“4E”评价法是政府能力评估在方法探索上的开端，标杆管理法预示着对政府能力全面评估的开始，平衡记分卡法有助于政府以长远的眼光对社会的发展提出愿景并作出战略规划，思考其在社会发展中应承担的使命，指导政府能力评估。

平衡计分卡（Balanced Score Card，以下简称BSC）是一种全面衡量企业健康状况和企业价值的综合企业管理评估方法。20世纪90年代，卡普兰（Robert S. Kaplan）和诺顿（David Norton）第一次提出用平衡计分卡的方法对企业管理进行测评，此后，BSC一直受到西方实业界和学术界的广泛关注。BSC是以公司战略为中心，将企业及其内部各部门的任务和决策转化为多样的、相互联系的目标，再将目标分解为多项指标的多元业绩评价系统。具体来说，它将组织经营任务的决策转化为四个维度的指标：财务、顾客、内部过程、学习和成长，将

❶ 李洋：《以汶川地震为视角看中国政府的危机管理》，《法制与社会》，2008年第8期，第198页。

组织战略分解为这四个维度的考察目标，每一考察目标分别设置几个独立的指标，多种指标组成了相互联系的一个系列的指标体系，这些目标和指标既保持一致又相互加强，构成了一个有机的统一体，从而达到财务指标与非财务指标、短期与长期、内部与外部、过去与未来之间的平衡，有利于实现组织的整体战略目标。

平衡计分卡的思想不仅适用于企业管理，它同样可以反映许多政府部门和其他公共部门的实际状况，但多运用于政府绩效评估。对于政府部门的能力评估来说，其指标体系的设计更强调一种“均衡”的理念，如长期目标与近期目标、部门竞争与协作、公平与效率、发展与稳定之间的均衡。而BSC的思维指标体系的多维度评估模式可以满足政府部门能力评估的这些要求。平衡计分卡在公共部门中运用的基本构建框架如图2所示。

通过这样的评估，以服务型政府为愿景的政府部门，从顾客角度对民众的需求进行了回应；从内部流程角度将民众需求落实为具体指标；从财务的角度提高了公共资源的使用效率；从学习和创新的角度保证了政府服务的可持续发展。

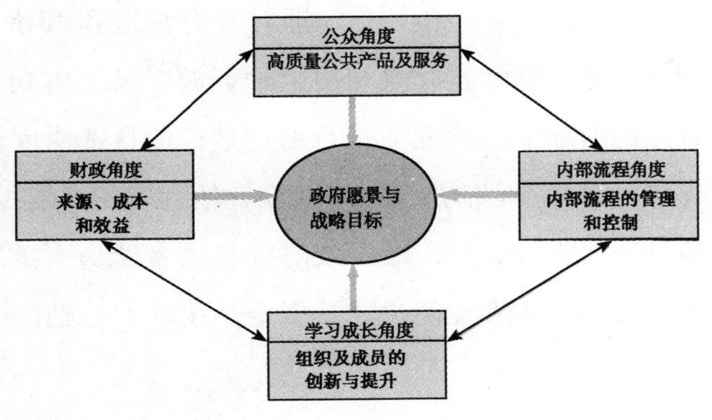

图2　公共部门的平衡计分卡评估基本框架

本文借鉴BSC评估模型框架来构建非传统安全政府应对能力评估的指标。由于政府服务的对象是社会公众，而在非传统安全应对中资源和环境是保障政府应对的重要方面，因此在指标体系构建中对BSC框架作适度调整，以符合非传统安全政府应对能力评估的实际。调整后的指标构建模型同样划分四个维度，分别是民众维度、资源环境维度、内部管理控制维度和学习成长维度。

2. 政府非传统安全应对能力评估目标和内容

(2) 评估目标

“政府效能的改善”（而非“奖优罚劣”）是政府能力评估的目标。因此，非传统安全政府应对能力评估的目标应该是在非传统安全应对职责上政府效能的完善和不断提高。具体来看，其评估目标可以分解为如下几个方面：首先，公共部门的价值导向引导其应对能力的评估目标，这些价值取向在非传统安全的应对过程中具体通过政府应对效率、危机管理能力、公共责任、对民众生命和财产利益的重视和保护程度、社会公众的满意程度等价值判断来实现；其次，以这些价值判断为基础，对非传统安全状态下政府的应对体系和应对能力做出评价，总结经验并发现其中存在的问题和不足；再次，完善非传统安全状态下政府的危机管理制度，提高政府在非传统安全领域的应急能力和恢复能力，防止同类问题的重复发生，并寻求进一步发展的机会。

(2) 评估内容

罗伯特希斯将非传统安全应对中的政府危机

管理概括为4R模式，即划分为缩减、预备、反应和恢复阶段。[1] 本文将事前的缩减和预备过程化作一个过程，从而将非传统安全应对中的政府管理分为事前管理阶段、实时管理阶段（即事中管理阶段）、事后管理阶段三个阶段。因此，对非传统安全政府应对能力的评估也应该包括这三个阶段政府管理机制和管理能力的全部内容，并在此基础上做出综合评价。同样，按照这三个过程管理阶段的划分，具体评估内容可以分为如下几个方面：

第一，制度性基础工作评估。将危机消灭在萌芽状态或者提前预防危机发生是最经济也是最成功的非传统安全政府应对管理方法。制度性基础工作评估主要涉及的就是危机发生之前政府部门预警机制和事前风险管理能力的评估。具体包括如下评估：风险与预警体系评估，即政府是否能够提前进行风险识别并发现潜在的风险，进而排除潜在风险；对没有排除的潜在风险是否有相应的预警管理机制，从而将危机消灭在萌芽状态或者尽量使危机损失减少到最小；公众危机意识评估，即政府是否能够培养并引导公众的危机意识，增强公众识别、应对危机的能力和信心；事前准备体系评估，即政府是否在非传统安全之前建立完备有效的应急预案和演习体系，是否具备危机应对的物质技术储备和物质管理体系；组织体系评估，即政府非传统安全应对的组织设置是否合理，组织及其成员是否具备相应的素质、能力和经验；法律体系评估，即是否有专门的法律和法规体系来指导和规范政府的危机管理，是否通过专门的法律来赋予和限定政府权责；信息系统评估，即政府在应对非传统安全过程中日常监测、信息积累、分析预测等方面的能力和效果，以及信息披露机制是否完备；决策指挥体系评估，即对政府相应的决策方法、决策咨询和监控系统、决策者能力、决策理论准备等进行的评估。

第二，实时应对能力评估。实时应对能力是在非传统安全发生过程中，政府根据危机发生、发展的状况及时反应、科学决策、合理应对，从而及时、有效应对危机，减少危机造成的损失，并恢复社会稳定和公众对政府信任的能力。由于非传统安全应对过程中时间的高度紧张性、信息的有限性、资源的极度匮乏性以及管理目标的动态权变性，所以实时应对能力评估中应该兼顾政府危机管理的合理性和合法性，统筹评估政府的应对能力和应对措施。这一阶段的评估包括如下方面：信息沟通能力评估，即非传统安全的识别、上报，以及政府应对过程中信息传递和不同部门沟通有效程度的评估；救援能力评估，即对政府减轻非传统安全造成的损失，保护公众生命财产安全的能力，以及相应的物质和心理救援体系的评估；社会参与评估，即对民众与民间组织参与非传统安全应对状况，以及与政府合作有效性进行的评估；国际合作评估，即对政府营造和引导国际舆论，争取和有效利用国际资源，以及树立良好的国际形象的能力进行的评估；信息透明度评估，即对政府信息公开和公众知情程度的评估；应急处理能力评估，即对政府应急决策能力、执行能力、媒体管理能力，及资金、技术、后勤保

---

[1] ［美］罗伯特·希斯著：《危机管理》，王成等译，北京：中信出版社，2001年版。

障能力等的评估。

第三，事后反馈机制评估。这是对非传统安全政府应对实际效果和政府能力持续改善方面的评估，包括政府危机管理实际效果和政府学习创新能力的评估两个方面。具体来说，事后反馈机制评估内容，可以从量和质两个方面进行细分。"量"的评估表明的是非传统安全政府应对效率，包括：投入和产出的比例评估，资金利用效率评估，危机管理中政府无形损耗及其变化趋向，以及危机后救援体制的评估等。"质"的评估表明的是非传统安全政府应对能力的持续改善与提高，以及社会公众的满意程度，包括：政府学习创新能力的评估，政府形象管理能力评估，及公众满意度评估等。具体来说包括：恢复能力评估，即非传统安全发生之后，政府维护社会稳定，迅速恢复人民生产、生活秩序的能力评估；反馈管理评估，即危机发生之后，政府反思和评价危机应对过程中的资源利用效率、民众满意程度、善后管理和形象恢复的能力评估；学习和提升能力评估，即政府从非传统安全中获利，调整组织和人员、改善危机管理机制、进行流程再造能力的评估。

3. 指标的筛选原则

为了利用所建立的指标体系对非传统安全的政府应对能力进行有效地评价，在构建指标体系和选取指标时必须遵守一些基本原则。许多专家学者已对评估指标的选取原则做过论述，结合非传统安全政府应对能力评估的特点，除科学性、稳定性、结构性等一般原则之外，还应该着重考虑以下基本原则：

第一，可操作性原则。指标体系中的指标应有可测性和可比性，操作使用方便，指标体系应尽可能简化，计算方法简单，数据容易获得，便于推广。

第二，概括性原则。非传统安全政府应对能力的概念具有深刻而丰富的内涵，这就要求描述和刻画概念的指标体系既要有足够的涵盖面，又要把握关键要素，不可能面面俱到。在指标选取上要尽可能全面而概括的反映此项评估三方面内容的各个侧面，对于主要内容不应遗漏。

第三，可靠性原则。指标的选取是进行科学评估的基础，指标的可靠性是指标体系构建过程必须注意的环节。为此，指标的选取必须有一定的理论基础做支撑，并通过相对合理的模型框架形成科学的指标体系。

第四，动态性和稳定性相结合原则。指标是一种随时空变化的参数，不同的事件或不同的发展阶段可能需要不同的指标，因此指标的选择要保留一定的弹性，同时，指标也应该要保证一定范围和一定时期内的稳定，以便进行评价。

4. 指标体系构建

指标体系的构建是非传统安全政府应对能力评估的基础与前提，指标设计的好坏直接影响到评估的可操作性和可靠性，因此，能力评估指标的设置必须在非传统安全政府能力评估理论基础的指导下，根据对非传统安全和政府能力评估相关理论的探索及理解，遵循指标设计的原则进行。

本研究将平衡计分卡的评估模型应用到非传统安全政府能力评估体之中，从政府应对非传统安全的战略目标出发，在 BSC 四个维度的范围内建立相应的指标体系。根据对非传统安全政府能力评估内容的分析基础，我们对平衡计分卡的四个维度做出调整，建立了非传统安全政府应对能力评估的指标模型框架。(见图 3)

依据这个模型框架，我们将设计包括民众、资源环境、内部管理与控制和学习成长四个维度的指标体系：

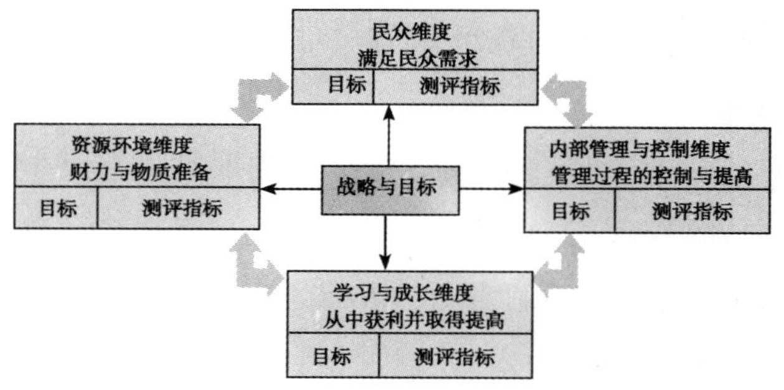

图 3　政府非传统安全应对能力评估的平衡计分卡

(1) 民众维度指标

该维度关注的是，在政府应对非传统安全的过程中，“人的安全”如何得到有效的保障。“人的安全”主要指每个个体的基本政治权利与生存权利应当得到有效的保护，这是与个体所处的国家安全和政治稳定密不可分的。该层次的主要指标便是民众安全需求满足的质量和水平。满足民众需求的主要因素便是政府部门优质高效的服务，因此能否把为民众服务的概念贯彻到非传统安全应对的每一个环节，培养民众危机应对的能力并引导其支持政府应对非传统安全的行为，是衡量政府非传统安全应对能力的重要方面。

由此，本文将这一维度的目标分为一个一级指标，即服务能力，它是政府应对非传统安全中为满足公众需求而提供的公共服务的水平和质量。在这个一级指标下设二级指标 3 个：第一，民众配合程度。在非传统安全发生时，民众是否信任政府，并给予政府行为积极的回应，是衡量政府能力的重要方面；第二，民众抗危机能力。在应对非传统安全方面，政府如何强化公民的危机防范意识，完善应对灾难的培训和实地演习等素质教育，都通过这一指标表现出来；第三，民众知情程度。公民的知情权是其不可剥夺的权利。政府利用公开的、为人们所熟知的渠道和方式向公众传递各种有利于组织协调运转、危机弱化或化解的信息，及时公布事实真相，才能保障政府应对措施的科学和应对行为的持续。

(2) 资源环境维度指标

该维度关注的是，政府是否有充足的财力和物质准备应对突如其来的非传统安全，如何利用现有的资源适应和改变危机的环境。在此维度之下，政府既要保证资源的数量，也要提高资源的利用效率，还要营造良好的环境以保障政府应对行为的及时有效。

资源环境维度的指标要涵盖非传统安全政府应对能力两个方面的评估内容。一是在非传统安全状态下，现有的物质准备可以支撑政府的应对行为，政府有能力实现有限资源的充分利用，从而实现在“不浪费有限资源的情况下提供充分的服务”以及“必须的服务随时可以保障”的目标。[1] 二是政府的应对行为能够与环境的变化相适应，并能够培养和引导充分利用现有公共资源和

[1] R. kaplan, D. Norton Ten balanced score card – measures that drive performance Havard Business Review, 1992, 70 (1): 71 – 79.

调动社会资源的环境，从而最大限度的保障国家利益和公民的生命财产安全。本文将这一维度的指标分为两个一级指标：

第一，资源保障能力是在非传统安全的应对中政府在物质资源方面的保障水平，以及对相应资源的利用程度。具体有三个二级指标对其进行分解。一是资源储备程度。这一指标描述，在政府应对非传统安全的过程中，其物质资源的保障程度；二是公共风险支出水平。这一指标表明，政府预防和控制非传统安全的财政开支在整个政府预算支出中的比例；三是资源整合调度水平。这表明政府对非传统安全应对资源利用的合理程度，包括公共资源和各种社会资源。

第二，环境保障能力是指政府行为与环境相适应，并适时引导环境发展的程度，包括信息利用、法律法规、政府形象等，包括四个三级指标：一是法制健全度。法律法规在非传统安全发生领域内的覆盖程度、完善程度以及可操作性直接关系到政府权责关系以及应对流程的规范程度；二是信息管理水平。信息管理贯穿于非传统安全应对的全过程，及时、充分、可靠的信息提供是防范和化解危机的主要手段。信息收集、处理和利用的水平决定着政府决策是否科学合理；三是政府形象维护水平。这一指标反映的是在非传统安全的处理中，政府在国内民众和国际社会建立、保持和恢复良好形象的能力；四是舆论引导水平。“新闻媒体是公众认知世界的桥梁，监督社会的公器”。[1] 非传统安全一旦发生，无论是民众还是媒体界都有迫切的知情权诉求。因此，政府要对新闻舆论进行合理的引导，“权威”“确切”的满足公众的知情权。

（3）内部管理与控制维度指标

该维度的目标在于加强非传统安全政府应对中各个流程的控制，提高政府应对的质量和效率。这一目标的实现，需要政府部门不断完善其内部控制和业务流程。这一维度的非传统安全政府应对能力评估，主要考核两个方面的内容：一是政府应对行为成本的最小化；二是政府应对行为效益的最大化。因此，这一维度范围内的评估涉及政府非传统安全应对的整个过程，是对政府组织的运行过程、运行内容以及运行结果进行全面评估的活动。

在这一维度本文设计了三个一级指标（预警管理能力、应变管理能力、恢复管理能力）和11个二级指标来评估这一维度范围内的政府应对能力。下面是各个指标设置的内涵介绍：

第一，预警管理能力即在非传统安全发生之前政府部门的预防和准备程度。下设四个二级指标：一是监测系统能力。这是指政府监测系统可以对政治、经济、社会、自然等环境进行观测，收集非传统安全可能发生的内部信息和外部环境信息，并将收集到的信息进行科学分析和识别，评估判断事件发生的概率和可能造成的危害程度，并对每一种可能性进行分类管理；二是应对计划完备程度。在应对非传统安全时，最重要的是未雨绸缪，在其发生之前就应制定完备的应急计划以对危机进行总体部

[1] 贺文发：《突发事件与对外报道》，中国传媒大学出版社，2008年版，第55～56页。

署。应对计划包括应对流程、应急预案以及相应的权责关系等。这一指标考察的是政府应对计划的可操作性和协同性；三是组织结构的合理性。反映了非传统安全应对中，政府组织结构设置的完备和合理程度；四是人员综合素质。反映的是在处理非传统安全方面，政府内部人员的综合能力和水平。

第二，应变管理能力是指政府随着非传统安全的发生和发展而采取合理应对行为的能力。下设四个二级指标：一是决策指挥能力。非传统安全应对决策指挥系统是指在非传统安全发生中负责对重大问题进行决策，并领导与指挥本行政区域内相关处理工作的体系。决策指挥系统能不能科学、合理、及时地做出反应和部署，是衡量一个国家和政府非传统安全应对能力的主要因素；二是协调配合能力。这一方面的能力包括政府纵向体系、政府横向体系以及政府与社会体系的协调和整合。一些国家的成功经验表明，非传统安全应对的成败关键在于是否有一套高效、和谐的综合协调机制；三是现场执行能力。判断政府部门非传统安全应对在执行控制方面的有效程度，关键就是能否高效贯彻决策指挥系统的决策，在最短的时间内调动各种社会资源来解决危机；四是国际合作能力。近年来许多非传统安全造成的危机都表现出国际合作应对的特点，能否有效展开国际合作已经成为各国政府成功处理非传统安全的一个必不可少的条件。

第三，恢复管理能力，即在非传统安全发生之后政府迅速恢复社会秩序的能力，包括三个二级指标：一是物质恢复能力。在一般情况下，非传统安全造成的损失必须通过一定的物质方面的重建工作加以减轻，包括：基础设施的恢复、公民生命安全的关注以及公民财产损失的补偿、恢复和重建等；二是社会恢复能力。这是指在非传统安全处理中，政府迅速恢复正常的社会生产生活秩序和自身形象的程度；三是心理恢复能力。非传统安全很容易造成民众身心巨大的创伤，恰当的心理干预和心理救助体现了现代政府更多的人文关怀。衡量心理恢复能力的关键是政府心理援助机制的完善程度。

（4）学习成长维度指标

该维度关注的是政府在非传统安全应对中反思、学习和提高的能力。政府应对能力能否持续得到改进和提高，取决于组织的创新和学习能力。在这一维度设定一个一级指标，即学习和成长能力，也就是政府部门通过非传统安全取得能力提高的程度。针对政府的得利状况，本文针对性地提出了四个二级指标：一是激励奖惩水平，即政府在非传统安全之后对内部组织和人员责任追究的合理程度；二是应对机制改造程度。这是用来衡量政府进行反思并持续改善非传统安全应对机制的能力；三是理论技术改进程度。该项指标是指政府不断改进现有的非传统安全应对理论和专业技术的程度；四是人员专业培训水平。此项指标用来评价政府对其内部人员针对非传统安全应对进行培训和演练的能力。

根据上述在 BSC 框架之下的政府非传统安全应对能力评估指标设置的论述，结合层次分析法的相关理论，可以构建出非传统安全政府应对能力评估指标体系（见表3）。

表 3　非传统安全政府应对能力评估指标体系

目标层		一级指标	二级指标
非传统安全政府应对能力	民众维度	服务能力	民众配合程度
			民众抗危机能力
			民众知情程度
	资源环境维度	资源保障能力	资源储备程度
			公共风险支出水平
			资源整合调度水平
		环境保障能力	法制健全度
			信息管理水平
			政府形象维护水平
			舆论引导水平
	内部管理与控制维度	预警管理能力	监测系统能力
			应对计划完备程度
			组织结构的合理性
			人员综合素质
		应变能力	决策指挥能力
			协调配合能力
			现场执行能力
			国际合作能力
		恢复管理能力	物质恢复能力
			社会恢复能力
			心理恢复能力
	学习和成长维度	学习成长能力	激励奖惩水平
			应对机制改造程度
			理论技术改进程度
			人员专业培训水平

五、政府非传统安全应对能力评估指标的权重设计

1. 问卷调研与数据的收集

由于非传统安全政府应对能力的评估是专业性比较强的一个领域，不同于一般社科类的调查研究可以大范围地覆盖大多数群众。对非传统安全政府应对能力评估的调查研究所面向的群体必须具备一定的专业背景，比如管理学、国际关系学、社会学、政府管理等，并且最好具有一定的社会阅历。

根据上述分析，本次对非传统安全政府能力评估调查问卷的发放范围是相关领域学者、政府公务人员、相关专业研究生和 MPA 学生，这一范围内的调查对象不仅具备一定的专业知识、对非传统安全和政府管理领域有着一定的认知和了解，而且作为具有一定社会阅历的人群，其大部分有一定时间的相关工作经验或者知识积累，具有较丰富的阅历，对国家的安全领域有着独到深入的认识和理解，完全符合本次调查研究所要求的条件。

本次调查共发放问卷 280 份，回收问卷 227 份，回收率为 81.1%，其中，有效问卷为 204 份，占回收问卷的 89.9%。调研对象分布结构是，专家学者比重为 5%，公务员比重为 37%，MPA 及全日制研究生比重为 55%，其他为 3%。

问卷调研的主要内容是非传统安全应对能力重要性打分以及“5·12”大地震中中国政府各项应对能力打分。问卷采用李可特 5 点量表的标准形式，问卷经多轮试测与完善基本符合研究设计的要求。在数据处理中，本文直接将问卷选项通过一定数学方法进行无量纲处理。

2. 基于 AHP 法的指标权重确定

(1) AHP 法原理

A. 层次分析法。层次分析法（The Analytic Hierarchy Process，简称 AHP 法）是美国著名运筹学家萨迪（T. L. Saaty）于 20 世纪 70 年代初期提

出的，[1] 从本质上讲，层次分析法是模糊数学的应用，是一种将人们的经验、逻辑、客观、理性和数学的推理完美结合的定量化数学工具和决策方法，是一种应用广泛的模型工具。[2] 具体步骤如下：[3]

B. 分析系统中各因素的关系，建立递阶层次结构

对同一层次的各因素关于上一层次中某一准则的重要性进行两两比较构造判断矩阵；

以判断矩阵 B 为例（表4）。

矩阵中元素相对重要性的比例标度及定义（表5）。

表4 判断矩阵 B

A	B_1	B_2	…	B_M
B_1	b_{11}	b_{12}	…	b_{1m}
B_2	b_{21}	b_{22}	…	b_{2m}
…	…	…	…	…
B_M	b_{m1}	B_{m2}	…	b_{mm}

表5 相对重要性比例标度及定义

标度（$f(x, y)$）	定义
1	因素 x 与因素 y 同样重要
3	因素 x 比因素 y 略重要
5	因素 x 比因素 y 较重要
7	因素 x 比因素 y 明显重要
9	因素 x 比因素 y 绝对重要
2，4，6，8	为以上两判断之间的中间状态
倒数	对于因素 B_i 和 B_j 作相互比较判断，得到一个值判断 b_{ij}，则 $b_{ij}=1/b_{ji}$

C. 计算同一准则下各要素的相对权重

在同一准则下求解各指标相对权重问题，在数学上也就是计算判断矩阵最大特征根及其对应的特征向量问题，在矩阵 B 中，即是 $BW=\lambda W$，解出最大特征根 λ_{max} 及对应的特征向量 W，将 λ_{max} 所对应的最大特征向量归一化，就得到 B_1，B_2，…，B_m 相对于 A 的权重值。[4]

计算判断矩阵最大特征根及其对应的特征向量的方法有多种，本文采用精确度比较高的方根法。具体计算方法如下：

①计算判断矩阵 B 的每一行元素的乘积

$$M_i = \prod_{j=1}^{n} x_{ij} \quad i = 1,2,\cdots,n \qquad \text{（式5-1）}$$

②计算 n 次方根

$$\overline{w_i} = \sqrt[n]{Mi} \qquad \text{（式5-2）}$$

③对向量 $\bar{w} = (\bar{w}_1,\bar{w}_2,\cdots,\bar{w}_n)T$ 进行规范归一化

$$\widehat{w}_i = \frac{\bar{w}_i}{\sum_{j=1}^{n}\bar{w}_j} \qquad \text{（式5-3）}$$

矢量 $\widehat{w}=(\widehat{w}_1, \widehat{w}_2, \cdots, \widehat{w}_n)T$ 即为所求的特征向量。

D. 一致性检验

由于客观事物的复杂性或对事物认识的片面性，透过所构造的判断矩阵求出的特征向量（权值）是否合理，需要对判断矩阵进行一致性和随机性检验，检验公式为：

$$C.R. = C.I./R.I. \qquad \text{（式5-4）}$$

---

[1] 赵焕臣、许树柏：《层次分析法》，科学出版社，1990年版。

[2] 周庆行、唐峰：《公共危机决策绩效评估指标权重研究——基于层次分析法》，载：《理论与改革》，2005年第6期。

[3] 孙建军、成颖、邵佳宏等：《定量分析方法》，南京大学出版社，2002年版。

[4] 孙建军、成颖、邵佳宏等，《定量分析方法》，南京大学出版社，2002年版，第164～165页。

C. R. （consistency ratio）——为判断矩阵的一致性比率；

C. I. （consistency index）——为判断矩阵的一致性指标；

$$CI = \frac{\lambda_{\max} - m}{m - 1} \quad （式 5-5）$$

$\lambda_{\max}$——最大特征根

$$\lambda_{\max} = \frac{1}{n}\sum_{i=1}^{n}\frac{(A\widehat{w})_i}{\widehat{w}_i} \quad i = 1,2,\cdots,n \quad （式 5-6）$$

式中（$A\widehat{w}$）$_i$ 为向量 $A\widehat{w}$ 的第 i 个向量

m——判断矩阵阶数

R. I. （random index）——判断矩阵的平均随机一致性指标

随着判断矩阵阶数的增加，决策者判断一致性的难度逐渐增大，平均随机一次性指标 R. I. 即用来衡量不同阶矩阵的一致性。❶ 本文根据上文所设置的判断阶数的数量来查找 1～5 阶判断矩阵的 R. I. 值，如表 6。

表 6　平均随机一致性指标

矩阵阶数	1	2	3	4	5
R. I.	0	0	0. 52	0. 89	1. 12
矩阵阶数	6	7	8	9	10
R. I	1. 26	1. 36	1. 41	1. 46	1. 49

当 C. R. <0. 10 时，即认为判断矩阵具有满意的一致性，否则，就需要对判断矩阵进行调整，直至具有满意的一致性为止。❷

E. 计算各个元素对系统目标的合成权重

上面得到的是一组对其上一级中某指标的权重向量，而最终要得到每个指标对总目标的权重，即所谓合成权重。假定经过计算，B_1，B_2，B_3，…，B_m 对一级指标 A 的权重为 b_1，b_2，b_3，…，b_m，三级指标层 C 中的各指标 C_1，C_2，C_3，… C_n，对二级指标层 B 中的指标 B_1，B_2，B_3，…，B_m 的权重分别为 W_{11}，W_{21}，W_{31}，…，W_{n1}；W_{12}，W_{22}，W_{32}，…，W_{n2}；…；W_{1m}，W_{2m}，W_{3m}，…，W_{nm}。则三级指标中的 n 个指标对一级指标 A 的权重值分别为 W_1，W_2，W_3，…，W_n，其计算公式为：❸

$$W_i = b_i \cdot w_{ij} \quad i = 1,2,\cdots,n \quad j = 1,2,\cdots,m \quad （式 5-7）$$

其中：W_i 表示三级指标层中第 i 个指标 C_i 对一级指标层 A 的权重；

B_j 表示二级指标层中第 j 个指标 B_j 对一级指标层 A 的权重；

Wi_j 表示三级指标层中第 i 个指标 C_i 对二级指标层第 j 个指标 B_j 的权重。

（2）政府非传统安全应对能力评估指标权重确定

A. 构造政府非传统安全应对能力层次结构

在论文第四部分构建的非传统安全政府应对能力评估指标体系的基础上，根据 AHP 法指标权重确定的步骤，依照目标层、准则层和要素层的对应关系排列，形成相对应的递阶层次结构，如图 4 所示。

❶ 迟娜娜：《城市灾害应急能力评价指标体系研究》，首都经济贸易大学硕士学位论文，2006 年。

❷ 孙建军、成颖、邵佳宏等：《定量分析方法》，南京大学出版社，2002 年版，第 167 页。

❸ 迟娜娜：《城市灾害应急能力评价指标体系研究》，首都经济贸易大学硕士学位论文，2006 年。

这里主要根据 n 个元素 U_1，U_2，…，U_n 对于某准则的判断矩阵 A，求出它们对于此准则的相对权重 W_1，W_2，…，W_n，并最终求出各个指标相对于评估目标的指标权重。在这一节，文章的分析要解决两个问题，一个是单项指标权重的确定，另一个是判断矩阵一致性检验。

a. 准则层（一级指标）相对权重的判断矩阵。B_1、B_2、B_3、B_4、B_5、B_6、B_7 分别代表政府应对非传统安全的服务能力、政府应对非传统安全的资源保障能力、政府应对非传统安全的环境保障能力、政府应对非传统安全的预警管理能力、政府应对非传统安全的应变管理能力、政府应对非传统安全的恢复管理能力、政府应对非传统安全的学习成长能力对确定非传统安全政府应对能力评估的重要性程度。矩阵中的重要性标度数据来自经过统计软件 SPSS 处理的问卷数据以及表 5 的相对重要性比例标度的参考。

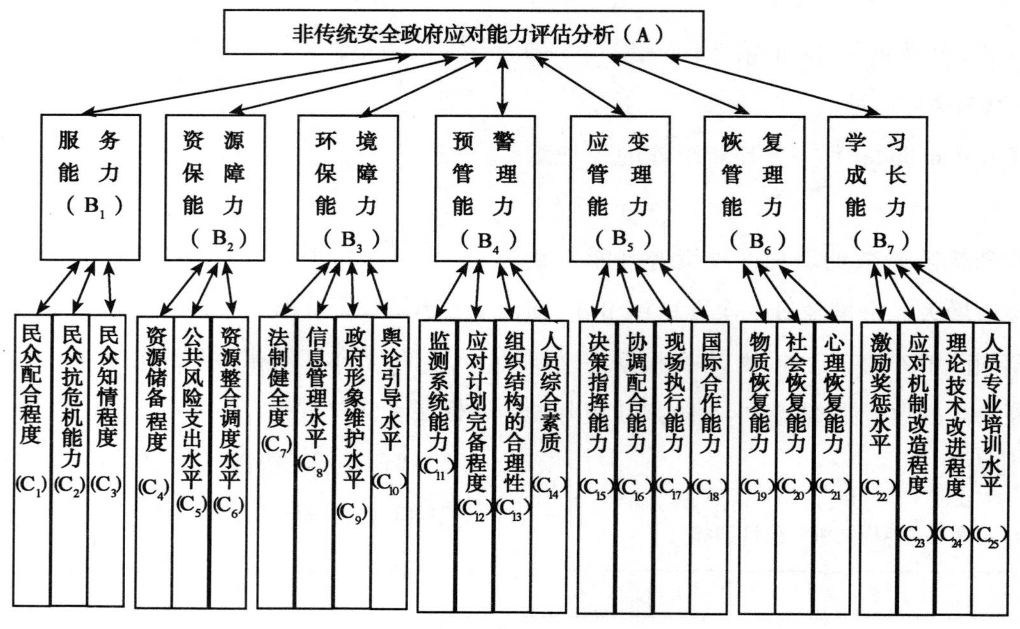

图 4　非传统安全政府应对能力评估的指标层次构造

表 7　准则层相对权重表

A	B_1	B_2	B_3	B_4	B_5	B_6	B_7	$\overline{w_i}=\sqrt[n]{\prod_{j=1}^{n}x_{ij}}$	$\widehat{w}_i=\frac{\overline{w_i}}{\sum_{j=1}^{n}\overline{w_j}}$
B_1	1	1	5/4	1	9/10	13/12	13/12	1.04	0.148
B_2	1	1	5/4	1	9/10	13/12	13/12	1.04	0.148
B_3	4/5	4/5	1	4/5	3/4	5/6	5/6	0.83	0.118
B_4	1	1	5/4	1	9/10	13/12	13/12	1.04	0.148
B_5	10/9	10/9	4/3	10/9	1	5/4	5/4	1.16	0.165
B_6	12/13	12/13	6/5	12/13	4/5	1	1	0.96	0.137
B_7	12/13	12/13	6/5	12/13	4/5	1	1	0.96	0.137

一致性检验：

$$A\widehat{w}=\begin{pmatrix}1&1&5/4&1&9/10&13/12&13/12\\1&1&5/4&1&9/10&13/12&13/12\\4/5&4/5&1&4/5&3/4&5/6&5/6\\1&1&5/4&1&9/10&13/12&13/12\\10/9&10/9&4/3&10/9&1&5/4&5/4\\12/13&12/13&6/5&12/13&4/5&1&1\\12/13&12/13&6/5&12/13&4/5&1&1\end{pmatrix}\cdot\begin{pmatrix}0.148\\0.148\\0.118\\0.148\\0.165\\0.137\\0.137\end{pmatrix}=\begin{pmatrix}1.037\\1.037\\0.825\\1.037\\1.158\\0.957\\0.957\end{pmatrix}$$

$$\lambda_{max}=\frac{1}{7}\sum_{i=1}^{7}\frac{(A\widehat{w})_i}{\widehat{w}_i}$$

$$=\frac{1}{7}(1.037/0.148+1.037/0.148+0.825/0.118+1.037/0.148+1.158/0.165+0.957/0.137$$

$$+0.957/0.137)=7.001$$

$$CI=\frac{\lambda_{max}-m}{m-1}=(7.001-7)/(7-1)=0.0002$$

由表5.3可知，当 $m=7$，R. I. =1.36

C. R_A. = C. I_A. / R. I_A. = 0.0003/1.36 = 0.0001 <0.10

由于C. R. =0.0001 <0.10，所以该判断矩阵具有满意的一致性。

指标排序权向量为：

$W_A=[W_{B1}\ W_{B2}\ W_{B3}\ W_{B4}\ W_{B5}\ W_{B6}\ W_{B7}]\ T$

= [0.148 0.148 0.118 0.148 0.165 0.137 0.137] T

b. 非传统安全政府应对服务能力的判断矩阵。C_1、C_2、C_3 分别代表民众配合程度、民众应对非传统安全的抗危机能力及民众的知情状况对非传统安全政府应对服务品质的重要性程度。矩阵中的重要性标度数据来自于经过统计软件SPSS处理的问卷数据以及表6的相对重要性比例标度的参考。

表8 非传统安全政府应对的公共服务品质指标相对权重表

B_1	C_1	C_2	C_3	$\overline{w_i}=\sqrt[n]{\prod_{j=1}^{n}x_{ij}}$	$\widehat{w}_i=\frac{\widehat{w}_i}{\sum_{j=1}^{n}\widehat{w}_j}$
C_1	1	4/3	5/4	1.19	0.393
C_2	3/4	1	9/10	0.88	0.290
C_3	4/5	10/9	1	0.96	0.317

一致性检验如上演示：

λ_{max} =3.0006　C. I_{B1}. =0.0003　R. I_{B1}. = 0.52　C. R_{B1}. = 0.0006

因为C. R. =0.0006 <0.10，所以该判断矩阵具有满意的一致性。

指标排序权向量为：

$W_{B1}=[W_{c1}\ W_{c2}\ W_{c3}]$ T

= [0.393　0.290　0.317] T

c. 非传统安全政府应对资源保障能力的判断

矩阵。C_4、C_5、C_6 分别代表民众配合程度、民众应对非传统安全的抗危机能力及民众的知情状况对政府应对非传统安全时资源供给和利用状况的重要性程度。矩阵中的重要性标度数据来自经过统计软件 SPSS 处理的问卷数据以及表 6 的相对重要性比例标度的参考。

表 9 非传统安全政府应对的资源保障程度指标相对权重

B_2	C_4	C_5	C_6	$\overline{w_i} = \sqrt[n]{\prod_{j=1}^{n} x_{ij}}$	$\widehat{w}_i = \frac{\overline{w}_i}{\sum_{j=1}^{n} \overline{w}_j}$
C_4	1	8/7	1	1.05	0.349
C_5	7/8	1	7/8	0.91	0.302
C_6	1	8/7	1	1.05	0.349

一致性检验如上演示：

λ_{max} = 3.000　C. I_{B2}. =0　R. I_{B2}. = 0.52

C. R $_{B2}$. =0

因为 C. R. =0 <0.10，所以该判断矩阵具有满意的一致性。

指标排序权向量为：

W_{B2} = ［W_{c4} W_{c5} W_{c6}］ T

= ［0.349　0.302　0.349］ T

d. 非传统安全政府应对环境保障能力的判断矩阵。C_7、C_8、C_9、C_{10} 分别代表政府应对非传统安全的法制健全程度、政府搜集和利用信息的水平、政府维护自身形象的水平以及对舆论的引导状况对良好的非传统安全应对环境的重要性程度。矩阵中的重要性标度数据来自经过统计软件 SPSS 处理的问卷数据以及表 10 的相对重要性比例标度的参考。

表 10 非传统安全政府应对的环境保障程度指标相对权重

B_3	C_7	C_8	C_9	C_{10}	$\overline{w_i} = \sqrt[n]{\prod_{j=1}^{n} x_{ij}}$	$\widehat{w}_i = \frac{\overline{ww}_i}{\sum_{j=1}^{n} \overline{w}_j}$
C_7	1	1	5/4	11/10	1.08	0.269
C_8	1	1	6/5	11/10	1.07	0.267
C_9	4/5	5/6	1	6/7	0.87	0.217
C_{10}	10/11	10/11	7/6	1	0.99	0.247

一致性检验如上演示：

λ_{max} = 4.000　C. I_{B3}. =0　R. $I_{B3.}$ = 0.89

C. R_{B3}. = 0

因为 C. R. =0 <0.10，所以该判断矩阵具有满意的一致性。

指标排序权向量为：

W_{B3} = ［W_{c7} W_{c8} W_{c9} W_{c10}］ T

= ［0.269　0.267　0.217　0.247］ T

e. 非传统安全政府应对预警管理能力的判断矩阵。C_{11}、C_{12}、C_{13}、C_{14} 分别代表政府的监测系统能力、应对计划完备程度、应对机构设置的合理性和公务人员综合素质对非传统安全预警管理的重要性程度。矩阵中的重要性标度数据来自经过统计软件 SPSS 处理的问卷数据以及表 11 的相对重要性比例标度的参考。

表 11 非传统安全政府应对预警管理指标相对权重表

B_4	C_{11}	C_{12}	C_{13}	C_{14}	$\overline{w_i} = \sqrt[n]{\prod_{j=1}^{n} x_{ij}}$	$\widehat{w}_i = \frac{\overline{w}_i}{\sum_{j=1}^{n} \overline{w}_j}$
C_{11}	1	12/11	7/6	16/15	1.08	0.270
C_{12}	11/12	1	16/15	1	0.99	0.248
C_{13}	6/7	15/16	1	10/11	0.92	0.230
C_{14}	15/16	1	11/10	1	1.01	0.253

一致性检验如上演示：

λ_{max} = 3. 946　C. I_{B4}. =0. 018　R. I_{B4}. =0. 89　C. R_{B4}. = 0. 020

因为 C. R. =0. 020 <0. 10，所以该判断矩阵具有满意的一致性。

指标排序权向量为：

W_{B4} = [W_{c11} W_{c12} W_{c13} W_{c14}] T

= [0. 270　0. 248　0. 230　0. 253] T

f. 非传统安全政府应对应变管理能力的判断矩阵。C_{12}、C_{13}、C_{14}、C_{15}分别代表政府应对非传统安全过程中的决策指挥能力、协调配合能力、现场执行能力和国际合作能力对政府应变管理的重要性程度。矩阵中的重要性标度数据来自经过统计软件 SPSS 处理的问卷数据以及表 6 的相对重要性比例标度的参考。

表 12　非传统安全政府应对应变管理指标相对权重

B_5	C_{15}	C_{16}	C_{17}	C_{18}	$\overline{w_i} = \sqrt[n]{\prod_{j=1}^{n} x_{ij}}$	$\widehat{w}_i = \frac{\overline{w}_i}{\sum_{j=1}^{n} \overline{w}_j}$
C_{15}	1	15/14	1	8/5	1. 14	0. 284
C_{16}	14/15	1	1	3/2	1. 09	0. 268
C_{17}	1	1	1	3/2	1. 11	0. 273
C_{18}	5/8	2/3	2/3	1	0. 73	0. 179

一致性检验如上演示：

λ_{max} = 4. 002　C. I_{B5}. =0. 0005　R. I_{B5}. =0. 89　C. R_{B5}. = 0. 0006

因为 C. R. =0. 0006 <0. 10，所以该判断矩阵具有满意的一致性。

指标排序权向量为：

W_{B5} = [W_{C15}　W_{C16}　W_{C17}　W_{C18}] T

= [0. 284　0. 268　0. 273　0. 179] T

g. 非传统安全政府应对恢复管理能力的判断矩阵。C_{19}、C_{20}、C_{21}分别代表非传统安全政府处理中危机破坏的物质恢复能力、社会秩序恢复能力以及受影响群体的心理恢复能力对政府恢复管理的重要性程度。矩阵中的重要性标度数据来于经过统计软件 SPSS 处理的问卷数据以及表 6 的相对重要性比例标度的参考。

表 5. 10　非传统安全政府应对恢复管理指标相对权重表

B_6	C_{19}	C_{20}	C_{21}	$\overline{w_i} = \sqrt[n]{\prod_{j=1}^{n} x_{ij}}$	$\widehat{w}_i = \frac{w\overline{w}_i}{\sum_{j=1}^{n} w\overline{w}_j}$
C_{19}	1	5/6	1	0. 94	0. 312
C_{20}	6/5	1	6/5	1. 13	0. 375
C_{21}	1	5/6	1	0. 94	0. 312

一致性检验如上演示：

λ_{max} =3. 000　C. I_{B6}. =0　R. I_{B6}. =0. 52　C. R_{B6}. = 0

因为 C. R. =0 <0. 10，所以该判断矩阵具有满意的一致性。

指标排序权向量为：

W_{B6} = [W_{c19} W_{c20} W_{c21}] T

= [0. 312　0. 375　0. 312] T

h. 非传统安全应对中政府学习成长能力的判断矩阵。C_{22}、C_{23}、C_{24}、C_{25}分别代表政府的激励奖惩水平、应对机制改造程度、理论技术改进程度和人员专业培训水平对政府学习成长能力的重要性程度。矩阵中的重要性标度数据来自经过统计软件 SPSS 处理的问卷数据以及表 6 的相对重要性比例标度的参考。

表 14　非传统安全政府应对学习成长能力指标相对权重

B_7	C_{22}	C_{23}	C_{24}	C_{25}	$\overline{w_i} = \sqrt[n]{\prod_{j=1}^{n} x_{ij}}$	$\widehat{w}_i = \frac{\overline{w}_i}{\sum_{j=1}^{n}\overline{w}_j}$
C_{22}	1	4/5	11/10	9/10	0.94	0.233
C_{23}	5/4	1	7/5	11/10	1.18	0.293
C_{24}	10/11	5/7	1	4/5	0.85	0.211
C_{25}	10/9	10/11	5/4	1	1.06	0.263

一致性检验如上演示：

$\lambda_{max} = 4.001$　C. I_{B7}. = 0.0002 R. $I_{B7.}$ = 0.89

C. R_{B7}. = 0.0002

因为 C. R. = 0.0002 < 0.10，所以该判断矩阵具有满意的一致性。

指标排序权向量为：

$W_{B7} = [W_{c22}\ W_{c23}\ W_{c24}\ W_{c25}]\ T$

$= [0.233\quad 0.293\quad 0.211\quad 0.263]\ T$

C. 政府非传统安全应对能力评估指标合成权重分析

上一节计算得出的同一层次下的指标相对于其上一级指标的相对权重向量，而要保证指标体系能够应用于实际的非传统安全政府应对能力评估，需要计算每个指标相对于目标层的权重，即合成权重。二级指标权重总排序为：

$$= \begin{pmatrix} 0.393 & 0.349 & 0.269 & 0.270 & 0.284 & 0.312 & 0.233 \\ 0.290 & 0.302 & 0.267 & 0.248 & 0.268 & 0.375 & 0.293 \\ 0.317 & 0.349 & 0.217 & 0.230 & 0.273 & 0.312 & 0.211 \\ 0 & 0 & 0.247 & 0.253 & 0.179 & 0 & 0.263 \end{pmatrix}$$

$$\times \begin{pmatrix} 0.148 & & & & & & \\ & 0.148 & & & & & \\ & & 0.118 & & & & \\ & & & 0.148 & & & \\ & & & & 0.165 & & \\ & & & & & 0.137 & \\ & & & & & & 0.137 \end{pmatrix}$$

$$= \begin{pmatrix} 0.058 & 0.052 & 0.032 & 0.040 & 0.047 & 0.043 & 0.032 \\ 0.043 & 0.045 & 0.032 & 0.037 & 0.044 & 0.051 & 0.040 \\ 0.047 & 0.052 & 0.026 & 0.034 & 0.045 & 0.043 & 0.029 \\ 0 & 0 & 0.029 & 0.037 & 0.030 & 0 & 0.036 \end{pmatrix}$$

一致性检验：

C. I_C = [C. I_{B1} C. I_{B2} C. I_{B3} C. I_{B4} C. I_{B5} C. I_{B6} C. I_{B7}] × W_A

= [0.0003　0　0　0.018　0.0005　0　0.0002]

× [0.148　0.148　0.118　0.148　0.165　0.137　0.137] T = 0.0028

R. I_C = [R. I_{B1}　R. I_{B2}　R. I_{B3}　R. I_{B4}　R. I_{B5}　R. I_{B6}　R. I_{B7}] × W_A

= [0.52　0.52　0.89　0.89　0.89　0.52　0.89]

× [0.148　0.148　0.118　0.148　0.165　0.137　0.137] T = 0.7307

$C.R_C = C.R_A + C.I_B / R.I_B = 0.0001 + 0.0038 = 0.0039 < 0.1$

满足整体一致性的要求。

因此，各个二级指标的合成权重为：

$W_1 = 0.058$；$W_2 = 0.043$；$W_3 = 0.047$；$W_4 = 0.052$；$W_5 = 0.045$；

$W_6 = 0.052$；$W_7 = 0.032$；$W_8 = 0.032$；$W_9 = 0.026$；$W_{10} = 0.029$；

$W_{11} = 0.040$；$W_{12} = 0.037$；$W_{13} = 0.034$；$W_{14} = 0.037$；$W_{15} = 0.047$；

$W_{16} = 0.044$；$W_{17} = 0.045$；$W_{18} = 0.030$；$W_{19} = 0.043$；$W_{20} = 0.051$；

$W_{21} = 0.043$；$W_{22} = 0.032$；$W_{23} = 0.040$；$W_{24} = 0.029$；$W_{25} = 0.036$

最后形成非传统政府应对能力评估指标体系及权重值（见表 15）：

表 15　政府非传统安全应对能力评估指标权重值

目标层	一级指标（B）	二级指标（C）	权重
政府非传统安全应对能力	服务能力（B_1）	民众配合程度（C_1）	0.058
		民众抗危机能力（C_2）	0.043
	资源保障能力（B_2）	民众知情程度（C_3）	0.047
		资源储备程度（C_4）	0.052
	环境保障能力（B_3）	公共风险支出水平（C_5）	0.045
		资源整合调度水平（C_6）	0.052
		法制健全度（C_7）	0.032
		信息管理水平（C_8）	0.032
	预警管理能力（B_4）	政府形象维护水平（C_9）	0.026
		舆论引导水平（C_{10}）	0.029
		监测系统能力（C_{11}）	0.040
		应对计划完备程度（C_{12}）	0.037
	应变管理能力（B_5）	组织结构的合理性（C_{13}）	0.034
		人员综合素质（C_{14}）	0.037
		决策指挥能力（C_{15}）	0.047
		协调配合能力（C_{16}）	0.044
	恢复管理能力（B_6）	现场执行能力（C_{17}）	0.045
		国际合作能力（C_{18}）	0.030
		物质恢复能力（C_{19}）	0.043
	学习成长能力（B_7）	社会恢复能力（C_{20}）	0.051
		心理恢复能力（C_{21}）	0.043
		激励奖惩水平（C_{22}）	0.032
		应对机制改造程度（C_{23}）	0.040
		理论技术改进程度（C_{24}）	0.029
		人员专业培训水平（C_{25}）	0.036

六、中国政府应对“5·12”大地震能力评估的实证分析

本章以中国政府应对“5·12”大地震为典型案例，在非传统安全政府应对能力评估指标分析的基础上，对中国政府应对非传统安全的能力进行综合评估和实证分析。

1. “5·12”大地震应对的背景分析

2008年5月12日14时28分，我国发生8.0级大地震，震中位于四川省汶川县，中西部的大部分地区均受到此次地震的影响。其中，四川、陕西、甘肃、重庆、云南等省市受到的破坏较为严重，受灾面积达10多万平方公里。“5·12”大地震震级达到里氏8.0级，最大强度达到11度，并带来大量次生灾害。地震诱发的滑坡、坍塌、泥石流、堰塞湖等次生地质灾害，造成交通、水利设施、旅游设施、民居等被埋、被毁、被损，给人民的生命财产带来巨大损失，对生态环境带来了严重破坏。地震造成7万人死亡，受伤37万余人，失踪近2万人。经济财产损失严重，51个县市区的直接经济损失为8437.7亿元；生产基础设施严重受损，相当数量的水、电、通信、医疗等设施遭到破坏。城乡住房破坏严重，有超过2.8亿平方米的居民住房严重破坏、倒塌或损毁。这次地震对我国的宏观经济发展环境造成重大影响，灾后重建和社会秩序恢复的任务十分艰巨。“5·12”大地震物质损失状况如表16所示：

表16 “5·12”地震损失总体情况

受损项目		51个县（市区）损失状况
直接经济损失（亿元）		8437.7
	工业企业直接经济损失（亿元）	961.8
	农业直接经济损失（亿元）	404.2
损毁公路（公里）		34125.0
受损水库（座）		1263.0
受损供电设施	输电线路（公里）	61524.0
	35千伏以上变电站（座）	250.0
受损学校（所）		7444.0
受损医疗卫生机构（个）		11028.0
受损农村居民住房	倒塌（万平方米）	10709.6
	严重受损（万平方米）	9432.2
受损城镇居民住房	倒塌或损毁（万平方米）	1187.9
	严重破坏（万平方米）	5836.2

数据来源：国家汶川地震灾后恢复重建总体规划文本（征求意见稿）

"5·12"大地震的发生直接考验着政府应对非传统安全的能力，是对政府价值理念、对人的安全的关注程度、资源运用与整合能力、内部管理和外部沟通以及政府自身成长发展等综合应对能力的总体考验。中央政府在这次地震应对中反应非常快，也比较全面地展示了自身在非传统安全领域的应对能力。地震发生十几分钟内国家地震局就发布了此次地震的正式消息。14 时 50 分，中国地震局启动一级预案；15 时 25 分，国务院总理温家宝便赶赴四川指挥抗震救灾；15 时 30 分 民政部紧急调拨 5000 顶帐篷支援灾区，之后中央各部委和直属机关几乎在同一时间启动各自分管领域的抗震救灾工作。12 日晚，中共中央政治局常委召开紧急会议研究部署抗震救灾工作，抗震救灾总指挥部成立；国家减灾委员会启动二级响应，军队随即也第一时间启动应急预案，并做好先期准备和随后的介入工作；专业救援队伍也于当晚迅速抵达受灾地区。一系列积极的应对行为，西方舆论逐渐正面报道中国政府在此次应对中的表现。但与此形成对比的是，政府基层组织在救灾处理中的表现不能令人满意，政府、社会组织以及军队的协调配合不够充分，政府对救灾捐助款项的使用受到公众质疑，政府在灾后重建的漫长过程中也逐渐暴露出许多问题。

鉴于此次地震的广泛影响，以及中国政府在这次地震应对中的表现，本文基于以下四方面原因选取"5·12"大地震为典型案例来评估中国政府应对非传统安全的能力：一是地震时非传统安全中自然灾害的一种，是非传统安全的典型事例。中国是世界上受自然灾害影响最严重的国家之一。在经济迅速发展的同时，中国的资源、环境和生态压力加剧，自然灾害防范应对形式更严峻。我国发生的自然灾害存在灾害种类多、分布地域广、发生频率高以及损失重的特点，因此对自然灾害的应对直接和全面地考验着我国政府应对非传统安全的能力；二是"5·12"地震对中国政府应对能力的考验超过新中国成立以来任何一次特大地震。此次地震不仅考验政府的预警、应变和灾后恢复能力，还因地震应对中政府内外的全面动员参与、国内外民族精神的强烈感情凝聚以及世界舆论的关注，从而对我国政府应对非传统安全的能力提出了更全面的要求；三是此次地震中中国政府上下动员，充分调动并配合军队和社会力量参与抗震救灾。因此，"5·12"大地震是中国政府应对非传统安全能力的一次全面展示；四是"5·12"地震的应对状况受到国内民众和国际舆论的广泛关注，政府对外发布信息较为充分及时。因为政府应对非传统安全能力评价的特殊性，要求调研对象对政府相关应对状况掌握比较充分的信息。而由于多方面原因，政府对许多非传统安全应对信息披露不充分，以这些事件为实例对政府应对能力进行评估具有较大局限性。因此，用"5·12"大地震作为典型案例进行应对能力评估研究，既方便问卷调研和数据收集，也能全方位地评估政府的应对能力。

2. 中国政府应对"5·12"大地震能力评估结果分析

（1）能力评估计算原理

加权求和法是指数合并的方法之一，也是应用最为广泛的方法之一，即将已计算得出的每一层指标权重与对应的单项指标分值相乘并合并，从而得到分值。计算公式如下：

先求出第 j 个评价对象的第 i 个指标的均值

$$E_{ij} = \frac{1}{n}\sum_{m=1}^{n} A_{ij} \quad m = 1,2,\cdots,n(n\text{ 为样本数}) \qquad (\text{式}6-1)$$

根据得到的 W_i 与，E_{ij} 计算应对能力值 P_i：

$$P_i = W_i E_{ij} \qquad (\text{式}6-2)$$

通过每项应对能力值的加总得到政府应对能力总值：

$$P_i = \sum_{i=1}^{n} W_i E_{ij} \qquad (\text{式}6-3)$$

由于 $\sum_{i=1}^{n} W_i = 1$，而 $E_{ij}\max = 5$，$E_{ij}\min = 1$（因为在本次调研问卷的设置中，每个指标属性的最大值是 5，最小值是 1，），因此应对能力值 P 介于 1 ~5，即 P∈［1，5］。

（2）能力评估计算分析

根据上一节计算原理的分析，通过实证调研获得的问卷数据求出非传统安全政府应对能力的每一项指标和，然后算出均值（式 6－1）。借助于统计软件 SPSS 与前一章中确定的指标权重求得每一项应对能力的值（式 6－2）。最后通过上一节加权求和法得出中国政府应对非传统安全的能力总值（式 6－3）。

本项问卷调查针对中国政府应对“5·12”大地震的状况，采用问卷打分的方式对政府的应对能力进行评价。打分赋值采用 5 分制，对每一项的应对能力用 1 ~5 分进行打分。

具体评分标准如表 17：

具体结果见表 18：

表 17　非传统安全政府应对能力评分标准

分值	1	2	3	4	5
应对能力	弱	较弱	一般	较强	强

表 18　中国政府应对非传统安全能力值

一级指标	二级指标	权重	问卷得分	综合得分	排序
服务能力	民众配合程度	0.058	4.20	0.24	1
	民众抗危机能力	0.043	2.53	0.11	23
	民众知情程度	0.047	2.75	0.13	20
资源保障能力	资源储备程度	0.052	3.10	0.16	14
	公共风险支出水平	0.045	2.78	0.13	18
	资源整合调度水平	0.052	3.72	0.19	6
环境保障能力	法制健全度	0.032	2.63	0.08	22
	信息管理水平	0.032	3.32	0.11	11
	政府形象维护水平	0.026	3.75	0.10	5
	舆论引导水平	0.029	3.82	0.11	4
预警管理能力	监测系统能力	0.040	2.27	0.09	24
	应对计划完备程度	0.037	2.17	0.08	25
	组织结构的合理性	0.034	2.65	0.09	21
	人员综合素质	0.037	2.93	0.11	17

续表

一级指标	二级指标	权重	问卷得分	综合得分	排序
应变管理能力	决策指挥能力	0.047	3.92	0.18	3
	协调配合能力	0.044	3.68	0.16	7
	现场执行能力	0.045	3.40	0.15	9
	国际合作能力	0.030	3.25	0.10	13
恢复管理能力	物质恢复能力	0.043	3.67	0.16	8
	社会恢复能力	0.051	3.97	0.20	2
	心理恢复能力	0.043	3.08	0.13	15
学习成长能力	激励奖惩水平	0.032	2.77	0.09	19
	应对机制改造程度	0.040	3.38	0.14	10
	理论技术改进程度	0.029	3.25	0.09	12
	人员专业培训水平	0.036	3.03	0.11	16
中国政府应对非传统安全能力				3.25	

（3）评估结果分析

由上一节的分析可以得到，在2008年“5·12”大地震中中国政府面对这一非传统安全的整体应对能力得分为3.25分。按照设计的评分标准可以看出政府在这次危机中的综合应对能力处于中等水平。总体来看，中国政府非传统安全的的应对能力已经开始形成涉及能力建设各个方面的初步应对体系，具备了一定的综合应对能力。但这一应对能力还处于培育和发展的阶段，在非传统安全应对的大部分领域，政府的能力都有待进一步提高和完善。针对此次“5·12”大地震的应对，本文将25项应对能力划分为能力较强、能力一般和能力偏弱三类来做具体分析。

第二，“5·12”大地震政府应对能力较强的指标。如图5所示，中国政府在此次地震中应对能力表现良好能力指标的问卷得分都在3.5分之上。从能力类型来看，政府所具备的较强的应对能力大都属于事件发生之后的实时应对和震后恢复方面，表明政府在地震之后的抗震救灾上有着良好的表现。这一方面是因为高度集中的社会主义体制可以集中力量办大事，政府可以迅速调动各种资源应对危机，并在危机后动员社会力量对灾后恢复工作给政府以有利的支持；另一方面是因为政府在决策指挥时对“人的安全”的关注，使得政府树立了良好的形象，获得大众舆论支持，从而为集中力量抗震救灾奠定基础。

第二，“5·12”大地震政府应对能力一般的指标。如图6所示，中国政府在此次地震中应对能力表现一般指标的问卷得分均在3~3.5分，表明政府这些方面的能力处于一般水平。这些方面的能力建设往往不可能在短时间的危机中得到完整的体现，需要政府长期地积累和持续发展。但是这些也是政府应对非传统安全过程中的基础能力，能够推动政府更加合理科学的应对非传统安全。

我国政府在抗震救灾中这些方面表现一般，很大程度上是由于此类能力的隐形特征使得政府和民众在非传统安全应对能力建设时对此关注不足。另外也不排除因为调研对象对政府这些方面的信息掌握不足，从而在打分的过程出现中间趋同的可能。

第三，“5·12”大地震政府应对能力较弱的指标。如图7所示，中国政府在此次地震中应对能力表现偏弱指标的问卷得分均在3分之下。其中在抗震救灾过程中政府人员应对素质、组织结构合理性、监测系统能力以及应对计划完备程度得分较低，说明政府预警管理能力不足。民众抗危机能力低说明政府对公众应对非传统安全常识的教育和训练不够。虽然抗震救灾中工作对政府危机应对状况的了解已经比SARS期间有明显改善，但仍然远低于公众的需求。此外，在此次地震应对中中国政府的应对缺乏成熟的法律体系规范，公共风险的投入也不足。

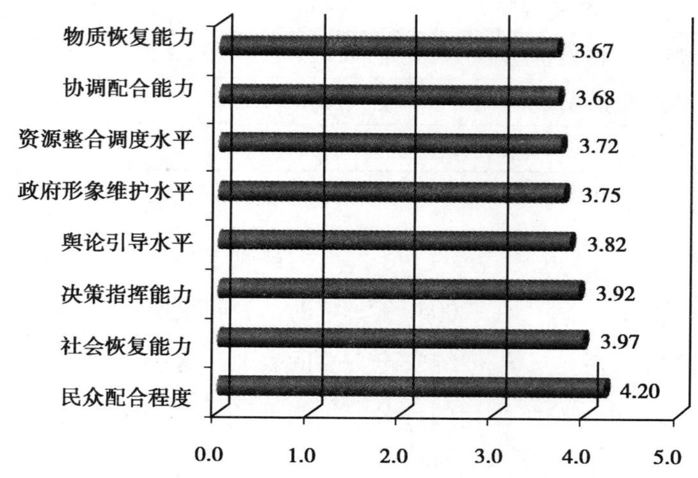

图5　较强水平政府应对能力得分

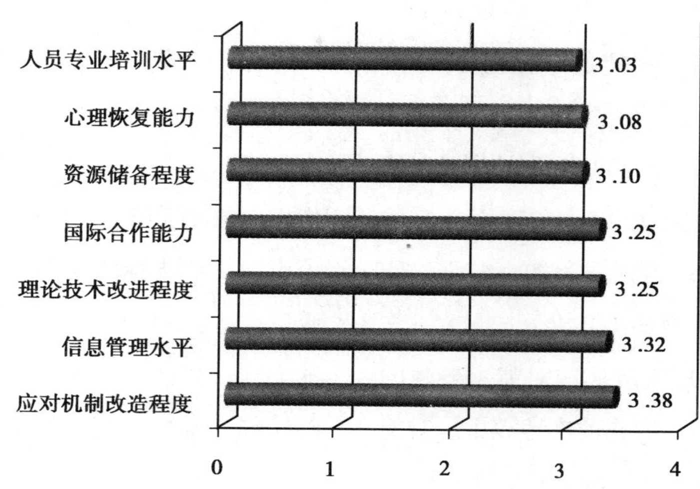

图6　一般水平政府应对能力得分

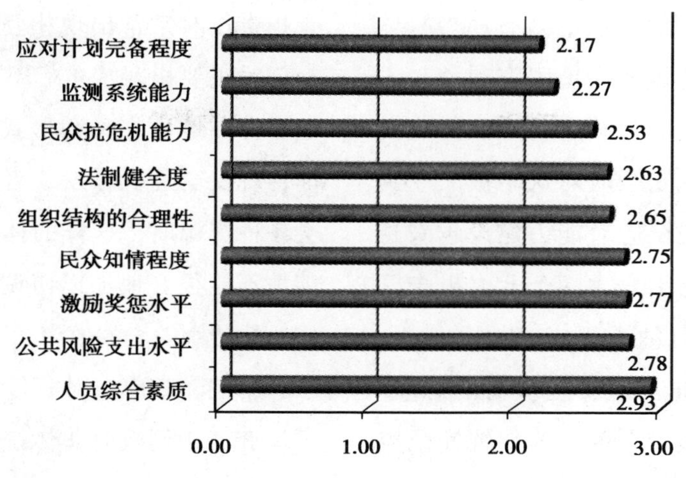

图 7　较弱政府应对能力得分

综合来看，在此次调研的 25 项政府能力指标中，获得较好评价的政府能力指标有八项，却有九项应对能力指标获得了一般以下的评价。此外，在此次地震中，政府展示了良好的动员和争取民众配合的能力（评价得分为 4.2 分）；而与此对应，在预警管理的监测系统、应对计划、组织结构和人员素质的指标上却存在着应对能力偏弱的特点。因此，中国政府应对此次地震的能力呈现总体能力偏弱且能力发展不均衡的特点。通过以上分析可以看出，从 2002 年 SARS 危机后，中国政府逐渐认识到了非传统安全应对的重要性，也在有意识地加强这一方面的能力建设。与 SARS 危机的应对相比，政府处理“5·12”大地震在事前预防、应对预备、快速反应和灾后恢复方面都已经具备了一定的综合应对能力。但与西方发达国家政府的应对能力相比，中国政府非传统安全的应对能力无论在理论上还是在实践中都不同程度的偏弱，政府应对非传统安全的体制尚在逐步建设和完善中。政府现有的非传统安全应对能力还不能满足人民群众的“安全”需求。因此，中国政府应对非传统安全的能力还不成熟。

3. 中国政府非传统安全应对能力建设的问题思考

通过对中国政府应对“5·12”大地震的实例分析，可以发现中国政府应对非传统安全的能力存在总体能力偏弱和能力发展不均衡的特点。值得指出的是，“5·12”大地震的应对也存在其个案的特殊性，因为事件的突发和巨大影响，政府势必对此次应对投入更多的关注，调动更多的资源，从而使得政府的整个应对能力得到比较充分的施展。同时，国内外舆论对地震影响的关注以及公众朴素感情的凝聚也为政府能力发挥提供了巨大支持。在面对金融危机、甲型 H1N1 流感、新疆“七·五骚乱”这类应对效果无法短时间显现的非传统安全危机时政府的应对能力往往显现出更多的问题和漏洞。综合上一章中的实证分析，结合现有的实践关注和理论追踪，本文将中国政府非传统安全应对能力的问题归纳为如下几点：

第一，政府应对非传统安全的意识淡薄。中国政府希望政府管理和公共服务能够“以民为本”，能够推动经济的可持续发展和人民生活安定富足。因此，面对危机时如何有效的保护国家利益和人民群众的生命财产安全便成为政府应对非传统安全的核心关注点。非传统安全应对从不被关注到进入国家战略，非传统安全应对能力建设越来越受到党和政府重视，党的十六大、十七大报告已经明确将非传统安全应对纳入了国家执政议程，这些都表明中国政府对非传统安全应对的态度。然而，虽然中央政府的应对态度是非传统安全应对意识的基础部分，但在将这种态度向现实应对能力转化的过程中政府还存在着许多的不足。如日本在阪神大地震之后，历次地震都没有再超过此次的损失和伤亡，而新中国在经历了唐山地震的巨大创伤之后却不得不再次面对汶川地震带给我们的破坏和痛苦。其中除了天灾的巨大破坏力之外，政府应对非传统安全的意识淡薄，看不到平稳镜像下隐藏的危机也是值得关注的因素。

第二，政府应对非传统安全行政管理体制存在缺陷。组织的合理高效是非传统安全应对中资源有效利用的保证。“发生重大突发性事件后，政府能否有效控制和处理这个事件，关键取决于是否存在反应灵敏、决策果断、指挥有力的核心协调机构。”❶ 中国的非传统安全应对组织体系大多是临时组建的，没有统一的非传统安全应对管理机构，政府组织在应对过程中缺乏专业性、机动性，也没有相应的人力资源来保障。由于非传统安全应对的特殊性，应对过程需要政府各个部门的整合联动和协调配合。但我国非传统安全应对的政府权责划分不清，管理事项条块分割严重，承担责任时常常出现相互推诿的状况。非传统安全应对主要由相应的行政领导决策协调，且应对过程存在地区主义和形式主义的问题。一旦重大非传统安全危机爆发或者多事件并发需要调动社会各种资源时，这样的体制往往使政府的政策和能力不能很好地加以协调，从而严重地影响政府应对非传统安全的效率。

第三，政府应对非传统安全能力建设和发展不均衡。中国政府非传统安全应对能力建设具有发展不均衡的特点，原因是政府对非传统安全应对能力的选择性关注和发展。中国政府现有的非传统安全应对能力是一种事后补救型的发展模式。政府非传统安全应对的着眼点往往是事件发生之后的应对和恢复，而在危机发生之前往往采取不作为或者多一事不如少一事的心态。非传统安全应对事前防范、适时应对、善后恢复以及事后提高四方面机制的综合协调往往只停留在形式上和政府书面报告之中，在政府应对能力建设的实践中远远没有落到实处。通过实证分析可以发现民众在“5·12”大地震中的抗危机能力偏弱，这与政府对公民相应的教育和训练缺乏不无关系。除此之外，现阶段我国政府的应对能力建设偏重于单一事件的个案应对，缺乏战略高度的非传统安全综合应对体制。一般的做法是危机发生之后，政府组建临时应对小组针对个案采取措施。这就造成了中国非传统安全应对缺乏条理，效率低下，宝贵的资源浪费在单一突发事件应对方式探索上。

第四，政府应对非传统安全的法律体系不健

---

❶ 黄天柱、胡税根：《政府危机管理体系的构建》，载：《银企咨询》，2008 年第 8 期，第 40 页。

全。从上一章的实证分析可以看出，中国政府在非传统安全应对中的法制健全程度在中等水平以下。政府在非传统安全应对中往往靠口号和觉悟来实现政府上下的协调以及对社会力量的动员；政府应对水平的高低往往取决于政府相应人员的个人素质和现场应变能力。政府应对行为缺乏健全的法律根据，应该做什么、不应该做什么，政府有很大的自由裁量随意性。地方政府在非传统安全萌芽产生之初，为了避免上级部门的问责和公众的指责，往往采取对外封锁、对内隐瞒的应对策略。现实中往往是社会舆论推动政府应对非传统安全，政府只对产生广泛社会影响的危机全力应对。如“三鹿奶粉”事件，直至中央政府介入之前，地方政府采取的都是瞒报信息、拒绝承认监管失职的策略。因为相应法律法规的缺失直接导致了政府的事后问责追究机制失灵。许多严重违背非传统安全应对规律的行为得不到追究，一些本应承担巨大责任的人常常能够逍遥法外。如“5·12”大地震中针对建筑质量的责任追究便因为法律体系的缺陷而难以持续地深入进行。

7　中国政府非传统安全应对能力建设的对策建议

“危机像死亡和纳税一样不可避免”❶，中国面对的非传统安全状况对政府的非传统安全应对能力提出了严峻的考验。面对复杂多变的安全环境，提升政府的非传统安全应对能力是降低危机损害的关键因素。目前，我国的非传统安全应对研究才刚刚起步，政府的非传统安全应对能力建设还有许多不完善的地方。尽管国情不同，但发达国家防治、应对非传统安全威胁，保护公民的人身权和财产权，维护国家安全的措施和经验值得我们学习和借鉴。通过对非传统安全政府应对能力评估指标体系构建及实证研究，我们已经总结了中国政府应对非传统安全能力建设的现状及存在问题。我国政府可以根据目前政府应对能力建设的现实和困境，有针对性地采取措施，从而持续提高对非传统安全的能力。

一是重视树立以“人的安全”为核心的新安全观。经济迅速发展和社会转型时期，中国政府更应该加强对非传统安全的关注，在传统安全已有基本保障和国家安全总体稳定的前提下，应该更加重视“人的安全”。政府要以“人的安全”为核心，强调树立以人为本、以社会稳定为基础的非传统安全观，培养现代公民安全文化，鼓励所有公民都积极关心和参与社会治理并提高公民的危机应对能力；另一方面，政府应该意识到公民个人既应该是享有安全的对象，也可能是制造非传统安全危机的主体。“个人需要从国内和国际社会稳定中获取安全感，但少数个人也可能因为某些社会尚难解决的现实问题而刻意制造对他人、对政府和国家的威胁。”❷ 2010 年 3 月 23 日，福建南平实验小学校园凶杀事件中 8 个幼小的生命为政府的非传统安全应对能力建设敲响警钟。因此，政府要增强自身的非传统安全应对意识，注重培养现代公民的责任意识，防微杜渐胜于临渴掘井。

二是不断完善政府应对非传统安全的管理体

❶ Steven Fink：Crisis Management：Planning for the Inevitable，June 19，2000.

❷ 余潇枫、潘一禾、王丽江：《非传统安全概论》，浙江人民出版社，2006 年版，第 74 页。

制和机制。在组织机构方面，政府应该设置非传统安全应对的专门管理机构，将非传统安全应对作为政府一项日常工作来处理，使其逐步走上正规化和专门化的轨道。首先是设立专业、高效的综合性应对管理指挥系统。美国于20世纪70年代建立以总统为核心的非传统安全应对机制，总统可以召开国家安全委员会讨论安全形势，也可以组成高层顾问团帮助总统合理决策。依据发达国家的经验，我国更需要设立由专业人员组成的专业高效综合的应对管理指挥系统，以全面应对各类非传统安全事件，从而提升危机应对能力。其次是建立健全的预警机制和高效的应对机制。美国总统直接领导的联邦紧急事务管理署（FEMA：Federal Emergency Management Agency）将全国划分为十个应急管理分区，设有紧急事态援助中心和FEMA训练中心，年资金预算拨款达30亿美元，配备2500多名全职员工和4500多名后备保障人员。因此，需要重点完善预警机制，建立高效的应对机制，这样才有可能灵活应对各种突发性的非传统安全事件。再次是有效利用先进发达的信息管理系统。良好的信息管理系统可以为非传统安全应对提供数据支持，在非传统安全应对中有助于防止信息获取的滞后和不足，可以防止信息的误传，还可以对非传统安全潜伏和发生期间的情况及时处理，在短时间内控制事态。

三是培养和提高公民的非传统安全意识和抗危机能力。国民意识的强弱直接关系到政府非传统安全应对的效果。许多国家不仅重视国民非传统安全意识的培养，而且时常开展系统化的演练和培训。在日本，人们从小就受到防灾的教育，孩子们在幼儿园、小学，不但要上地震知识的必修课，还经常参加全民学习活动，各街区都能看到避难场所的标识。所以每到地震、台风来临，人们都能镇静自如。澳大利亚的防灾教育深入人心，政府不仅设立了全国灾害管理学院，培养非传统安全应对的专业人才，而且不断对百姓宣传非传统安全应对知识，如向每户居民发放有关反恐的资料，指导人们在发生恐怖事件时如何应对。韩国政府还专门设立防灾培训的“全国防灾日”，在这一天举行全国性的“综合防灾训练”，通过防灾演习让政府官员和普通百姓学会防灾，提高应对灾害的能力。❶

四是政府采取有效措施保证各种非传统安全应对能力的均衡发展。在遇到重大突发事件时，政府机构要能形成统一协调、统一调动各种应对资源的整体合力。要改变“救火式”的非传统安全应对模式，加强非传统安全应对的事前防范和学习成长能力建设。凡事预则立，不预则废。事前预警和防范能力是非传统安全应对能力的关键部分，具有非常重要的地位。在非传统安全发生之前以及开始之后的前兆阶段，破坏较小且属于量变阶段，是解决危机和消除破坏的最佳时期。同时，非传统安全之后的反思和改进则是政府真正实现能力提高的核心部分。没有事后的总结，政府的应对能力就会仅仅限于针对每一个个案的缝缝补补，不能形成整体性的非传统安全应对。诚然，这两方面能力的提高往往不会出现迅速的效果转化，花费的时间、精力也比“救火式”的

❶ 王德讯：《国外公共危机管理机制纵横谈》，载：《发展》，2006年第1期。

能力建设要大。但是倡导“使用少量的钱预防，而不是花大量钱治疗”❶ 正是非传统安全应对能力建设的核心观念。

五是建立健全非传统安全应对法律法规体系。制定完善、系统的安全法律法规体系是能力提升的基础。实践证明，将非传统安全应对纳入法制化的轨道，有利于保证突发事件应急措施的正当性和高效性。美国有以《国家安全法》《全国紧急状态法》《反恐怖主义法》和《联邦应急计划》等为核心的安全法律法规体系；俄罗斯有以《俄罗斯联邦紧急状态法》《俄罗斯联邦战时状态法》《紧急事件和救援服务以及救援者的地位法》和《紧急事件管理法律保障计划》为核心的安全法律法规体系。到目前为止，日本共制定有关非传统安全和危机管理（防灾救灾和紧急状态）的法律法规 227 部。这些国家都有健全的各类单项法规措施来应对各种具体的突发性灾难，使非传统安全在单项具体法规的框架内得到处理和解决。虽然这些法律名称各异，但其目的和内容却大致相同，就是保障政府有充分的权力，以便快速应对非传统安全，将突发性灾难所带来的损失降低到最小。从发达国家的经验来看，为有效应对非传统安全，首先要开展的工作就是制定相关的法律，从而使得政府拥有非传统安全应对的明晰权力，统一规定政府职责，确定依法处理紧急状态和危机情景的法治原则。非传统安全应对的法制体系一方面要明确政府权力，保证政府在应对过程中指挥和行为的权威性、主动性，以及对资源整合运用的能力；另一方面保证政府在非传统安全应对行使特别权力时，要做到依法行政，从而减少社会恐慌，保持社会稳定。法制的健全要实现法律体系的全方位涵盖，不仅囊括非传统安全宏观领域的立法，还应制定微观领域中具体管理环节的实施细则。同时，政府应保证法律体系的协调统一，要对现有应对法律法规进行清理，统一和协调各层次、各领域的非传统安全应对法律规范。此外，政府还要确保非传统安全应对法律的可操作性，防止执行层面的有法不依。

六是加强非传统安全应对的国际合作。任何国家的政府都不是万能而是有限的，其并不能独自处理所面对的全部非传统安全，也需要国家间的合作以及外国政府和机构的援助。“在对危机的处理上，尽管世界各国存在地域和意识形态上的差异，但反应是相似的”,❷ 必要时需加强国际合作。例如始于英国，后来蔓延整个欧洲的“疯牛病”危机，有关政府与世界卫生组织积极配合，各国专家共同调查传染关系以及处理方法，从而有效控制了疫情。在加强国际合作的同时，世界许多国家的政府都注重对非传统安全相关理论的研究，并设立专门的机构。比如美国的行政管理学会的危机管理分会、欧洲的 CRISMART 等，就对古巴导弹危机、疯牛病等危机进行过深入的研究。❸

政府非传统安全应对能力建设直接关系着人的安全、社会的安全和国家的安全，是任何国家都要重视的中心问题。传统政府主要面临的是主

---

❶ ［美］戴维·奥斯本、特德·盖布勒：《改革政府》，上海译文出版社，1996 年版。

❷ 斯蒂尔曼：《公共行政学》，中国社会科学出版社，1989 年版，第 184 页。

❸ 胡税根、余潇枫等：《公共危机管理通论》，浙江大学出版社，2009 年版，第 334 页。

权危机的应对，现代政府除了面临主权危机的应对以外，更重要的是面临非传统安全和公共危机的应对。因此，中国政府在新的时期要加强对非传统安全政府应对能力建设的关注和重视。无论是非传统安全理论研究还是政府实践，最终的意义都应该落在对人的关注上，关注如何保障每一个鲜活个体，关注保障安全权利和自由政府能力的持续提高。因此，我国政府在未来应更重视非传统安全问题的应对，更好地保障公民的个体安全和社会安全，这有助于提高政府的执政能力和合法性，也有助于国家的未来发展和社会的长治久安。

人口数量与中国发展安全

原华荣　王凌艳*

【摘要】人口数量是决定人类社会和生物圈命运的“序参量”。“老龄化并非衰亡”而只是“疥癣之疾”；人口数量过多严重威胁“种际平等”“代际平等”和“种内平等”属“心膂之忧”。缩减人口规模是发展安全能力建设，增加选择机会，保证资源、生态/环境、粮食安全的根本和“最便宜的反应策略”。

【关键词】人口数量，“序参量”，缩减人口，发展安全，关键

一、发展安全

（一）从传统安全到非传统安全

1. 从“传统安全”到“非传统安全”

在全球变化背景下，由资源枯竭、生态/环境退化和生物灭绝引起的“发展安全”问题日益凸显。莱斯特·布朗即意识到：对国家安全的威胁已由“传统的”军事方面扩展到“非传统的”资源、能源、生态、环境等诸多领域。对很多国家来说，这些威胁，如“沙漠扩延或土壤侵蚀可能比入侵敌军更能威胁国家的安全”❶——认为现代社会不可能崩溃是一种危险的幻想。❷由是，他主张重新定义国家安全并呼吁：把安全防范的重点由传统的人与人的关系方面，转向“非传统的”人与自然关系的领域；减少军备开支，把投资的重点转向人口控制、资源/能源安全和生态/环境保护，即发展的可持续性上来。❸

2. 环境问题的的关联性

“今天吃的白面包，明年春天可能会在堤坝上冲开一个缺口而淹没新奥尔良。”

对这一变化早有认识并特别强调环境问题关联性的是威廉·福格特。他在《生存之路》（1949）中就写道，“人类由于过度生育和滥用土地已陷入了生态陷阱”❹——“今天吃的白面包，明年春天可能会在堤坝上冲开一个缺口而淹没新奥尔良”。❺而那些滥用土地的人，则在为城市提

* 原华荣：浙江大学中国西部发展研究院教授、博士生导师；王凌艳：兰州职业技术学院讲师。

❶ ［美］莱斯特·布朗：《建设一个持续发展的社会》，祝友三等译，科学技术文献出版社，1984 年版，第 289 页。

❷ 同上书，第 101 页。

❸ 同上书，第 290 ~ 291 页。

❹ 汪士铎：《汪悔翁乙丙日记》（邓之诚辑录），文海出版社，1936 年版，第 267 页。

❺ 同上书，第 268 页。

供粮食、纤维、木材的同时，也由于对资源的破坏而把自己变成了“生态难民”。❶

（二）发展安全

1. 发展安全

“发展安全”指各发展要素自身的安全和对安全发展的保证——支持而不是显著制约发展。由发展的可持续性所规定的“发展安全”，其宗旨在于通过对各发展要素状况及其相互关联的监测、预警、调整，保证各发展要素自身的安全——有保障的供给或稳定，进而对生存和发展的持续支持。与防范军事威胁的传统安全相比，“发展安全”或“非传统安全”包括：国土安全、社会安全、资源安全、生态/环境安全和人口安全。

2. 国土安全

国土安全源于国土要素变异对人类、生物活动的影响，指通过监测、预警、预防和应对，避免国土要素大变异的发生，或把不可抗拒变异对生存和发展的危害减低到最小程度。主要包括覆被变化（森林、湿地减少，土地荒漠化）、气候变化（温室效应及其影响）、灾害性天气（沙尘暴、暴雨、降温、大风）、洪涝、生物灾害（生物入侵、种群暴发、病害、虫害）、滑坡、泥石流、火山、地震、海啸，以及大型工程安全等。

3. 社会安全

社会安全源于国家、民族、宗教、政党、阶层、群体间的矛盾和冲突，指通过协商、调解、社会保障，避免矛盾的激化或把冲突降低到最小程度，保证社会的安全稳定、和谐，为生存和发展创造良好的社会环境和条件。社会安全包括国防安全、国家安全和社会安全（狭义）三个方面。

4. 资源安全

资源安全指资源供给对生存和发展需求的持续满足。可区别为资源安全（狭义，水、土地、生物、矿产等），能源安全、粮食安全等。能源安全的基本要义除有保障的供给外，还有对环境，特别是对大气环境的低污染。在当代，对生存和发展不可或缺的，且供给受到越来越大限制的资源主要有水、土地、粮食、能源和为工业所需的各类重要矿产。

5. 生态/环境安全

生态/环境安全指人类活动造成的冲击力被控制在环境承载力之内——消费小于“临界土地承载力”，污染远小于环境的自净/消纳能力。包括生态安全和环境安全。对生态安全来说，是生物多样性的保持和生态功能的正常；对环境安全来说，是环境各要素组分的稳定和环境功能的正常。

（三）人口安全

人口安全源于人口数量、质量、结构变化对自然、生物和人类社会发展的影响。指通过数量、结构的调整和质量的提高，保证生物的生存和对人类发展的支持。包括数量安全、结构安全、遗传安全、生存安全和人力资源安全等。

1. 结构安全。

结构安全分性别和年龄结构安全。性别结构安全指通过社会的宣传、干预，避免出生人口性别比的人为（B 超和选择性流产）上升，进而婚龄性别比失调对社会生活带来的危害（性犯罪、拐卖妇女和儿童），或尽可能地把这种危害减小到

---

❶ 汪士铎：《汪悔翁乙丙日记》（邓之诚辑录），文海出版社，1936 年版，第 101 ~ 106 页。

最低限度；年龄结构安全指通过对出生人口数量的调整，把人口年轻化/人口老化对社会生活、经济发展带来的负面影响减低到最小程度。

2. 人力资源安全

人力资源安全指通过教育、培训、引进、福利，提高国民文化、科技素质，累积人力资源，培育人力资本，保证对发展的支持和社会对专门人才的需求，以及对特殊、关键科学家的保护。

3. 遗传安全

遗传安全指通过优生（禁止近亲婚配、生殖健康、出生缺陷干预等）杜绝遗传缺陷、残疾胎儿的出生，避免遗传病的扩散，降低遗传缺陷率，提高国民遗传素质；同时，保证种族遗传基因（密码）的安全。

4. 生存安全

生存安全包括公共卫生安全和难民等问题。公共卫生安全指通过对烈性传染病（如鼠疫、霍乱、SARS、甲型 H1N1 流感等）的调查、研究，疫源控制，预防、隔离和应急系统的建立，避免其之传播或使之迅速得到控制，从而把对生命的损失和造成的恐慌、社会混乱减低到最小程度；同时，通过全民健身，易感人群保护（自我、社会）和公共卫生措施等，控制和降低一般传染病（流感、肝炎、梅毒、艾滋病等）的发病率，并对之进行积极治疗以保证公共卫生安全。

由战争、环境灾难等对群体生存直接构成威胁的问题，如战争难民、生态/环境难民等，则由于全球（气候、覆被）变化引起的生态/环境恶化、水资源危机、粮食危机，进而共同体之间冲突的上升而日益凸现，成为人口安全的重要内容并进一步强化着公共卫生安全问题。

5. 人口数量安全

人口数量安全指对自身繁衍、社会劳动力/兵源需求的最低数量保证，和为最大限度减轻人口对资源、生态/环境存量压力而对“临界土地承载力”的不超越。当代人口数量安全的根本，便在于最大限度地缩减人口规模。

二、人口数量与人口安全

（一）数量与质量

1. “人多而气分，赋禀遂薄”：人口的质量与数量反相关

“古者户口少而皆才智之人，后世生齿繁而多窳惰之辈”（马端临，《文献通考·自序·户口考序》）；“穷汉生一群，……直似飽糠牲”（王梵志，《王梵志诗文校辑·卷五》）——随着人口“孳乳过多”带来的质量下降，人们清楚地认识到：“既庶何以富之乎？”[1]（汪士铎），“人口数量与人口品质处于反对地位。”[2]（陈达），对此的历史见证是：在传统农业的极限内，人口数量的增加把以高人均土地占有量和农业剩余率（余粮率）为基础，由气势恢弘秦代兵马俑所展现的所宇轩昂，出则骑马佩剑、入则扶犁耕田的中国古代农民，变成了鲁迅先生笔下多子、水旱灾害、半年糠菜半年粮的浑僵、木讷的润土。

对人口质量与数量的这种反向关联，汪士铎

[1] 陈达：《人口问题》（节录），载：《人口问题资料》，商务印书馆，1962 年版，第 90 页。

[2] 同上书，第 168 页。

的解释是："人多而气分，赋禀遂薄。"❶ 即人均物质、文化生活资料消费水平——人口质量的物质规定——随人口增加而减少。驯化与野生物种对一定可获得资源的不同配置，也体现着数量对质量的规定和二者的反向关联：果实累累的桃树，在耐寒、耐旱上远小于其果实小而少的野生品种；以出肉或产崽为"己任"的家猪，其抗逆性也远无法同野猪相比。❷ 中国"控制人口数量，提高人口素质"基本国策的高明之处，即在于对人口质量与人口数量反向关联的体现。

2. 欲"提高人口质量"，必先"控制人口数量"

欲"提高人口质量"，必先"控制人口数量"是人口质量与数量反向关联的规定，或对之的进一步证明。如诺贝尔奖获得者在少数国家/少量人口中集聚，而与多数国家/众多人口的无缘。据笔者统计：在1901～1960年的60年中，计有29个国家（按国籍）的319人（320人次，居里夫人一人获奖二次）获得了诺贝尔奖。其中，美、英、德、法、瑞典、瑞士、荷兰、意大利、丹麦和前苏联居前10位，计276人占87%；前六位国家242人占76%；前三位的美、英、德180人占56%；前两位的美、英133人占42%，第一位的美国83人占26%。❸

陈长衡"欲得大木，则植木宜疏"的论断，则是一个精辟的"类比"和阐释："国家之求人才，犹治森林者之求大木也。治森林者欲得大木，则植木宜疏，然后得地宽，受日足，根干敷荣，枝叶畅茂，巍然立地参天，以成大树。若夫种植太密，则不能畅茂敷荣，甚或憔悴枯槁，丛遝以死。是以欲每株皆成才，莫如少其株数，庶各有成长之机会。人类亦犹是也，人口太密，孳生太繁，则个人难期发达，人才难望众多。欲发达个人，增多人才，舍减少生育，其道无由。必生育减少，人口不至太稠，然后个人之衣、食、住三用始丰，德、智、体三育始备。斯宾塞所谓个人发达与生育繁多成反比，盖谓此也。"❹

（二）数量与结构

1. 数量和结构："心膂之忧"与"疥癣之疾"

从问题层面来看，人口数量过多属"心膂之忧"，"老龄化并非衰亡"而只是"疥癣之疾"。其一，人类文明的兴衰史表明，人口数量过剩招致生存危机——中国历史上的12次王朝更替和大动荡，10次即发生在人口高峰或稍后——而属"心膂之忧"；"老龄化并非衰亡"而只是"疥癣之疾"，中国的老龄化程度（10%）与发达国家（20%左右）相比仍不算高，并未掉进"老龄化陷阱"而处于寒冷的"人口冬天"。其二，从资源枯竭、生态/环境的总体退化到对经济胁迫越来越强的"资源—环境瓶颈"，从巨大的劳动就业压力到社会保障的"捉襟见肘"……中国正处于会"烤焦"一切的"人口夏天"。社会和发展面临的几乎所有问题，都与过多的人口数量有关。德国柏林人口发展研究所所长赖纳·克林霍尔茨指出：中国发展面临的根本问题，是资源、人口"瓶颈"

❶ 陈达：《人口问题》（节录），载：《人口问题资料》，商务印书馆，1962年版，第120页。

❷ 从人类某一方面（如高产出）需要看来的"优良品种"，实际是生存能力（抗逆性）极度下降的品种。

❸ 蔡华文、段玉然、王强、余暇：《诺贝尔奖金获得者传》（三卷本），湖南科学技术出版社，1988年版。

❹ 陈长衡：《中国人口论》（节录），载：《人口问题资料》，商务印书馆，1962年版，第10～15页。

而非“人口结构变化”。

2. 人口数量控制对年龄结构调整具优先性

从层级—尺度理论看，人口数量控制对年龄结构调整具优先性：

第一，随着系统层级的提高和尺度的增大，人口数量的重要性增加并成为决定人类和生物圈命运的“序参量”，年龄结构的影响减小并趋于消失。

在人口系统中，数量同结构同等重要，人口老化不可取，老龄问题要避免；在“人口—经济—社会”系统中，具“规模效应”“分母效应”而与就业压力、经济发展、资源短缺、社会保障等问题紧密关联的人口数量，对系统的影响便大大超过了作为老龄问题、劳动力老化等问题成因的年龄结构老化而成为决定人类命运的“序参量”；进入人与环境层级，起作用的人口因素只剩下作为决定生物圈命运“序参量”的人口数量，年龄结构的影响已不见踪影——当承载量超过轮船的吨位时，其沉没便成为一种必然——不论上面坐的是男人还是女人，老人还是小孩，绅士还是乞丐，教授还是白痴……

第二，解决人口数量控制问题对调整年龄结构具优先性。

人口系统是人类系统的子系统，人类系统是自然系统的子系统——人口数量控制属于解决人类与自然关系的高层级/大问题，人口年龄结构调整属于解决人口系统中人口结构老化的低层级/小问题。根据层级－尺度理论关于高层级系统对低层级系统的逐级控制、逐级制约（“逐级控制”原则）和在目的性上的包容（“包容原理”），进而解决高层级问题对低层级问题的优先性规定（“优先性”原则），人口数量控制对人口年龄结构调整的优先性和第一性，便是一种逻辑的必然。

第三，控制和减少人口数量是保持生物圈稳定的必要条件，提高出生率以调整人口年龄结构将招致混乱并有可能导致人类社会的崩溃。

控制和减少人口数量是保持生物圈稳定的必要条件，也符合对问题“系统内解决”的原则；提高出生率以调整人口年龄结构因造成对控制人口数量的冲击而是一种必然危及生物圈，乃至会导致人类社会崩溃的，具极大破坏性的“系统外解决”——通过“超额”捕食羊群解决“狼口”的过剩。正如马丁·萨戈雷斯所尖锐指出的：“用提高出生率来改变人口老化问题，是一种无知和不负责任”的主张。

提高出生率以调整人口结构是一种“饮鸩止渴”的选择，坚持“数量控制与结构调整并举”❶将为中华民族招致毁灭性的灾难。所以，必须把对年龄结构的调整，严格地限定在人口数量控制允许的范围之内。

（三）人口数量与人口安全

1. “生态学悖论”：一个既是雄鹰又是麻雀的物种

人类是一个体型大、寿命长、能耗强度高/生存力强的超级 K－对策物种。按照生物数量与体型、生存力、存活时间的反向关联，和 K－对策物种“小种群”的生存模式，只能有极少的数量才

---

❶ “既有效控制人口数量，又显著缓解人口老化”是一个内涵两个相反目标的假命题——有效控制人口数量要求降低出生率而必然加剧人口老化；显著缓解人口老化要求提高出生率而必然冲击对人口数量的有效控制。

能保证生态对策的“关联适应”，进而避免“稳定平衡原理”带来的死亡打击而存活。对生态对策“关联适应”的破坏和“小种群”生存模式的违背——大体型、高耗能、长寿命与庞大数量并存——则把人类变成了一个生态学上的“怪胎”：体型、耗能强度、寿命上的K－对策物种，数量上的r－对策物种——一个既是雄鹰又是麻雀的物种。

2. 人口数量与“种际平等”

生物多样性是“种际平等”的基本展现和保证——维护生物多样性就是维护“种际平等”。生物多样性的维护，是通过食物链、食物网上营养关系的限制，进而各取食环节、营养级之间各生物物种数量的动态平衡实现的。撇开对自然的攫取和掠夺，单是脱开营养关系限制的数量，就足以使“生命之网”变得破碎、生物多样性减小而导致人与生物的不平等。

3. 人口数量与“代际平等”

K－对策物种的“代际平等”为以“小种群”为关键生态对策的“小种群—代际共享”机制所保证——小规模的种群避免了上一代与下一代的生存资源竞争；r－对策物种的“代际平等”为以“短存活”为根本生态对策的“短存活—分代利用”机制所保证——短的寿命避免了上一代与下一代的生存资源竞争。

人类因“大种群”破坏了资源的“代际共享”机制；由于“长存活”破坏了资源的“分代利用”机制——由是，代际关系便处于无法解决的困境之中：长寿规定了对“代际共享”机制的维护——而为维护“代际共享”机制所必须的对自然资源利用的扩大和强化，则在加剧了人与自然不平等的同时，又因对后代生存资源的减少而破坏着人类社会的“代际平等”。

4. 人口数量与“种内平等”

人类社会的不平等是一个客观存在——不论我们用什么理论去做解释：或阶级学说，或能力差异，或人类在本质上就是一个种内不平等的物种……而人口数量增加对不平等的加剧，同样是一个不争的事实和逻辑的必然：在任何一种不平等理论下，“分母效应”对人均生存资源的减少，都会推动“种内斗争”而加剧不平等——即使在“种内平等”的生物界也难以避免，如冰川消融导致的北极熊食子，草原上极度干旱时发生的“羊吃羊”（牧民们为此给羊穿上衣服）。除制度改革（尽可能公正地分配“蛋糕”）外，通过“把蛋糕做大”的“不二法门”以追求“社会公正”，也同样会进一步扩大向自然的索取，由之破坏“代际平等”加剧人与自然的不平等。

5. 庞大的种群规模是对人口自身安全的最大威胁

因代际、种内不平等而使社会陷于危机并处于其中的人口，因与生物不平等而使自然陷于危机并处于其中的人口，必然是不安全的——于是，一个因数量过多而把人变成“生态学悖论”的人口，便构成了对自身安全的最大威胁。

三、人口数量是发展安全的关键

（一）人口与资源和生态/环境安全

1. 需求压力和供给能力的“自削弱”：对当代资源安全的根本挑战

不断加剧的供需矛盾是对当代资源安全的根本挑战。供需矛盾的形成和“剪刀差”的不断扩大，一方面因为庞大且增长着的人口数量和膨胀着的欲望所强化的巨大的需求压力——这是最为根本的；另一方面因因资源供给能力急剧的自削弱。资源供给能力的自削弱来自两个方面，一是有限、不可更新资源因“跷跷板效应”的减少——化石能源、地质矿藏存量与利用规模反相关；一是有限、不可更新资源在需求压力下因不可避免过度利用——如对庞大人口“基本需求”的满足——的破坏和退化。

对资源安全的挑战还来自：人口、经济与资源、能源在一定程度上的地域脱耦——由农耕形成的人口、经济与水资源、耕地、草原的地理关联和空间耦合，为资源基础大大改变了的工业化所打破；为各国家、民族为保证资源安全所推动的地缘政治的发展，即由地理要素——海洋、陆心、陆缘向能源、水资源、粮食和战略（矿产）资源的转变，❶ 也大大增加了资源安全的风险。

2. 人口与资源和生态/环境安全：五大因子、四个主要关系和六种效应

在人口与资源、生态/环境的关系中，存在五大因子、四个主要关系和六种效应。五个重要因子是：人口——总量、密度；消费——总消费、人均消费；经济——总量、人均产值、经济密度（万元/km^2）；资源——总量、人均资源量、资源密度（t/km^2）；污染——总量、人均排污量、排污强度（t/km^2、$10^4m^3/km^2$）。

四个方面的主要关系是：经济与资源耗费正相关；资源耗费与污染排放正相关；经济总量与污染排放正相关——时间节约的本质和资源节约的“天花板效用”，使技术只能削弱而不能在根本上改变上述各种“正相关”，由之规定了“循环经济”“低碳经济”对保证发展安全的有限性。在人均经济产值或人均消费一定时，人口总量、人口密度与经济总量、经济密度，进而资源耗费和污染排放正相关。由是，在各因子之间，便建立了如下途径的关联：人口总量/人口密度、人均消费→经济总量/经济密度→资源耗费总量/资源密度→污染总量/排污强度。在这一关联中，发生着人口的六种效应——“规模效应”“分母效应”“密度效应”/“阈密度效应”（对生物而言）“基本需求效应”“跷跷板效应”和“临界效应”。

这一关联所表达的是：人口越多、消费越高，所必需的经济规模便越大，进而，耗费的资源便越多，产生的污染便越严重——“物质不含糊”，这是一个“技术魔棒”也无法左右的过程。尼古拉斯·乔治斯库·罗根就此写到：“在我们制造出‘更好更大’的冰箱、汽车或者喷气式飞机的同时，不可能不产生同样‘更好更大’的废弃物。”❷ 这不仅是逻辑的，而且也是发生在世界各地区和国家的现实情况，仅从耗能、污染强度看，不少国家和地区已成了“燃烧的大地”和“污染的天堂”。

（二）人口数量是发展安全的关键：“序参量”和“人口序参量”

1. “序参量”和“人口序参量”

哈肯认为，通过组元（如激光中的电子）的协同作用（电子的同向震荡）而把单个组元组织

---

❶ 对制海权的追求，服务于对能源、资源的控制。

❷ ［美］尼古拉斯·乔治斯库－罗根：《熵定律和经济问题》，载：［美］赫尔曼·戴利、肯尼思·汤森：《珍惜地球——经济学、生态学、伦理学》，马杰、钟斌、朱又红译，范道丰校，商务印书馆，2001年版，第96页。

起来所形成的，反过来又支配着各个组元的“序参量”（激光中的光波），是决定系统性质和演化方向的状态变量。❶ 而作为系统“序参量”的人口总量，则通过对系统的支配规定着人口的各种现象、结构、质量乃至每一个人的命运——“在所有已讨论过的情况中，序参数与个体之间存在着一种特殊的关系，……即与某一物种的个体数目相关联。……在这些数量细节的后面隐藏着无数个个体的命运，它们是由总人口这个序参数虽然只是总体地，却又是极其严格地决定的”。❷

环境条件差（低经济密度）而人口稀少（3人/km^2）的澳大利亚，在发展上对环境条件良好（高经济密度）但人口极其稠密（超过1000人/km^2）的孟加拉国的巨大优势，即是“人口序参量”支配人们命运的典型例证。而且，“人口序参量”不仅支配着人类的命运，更为重要的是，它还决定着生物圈——地球上所有生命的未来。

这里要强调的是：日本等人口密度高、资源贫乏国家和地区经济的成功，并不会对“人口序参量”的普适性构成丝毫影响——日本只是一个特例——用别人的资源（不道德）发展自己的不可仿效的特例。

2. 人少的优势和21世纪的赢家

人少地广、人口—资源比高是美成为世界大国的基础——少量人口使美国成为世界最大的粮食供应国——提供约50%左右的贸易谷物，世界上有100多个国家依靠从北美进口粮食。1988年，美国谷物的消费超过了生产，原因是当年谷物产量因严重的干旱减少了1/3，大体上与常年谷物的出口量相当。❸ 这里的问题是，若美国人口同中国或印度一样多，还会有剩余谷物出口吗？显然，低密度的人口既为美国提供了选择机会，也为世界提供了选择机会。

1990年苏联的解体，使人们普遍对俄罗斯的前途担忧。但时隔不久，俄罗斯便在内外不看好的氛围中，迅速而令人瞩目地崛起了——以国际能源的强势需求为背景，利用石油（约一半产量用于出口）和天然气。这里同样有类似问题：若俄罗斯人口同印度或中国一样多，还会有多少石油和天然气可供出口吗？石还会是一张坚挺的“王牌”吗？——不能忘记的是，除了石油和天然气，普京的底气、俄罗斯往日雄风的重振，还在于它只有少量的人口。

“谁是21世纪的赢家”是一个颇受人们关注的问题——以人均资源，特别是人均可更新资源拥有量为判据，即从发展的持续性看，未来最具发展潜力的国家或21世纪的“赢家”，既不是欧洲、日本，也不是中国和印度，而是人均可更新资源量居世界前列的美国、俄罗斯、加拿大、澳大利亚和巴西，而五国中最具发展潜力的则是俄罗斯——既拥有辽阔的土地和大量可更新资源，又是各类工业化所需资源最为丰富的国家。

（三）发展安全的能力建设：缩减人口规模以增加选择机会

1. 人口的“基本需求效应”

人口的“基本需求效应”源自基本需求的

❶ ［德］赫尔曼·哈肯：《协同学——大自然构成的奥秘》，凌复华译，上海译文出版社，2001年版，第60～61页。
❷ 同上书，第78页。
❸ ［美］保罗·艾里奇，安妮·艾里奇：《人口爆炸》，张建中、钱 力译，钱炜校，新华出版社，2000年版，第1页。

"刚性"和基本需求品（如食物）生产的如下特征特征：一是生产资料（土地、水、热量，及其空间组合等）的有限性——稀缺、易耗竭和低更新；二是生产的艰巨性——1950～2000年，全球经济产出增5.6倍，食物产量仅增1.9倍。❶三是生产过程的巨大外部性——扩大耕地，投入化肥、农药，修建水利工程加剧着生态/环境退化；土地的退化迫使人们进一步扩大耕地和增加投入，形成相互强化的恶性循环；人口的增长，又进一步推动着这一恶性的正反馈循环——发展中国家生态/环境的破坏，如热带地区1980～1995年的森林滥伐，41%～48%是由于人口增长。❷

2. 粮食安全

在最根本的层级上，粮食安全是一个人与自然关系范畴的"供给保障"或"供求关系"问题。从需求看，是人口和消费增长的持续压力；从供给看，是全球变化（气候、覆被）带来的农业生产能力、粮食产量预期的大幅下降（lPCC），这一下降，又将为耕地因生物燃料生产占用的大量减少，和"石油农业"向"有机农业"的必然转变所推动——随供需剪刀差扩大而来的，则是世界性的粮食危机（已来临），越来越多的国家、地区需要进口越来越多粮食，全球谷物市场的萎缩和对美国、加拿大等少数谷物供应国依赖的增加。是故，从全球市场供给、必然的贸易纠纷和不可能排除的国际政治问题看，世界养活不了中国（大量进口），中国只能自己养活自己❸——而中国同样极为严峻的粮食安全情势，又使"自己养活自己"面临着根本性的挑战：

其一，由庞大且增加着的人口所构成的需求压力。其二，使国人趋于乐观的近30年来全国粮食总产的稳定和增加态势——这在很大程度上受益于气候变暖的早期效应，特别是农牧分界线北移和垦殖规模的扩大，东北地区粮食在土壤肥力下降情况下的增产即在于此。❹ 其三，全球变化将导致种植业生产能力总体下降，粮食产量大幅减少——据《国家气候变化评估报告》，到2030年，种植业生产能力在总体上减小5%～10%；至21世纪后半期，主要农作物，如小麦、水稻、玉米产量最多可减产37%。❺

2. 缩减人口规模：增加选择机会/保持灵活性的"最便宜的反应策略"

斯洛勃德金指出：进化是一场"生存的扑克游戏"，目的并非是为赢得大把钞票，而只是能继续玩下去。❻ 普洛格、贝茨接着写道："既然生存的扑克游戏的宗旨仅仅是继续玩下去，而不致被淘汰出赌桌。那么，增强生物体应付可能出现的食物供给、生存空间等挑战的能力的手段才是第一位的。对一种雄心勃勃的生物体最好的忠告是：保持灵活性"。而保持灵活性"最好的对策是尽可

---

❶ ［美］莱斯特·布朗：《B模式：拯救地球 延续文明》，林自新、暴永宁译，东方出版社，2003年版，第4页。

❷ 周广胜、王玉辉：《全球生态学》，北京：气象出版社，2003年版，第215页。

❸ ［美］普洛格、贝茨：《文化演进与人类行为》，吴爱明、邓勇译，黄坤坊审校，辽宁人民出版社，1988年版。

❹ 编写委员会：《气候变化国家评估报告》，科学出版社，2007年版，第197～198页。

❺ 同上书，第296页。

❻ ［美］普洛格、贝茨：《文化演进与人类行为》，吴爱明、邓勇译，黄坤坊审校，辽宁人民出版社，1988年版，第121页。

能最便宜的反应策略”。[1]

“保持灵活性”即增加选择的机会。在有限性或可供资源量一定情况下，选择机会的多少，与反应策略对资源的消耗，或“昂贵”程度密切相关：应对策略愈“廉价”，消耗的资源便愈少，选择机会便愈多；应对策略愈“昂贵”，消耗的资源便愈多，选择机会便愈少。而选择机会的多少，则规定着可持续性的强弱。由是，应对策略愈“廉价”，选择机会便愈多，可持续性便愈强，即继续玩下去的可能性便愈大；反之，应对策略愈“昂贵”，选择机会便愈少，可持续性便愈弱，即继续玩下去的可能性便愈小。

选择“昂贵”而抛弃“廉价”的原因，既在于“廉价”在人们看来的“低效率”而与其对效率追求的相左；更为重要的也许是，人口和欲望压力对“廉价”的拒绝和排斥——“廉价”的应对策略无法提供对大规模人口和膨胀着的欲望的支持。农业对牧业，传统农业对原始农业，“石油农业”对“有机农业”的相继替代，或我们所谓的“进步”表明：人类的文明史是一个随人口数量增加和欲望膨胀，“昂贵”应对策略拒绝和排斥“廉价”应对策略的历史，即选择机会不断减少的历史。是故，缩减人口规模便成了增加选择机会、保持灵活性以保证发展安全“最便宜的反应策略”。当然，也是唯一和最为根本的应对策略。

对缩减人口规模作为保证发展安全根本性的典型例证是由人口爆炸性增长的后果提供的。17世纪末，被引入爱尔兰的马铃薯为生活在不幸之中的200万人口带来了“福音”——更高的土地生产力和更多的食物。由此，爱尔兰的人口便疯长到1845年的800万。是年，马铃薯因遭枯萎病而歉收，于是，“福音”变成了灾难，降临于爱尔兰的大地：在1845～1848年的大饥荒中，200万人被饿死，200万人移居国外。活下来的400万人，则牢牢记住了这难以忘怀的惨痛教训——尽管爱尔兰是个天主教国家，但从那时起，人们便通过大大提高结婚年龄而大体保持了人口的稳定。[2]（博尔丁，《印象》，1956）

中国社会的规模，在历史上因气候对农业的制约——小麦、水稻、粟、黍等要求较好的水、热和土壤条件而只适于在平坝和浅丘坡地种植——而受到严格的控制。17、18世纪以来优良品种——耐旱、耐寒、耐瘠的玉米、番薯、马铃薯的普遍和大规模种植，使农业突破了气候、地形的限制而向“边缘地区”扩张，[3]极显著地提高了粮食产量，带来人口的爆炸性增长——由16世纪中叶的1.66亿，迅速地增加到19世纪中叶（1851年）的4亿多。20世纪50年代以来的“石油农业”，则导致了人口的第二次爆炸性增长——数量更为迅速地扩张到14亿。而支持人口爆炸性增长的优良品种、扩张的食物系统和“石油农业”，则使中国的生态/环境遭到了根本性的全面破坏并不断恶化。

---

[1] ［美］普洛格、贝茨：《文化演进与人类行为》，吴爱明、邓勇译，黄坤坊审校，辽宁人民出版社，1988年版，第122页。

[2] ［美］加勒特·哈丁：《生活在极限之内——生态学、经济学和人口禁忌》，戴星翼、张真译，上海译文出版社，2001年版，第256～257页。

[3] 蓝勇：《中国历史地理学》，高等教育出版社，2003年版，第251～254页。

学术争鸣

创造性介入：中国外交的短板与解决方案

王逸舟*

迄今为止全球体系确实一直受到西方强国的支配，其中确实包含大量不公正不合理的成分，但这不是中国拒绝参加全球治理进程的充分理由，而恰恰应当是中国人提出适合多数国家利益和要求的全球治理目标步骤的机会。中国期待的和更多参加的全球治理，应当充分吸收过去很少发声但却代表实际人口多数的国际社会大多数成员的提议，应当纳入新兴的非西方大国的集体表达，应当有中国自身的改造措施。

所谓的中国"积极介入"的立场，并不是否定过去在这些问题上的已有原则与说法，而是促使我们涉外部门和人员更加广泛地征求各方面意见，更加仔细地权衡不同方案的利害关系，在国际谈判中更加主动地提出动议和修改意见。从哲学高度讲，由西方主导的全球体系和全球治理过程，转向一种更加均衡、合理和公平的样式，可能有快速质变的路径，即摧毁性、破坏性、革命性的措施（如毛泽东时代中国人的选择），和另一种以量变带动质变的思路，即比较温和、渐进、改良的方法（这正是邓小平时代的核心）。

中国对外事务中的"创造性介入"，必须注意和遵守以下原则：首先，在任何情况下都要参照联合国宪章的基本精神，讲求介入过程的国际合法性；比如说，必须得到联合国多数成员的认可，特别是安理会的某种授权（至少是默许和不反对）。在各个专门领域，如海洋外空、气候环境、能源资源、人权政治、经社教育等，还应当参照不同的专门国际法律文书和实践先例，使中国可能的介入行为有理可依、有据可查。中国作为全球事务里的新来者，尤其要注意学习各种国际法和国际惯例，观摩分析老牌西方大国的经验教训，努力与自己的行为及宣示与公认的国际准则对接而不是冲撞。师出有名才能得道多助。其次，中国的"创造性介入"，一定要尊重被介入对象的权利与尊严，尊重国家主权原则和各国人民的自主选择原则。比如说，要得到主权国家合法政府的邀请，受到介入对象民众中多数的欢迎；在缺乏唯一和公认的政治权威的情况下，也要力争获得尽可能多数的政治势力和民意的接受（例如中国近些年在苏丹的角色）。当中国的利益受到直接威胁或损害时（如近期发生在利比亚的情形），或者当中国的国际角色与当事国的政治意愿发生矛盾

* 甘均先摘编自：王逸舟：《创造性介入：中国外交的短板与解决方案》，载：《东方早报》，2011年8月30日，第A14版。

时（如中国参加的有关伊朗核问题的大国协商），中国的“创造性介入”要选择好时机，避免被其他大国捆绑裹挟，坚定地采取自主表态、自主进入或撤出的立场，同时耐心细致地与对立方保持接触，两面下注，对冲或缓解针对中国的压力。

在军事配合外交参与“创造性介入”行动方面，需要指出两个值得重视和改进的地方：首先，军事不只是武器和战略方面的内容，更有准确研判对手、掌握宏观大局的要求。避免误判，防止“囚徒困境”（即对安全形势和对手的不了解），反对仅凭借旧习惯对付新情况的狭隘经验主义，是我军参与国际行动时特别应当注意之处。其次，适应国际范围非传统安全威胁突起的新形势，培养应对非战争性的多种军事行动的能力，是中国人民解放军创造性介入国际事务的一项重要任务。另一方面，由内战诱发的国际紧张与对峙，由国家武装力量对国际恐怖势力之类的非国家行为体的较量，表现出增多的趋势。对此我们的军事规划部门（特别是涉外部队）应当有充分的认知。总之，推动海外练兵、发展和改进远投装备、利用国际组织尤其是联合国的合法性对我海外重大利益的保护，这几方面必须统筹考虑、有机结合。

超越和平崛起——中国实施包容性崛起战略的必要性与可能性

王义桅[1]

中国与世界关系的新变化需要我们实施不仅包容西方的和平崛起，而且要包容其他新兴国家发展、有效代表发展中国家发展的“包容性崛起”新战略。包容性崛起的三大支柱是实现文化、体制与环境的三包容：其一，兼收并蓄的包容性战略文化。为解决中国发展途中知识与权力的不匹配，我们必须倡导文明的兼收并蓄，慎谈“中国模式”，发展包容西方的战略文化。包容西方，并非意味着就封锁我们改革的方向，而是相互学习、借鉴，实现共同发展、和谐发展与包容发展。其二，统筹兼顾的包容性战略体制。外交是内政的延伸，但在全球化时代，内政与外交日益不可分。为此，外交应超越内政制约，超越国家利益与国际社会的二分法，建构统筹内政—外交、权力—价值、利我—利他的包容性战略体制。其三，宽松和谐的包容性战略环境。建构包容性战略环境关键是超越现代化的赶超思维，再次确认中美关系“重中之重”的地位及厘清它对内政的意义和在改革开放进程中的全局意义。夸大自身实力、看低美国实力将会酿成历史的悲剧。

包容性崛起与和平崛起的区别有三个方面：一是和平崛起解决的是让西方包容中国崛起的问题，包容性崛起解决的是中国如何包容西方，减少崛起阻力的问题；二是和平崛起着眼于从新兴国家崛起中脱颖而出，包容性崛起着眼于如何解决与新兴国家同时崛起的矛盾，从而有效构筑持续崛起的战略保护带；三是和平崛起旨在开创发展中国家史无前例的成功范例，包容性崛起旨在国际新秩序中如何包容发展中国家权益。包容性崛起是介于和平崛起路径与和谐世界目标之间的道路，要解决的问题是如何通过中国的和平发展实现持久和平、共同繁荣的和谐世界。因为共同利益、共同安全、共同价值无法一步到位，只能从利益、安全与价值的包容性入手，实现中国与世界的包容和谐。包容性崛起战略实质是让世界从中国崛起中普遍受益，实现权力共享与责任共担，有利于形成国际共识，既让世界包容中国的发展，也让中国包容世界的发展。包容性崛起的目标是让世界对中国的发展道路不仅欣然接受、热情帮助，而且真诚欣赏。调整自己的心态总比

[1] 甘均先摘编自：王义桅：《超越和平崛起——中国实施包容性崛起战略的必要性与可能性》，载：《世界经济与政治》，2011 年第 8 期。

调整别人的心态容易。

这样，从认识论而言，包容性崛起改变了和平崛起自我宣示的单向思维，改变了片面追求利益最大化的理念，积极塑造主客体互动的包容性思维，追求适当而兼容的利益，改变中国与外部世界的二分法，形成中国与世界互动建构、相互学习适应的局面，塑造“中国崛起也是我的崛起”“中国为我们在崛起”等印象，让外界在中国崛起中看到自己的影子，实现其愿望，满足其安全感、幸福感、成就感。如果实现了这一点，其他国家自然就很欢迎并主动帮助中国崛起了。以“包容性崛起”坚持和完善和平崛起，既具必要性，又具可能性：

其一，必要性。美国虽无法长期主导世界，但在相当长的时期内，它仍将成为国际社会最有影响力的阵营。中国长期面临着来自西方的利益冲突、权力转移与意识形态压力。若不包容西方，则会面临西方联手遏制，自身发展道路的阻力将越来越大，可能最终无法实现和平发展道路目标。新兴国家、周边国家和发展中国家关系，作为中国崛起的战略保护带、战略依托与战略基础，我们更需包容其权益与意志，对冲中国与美国和西方国家关系的风险。

其二，可能性。当今世界，互动建构成为国际关系尤其是大国关系主旋律。没有固定的敌友，菜单式合作、竞争性合作成为常态。在国际秩序重建过程中，尽管西方国家的自信心不断下降，但价值优越感却依旧持续。同时，西方也并非铁板一块。围绕国际机构让权、国际贸易让利给新兴国家，西方内部矛盾加剧，给中国实施对西方的包容战略提供了战略空间。从本质而言，“包容性崛起”是积极的韬光养晦战略，努力倡导发展为了世界、发展依靠世界、发展成果由世界共享的理念，旨在实现全面、协调、可持续发展道路，这是科学发展观在中国与世界关系上的具体体现。包容性崛起需解决中国与世界的利益矛盾、权力竞争、责任纠纷与价值冲突，具体内涵包括：

其一，利益共赢。从利益而言，重点在发展中国家让利、周边国家互惠、新兴国家共赢、发达国家赢利。为此，要避免泛化“核心利益”提法，在继续做好互利共赢这篇大文章的同时，探讨建设共同安全机制。

其二，权力共生。从权力而言，重点在为发展中国家争权、给周边国家放权、与新兴国家让权、和发达国家共权，不断改善我们自身的权力结构，提升结构性权力。为此，要少提权力东移，多强调权力分散；淡化国家崛起，重视社会觉醒。

其三，责任共担。从责任而言，重点在为发展中国家承担责任、与周边国家共谋责任、与新兴国家分担责任、与发达国家共担责任，在有效承担国际义务的同时照顾利益攸关方。

其四，价值共享。从价值而言，重点反映发展中国家意志，挖掘与周边国家共同历史传统，凝聚新兴国家共识，与西方寻求价值共享面。公共外交主题也要从和而不同转到殊途同归上面来。为此，我们要淡化中国模式，突出发展道路的包容性、普适性，更多展示中国传统文化底蕴。

混沌理论在非传统安全治理研究中的应用——兼论索马里海盗问题

陈世瑞❶

非传统安全是一个复杂性范畴，涉及多个领域，其所要关注的是“和谐与发展”的问题，是如何实现与维护“人的安全”与“社会安全”。因此，如果以整个人类社会的持续和平与良性发展作为安全的根本出发点与归宿，那么人类社会就能够最终达到“优态共存”式的具有真正安全意味的和谐状态。从系统的角度对非传统安全进行综合的、全面的系统管理是非传统安全问题治理的内在本质要求。从非传统安全的性质来看，非传统安全问题具有不确定性、破坏性、复杂性、扩散性、突发性、动态性、可转化性等特点，并呈现跨国化、网络化、多样化等特征，上述种种，都表明非传统安全问题及其演化具有明显的非线性的混沌现象特征。

混沌理论相关研究表明：在现实中非传统安全威胁并非是一个线性系统，它依赖于诸多复杂因素，依赖于这些因素之间的相互作用力，是一个复杂的非线性系统，是混沌的。复杂现象具有内在规律性，可来自简单的、确定的规律；有些似乎强烈相关的因素之间其实并不存在任何直接的联系；小的不起眼的原因也会形成惊人的结果（蝴蝶效应）；复杂现象自身能产生“虚假信息”。混沌理论为非传统安全治理研究提出了两个最基本的复杂性范式：即一方面，简单系统能够展现复杂行为；另一方面，复杂系统受简单规则驱动。因此，混沌也是可以驾驭的，是可以管理的。混沌管理的目的就是根据非传统安全威胁的演化机制，介入非传统安全的自组织过程，控制非传统安全混沌发生的条件或规模，改变其动态行为，以达到化解危机，转危为安，实现人类社会的可持续发展。

1. 调整非传统安全的混沌吸引子。一个系统可以同时存在几个吸引子，存在几个吸引子域，该情况下，对系统未来状态的预测就很困难，因为给定系统的初始条件，并不清楚会导致系统进入哪一个吸引子中。反之，如果已知系统的吸引子域，那么就可以通过调整初始条件使系统的运动进入预定的吸引子中。因此，当非传统安全威胁出现时，只有改变吸引子在状态空间的位置和吸引子的类型，才能最终改变系统的终极状态，

❶ 甘均先摘编自：陈世瑞：《混沌理论在非传统安全治理研究中的应用——兼论索马里海盗问题》，载：《人力资源管理》，2011年第10期。

所以要改变非传统安全威胁的运行状态，就要对非传统安全混沌吸引子设法加以控制。以索马里海盗为例，其实质是国家治理失败所出现的一种“失败外输”现象。因此，其存在的吸引子有索马里国内治理、地区治理（东非七国、非盟等）、全球治理（联合国主导）、大国干预（如美国等）等。由于其内力已失，国家的中央权威已经崩溃，无法维持法治、推进人权和提供有效的治理，外力的输入必要性就凸显出来。因此，外力干预是引导索马里走向秩序的重要路径。以联合国为主导的国际干预一方面要根据索马里政治、经济、文化状况，以及各族群、教派力量对比与各方要求，开展斡旋和调解，达成妥协，尽可能恢复国内秩序，恢复其经济与政治基础。另一方面，加强对索马里的人道主义援助。国际社会必须认识到，对索马里的人道主义援助是一项“国际公益”，帮助索马里人民填饱肚子、有事可做，自家仓库的粮食才会更安全。最后一点，但并不是不重要的，对海盗的打击，绝不能手软，任其肆意为非作歹，致使“海盗财富效应”扩大，成为决策索马里走向的吸引子。

2. 把握非传统安全问题的分叉点。分叉点是一个系统状态的分裂发生点，系统新的发展方向的生成点。分叉是系统整个演变过程的一部分，它可作为系统渐进变化的一部分，也可作为系统突然变化的一部分，它还可作为系统进化方式的一部分。沌分叉点正如危机管理理论中的“危机”，危险与机遇的转折点，当前的分析家们更多看到非传统安全威胁，而对于非传统安全问题带来的机会认识不足，索马里海盗一方面是全人类的公敌，另一方面，也给了世人一个重新认识世界的机会。非传统安全是一个动态性概念，它体现了安全现实的变化和安全理论的拓展，是对应于全球化时代世界格局转变，在军事、政治领域之外产生大量严重危及国家与人类社会整体的威胁和危险而形成的区别于传统安全的理论关照与现实关注。伦理向度上，表现为较强的全球中心主义，全球一体化的发展势必使人们的视野从民族、国家、地区转向全球，形成一种“全球认同”。如果说这种理论研究只是一种理想模式的探讨的话，那么索马里海盗问题则给了世人一个警示：全球命运共同体正在凸现，索马里人道主义危机从一定意义上促进了共同体意识的形成，为非传统安全领域合作提供了广阔的空间，非传统安全威胁治理需要国际社会超越传统国际政治的狭隘视野，一个国家不应囿于精细的利益考量，以“零和”原则为基础进行权力之争。

3. 减弱反馈作用。系统不稳定根源于其内部存在大量的正负反馈活动过程。非传统安全治理难度大，主要原因也在于其强烈的正负反馈，非传统安全问题古已有之，而且许多问题根植于各国自身政治、经济、文化的深层土壤中，在旧的国际格局下，被当前突出的问题所掩盖，在国际格局发生质的变化后，以及全球化相互依存关系日益加深的背景下，所掩盖问题一经爆发，则愈演愈激烈，展现出来是“强者恒强、弱者恒弱”正、负反馈机制的作用。混沌理论让我们认识到，开头小小的差异，结果可能是极大的差异。而一旦处在这种反馈环中，则循序渐进的改变通常摆脱不了宿命。如果没有系统外的干预，这样的反馈机制很难摆脱。因而要打破或减弱这种反馈机制，必须从新的角度突破，而不是在现有的系统之内设法补救。从这层意义上讲，索马里海盗问题需要外力干预，全球协力防、消于海洋，全力除患于陆地，在海上恢复秩序，在陆上恢复正常的社会生活，以实现索马里社会大换血，增强其自身造血能力。

4．建立预警机制。对初始条件敏感是混沌系统的典型特征，其主要观点就是初始条件的微小差别可能导致最终结果的极大差别，或者说，起初小的误差可能引起灾难性的后果。正所谓“差之毫厘，失之千里”，这就充分暗示我们控制预测和建立预警系统的重要性以及预期正确后会有丰厚的回报。预防、减少非传统安全威胁的关键在于建立预警机制，以“全球中心主义”伦理向度的非传统安全威胁治理，则要在全球实行预警机制的共建、共享。

《非传统安全与当代世界》译丛书评

国际安全研究的演化与中国

——《国际安全研究的演化》书评

朱锋 *

安全研究从20世纪50年代中期以来，一直是国际关系学科中最重要的研究和教学领域。巴里·布赞教授则是当代国际安全研究领域响当当的人物。在过去30年的学者生涯中，他的研究不仅丰富了国际安全研究的视角，最重要的是，开拓了国际安全研究一系列新的研究议程。对其学术盛誉最重要的注脚，莫过于学术界公认他是国际安全研究中“哥本哈根学派”（Copenhagen School）的重要开创者之一，在国际安全研究领域树立起了自身学术成就的独特旗帜。《国际安全研究的演化》是巴里·布赞教授与丹麦哥本哈根大学政治科学系琳娜·汉森副教授通力合作，于近年推出的一本力作。经由浙江大学非传统安全与和平发展研究中心主任余潇枫教授精心翻译出版，无疑将成为中国国际安全研究学界一本重要的参考作品。本书的结构、内容和所归纳与梳理的问题，对中国国内学术界来说，是一笔必须借鉴和学习的知识和精神财富。

一、中国崛起需要中国也建立和发展多元化的安全研究议程

本书是一部有关“二战”以后国际关系学界中“安全研究”的学科发展史。正如该书的标题所阐明的，这是一本总结、梳理“国际安全研究”如何演化的书籍。对于广大中国读者来说，阅读此书不仅能了解“国际安全研究”的形成与进展，更重要的是，了解安全研究的演化路程，也是拓展我们安全视角的重要动力。

随着中国崛起，中国的国家安全问题越来越被广大读者所关注。中国国内学术界和媒体近10年来对如何定义中国的国家安全、如何审视中国今天崛起进程中面临的安全挑战、如何发展中国国家安全维护的手段以及如何理解中国的国家安全战略等诸多问题展开了广泛而又热烈的讨论。然而，“安全”这一概念如何定义，如何来有效地维护、保障和实现一个国家的安全需求，国家安全利益的实现如何建立起长期的、可靠的基础，特别是“安全”如何同“发展”“治理”等概念建立起内在的联系，这些问题，比单纯从政治、军事及传统的战略层面思考的安全议题复杂得多。

同样，“中国崛起”已成为今天全球安全研究的热门课题。其原因不仅是西方国家对中国崛起将改变国际体系内利益的再分配，并将导致西方

* 朱锋：北京大学国际关系学院教授、博士生导师，北京大学国际战略研究中心副主任。

传统的心理优势等认知因素的转变，更重要的是，“中国崛起”触动了安全研究领域内一项最古老的理论命题，那就是“大国崛起”以及由此而出现的“权力转移”（power transition）从人类历史来看，常常是造成冲突和战争最重要的根源。因此，“中国崛起”并不必然带来鲜花、掌声和鼓励，相反，“中国崛起”由于造成了国际关系中权力结构和利益结构的再分配，其结果是相当部分的国家对中国充满了疑虑、猜忌、怀疑，给予中国更多的是批评、指责，甚至是非难和防范。21 世纪世界政治最大的话题之一，可能将是如何让中国赢得更多安全的同时让世界也变得更加安全。

假如我们对这一话题感兴趣，假如我们坚信 21 世纪中国能够真正实现“和平崛起”，我们的思考和目光就不能简单地停留在国家层面的安全需求和安全应对，我们还需要了解安全研究的历史和发展，了解学术界学者的研究和努力，究竟给我们带来了什么样的分析工具，以便让我们可以更加全面和客观地审视和判断中国正在面临的安全挑战。

今天，国际关系领域内研究的安全问题，可以大致分为“传统安全”和“非传统安全”。这已经成为包括中国国内学术界在内的普遍的国际共识。“传统安全”问题是指军事、政治和外交手段来应对和实现的安全问题，如领土主权的完整、避免受到其他强国的军事干预和军事胁迫、建立起强大的国防力量来保障国家在各国间的力量对比中享有相对稳定的安全感、发展什么样的军事能力和军事原则以便预防冲突和保持必要的选择，以及如何在对外关系和在国家的战略目标的追求过程中有效、合理以及战略性地运用国防手段，等等。“非传统安全”威胁则主要是指非军事性质的安全挑战，这些挑战如果不能有效和及时地应对，同样将会实质性地损害一个国家的安全努力，弱化该国在传统领域内的安全努力，并将造成严重的不安全后果。例如，网络安全、经济和金融安全、环境安全、水资源安全、食品安全、打击和严防恐怖主义、分离主义和极端主义，以及生物安全、公共健康安全，等等。与此同时，对任何一个国家来说，安全威胁的来源，不仅是“国际的”，同时也是“国内的”；安全的主体，不仅是“国家的”，也是“社会的”和“个人的”。

安全的分类、定义和研究议程，从“传统领域”走向“非传统领域”，这不仅是冷战结束后全球化时代国际局势发展的结果，是人类社会发展到今天、安全概念和内涵都扩大和深化的结果，更是在各种现实的社会生活中，安全的挑战和构成不安全的根源事实上多样化、多元化和复杂化的结果。虽然国际关系学界对安全研究的争议从来没有停止过。这种争议不仅反映了不同的研究取向、学者们所遵从的价值以及研究方法，更重要的是，这些争议说明了独立的、深刻的学术研究对于丰富和多面性的人类社会所特有的“探究”能力。本书显然将为中国读者打开科学认识安全问题的“新视窗”。

二、“国际安全研究”是如何演化的

巴里·布赞和琳娜·汉森写这本书，用他们自己在书的《自序》中所说的，是得到了约瑟夫·奈和林恩－琼斯的启发。这两位新自由主义国际关系理论的大师级学者在 1988 年就指出，还没有一部国际安全研究的思想史著作。这本《国际安全研究的演化》是为了填补这一空白。两位作者这么说未免有点过。

事实上，在他们这本作品之前，已经出现了一系列有关国际安全研究的系谱学总结和介绍性的图书出版。这些书籍中有代表性的包括：爱德华·克罗德兹杰的《安全与国际关系》、特里·特里夫等人共同合作的《当代安全研究》、朗尼·李普舒尔茨主编的《论安全》，以及俄赛尔·爱定里与詹姆斯·罗森瑙合作编辑的《全球化、安全和民族国家》。❶ 这些书籍都从国际安全研究的学科发展和研究议程发展等诸多方面，分析和讨论了国际安全在概念、主体和研究议题等诸多领域内的新变化。然而，这些书的缺陷要么是偏重于理性主义的安全议程，要么过分强调 80 年代末欧洲兴起的“规范主义”（或者说“后实证主义”）的安全研究，都没有将这两大安全研究的分支——重军事、政治和外交研究的“美国主义”与重安全威胁的国内因素和社会视角的“欧洲主义”进行有效地整合，更没有从安全研究的学科发展史的角度出发，有说服力地概括和介绍“美国主义”与“欧洲主义”的差异与联系。

例如，爱德华·克罗德兹杰的《安全与国际关系》是剑桥大学出版社出版的国际安全研究的权威教材。但这本书的特点是希望以美国的安全研究范式为主体，来合并和兼容欧洲的后现代主义、后结构主义、理念主义等新的社会科学方法论为核心的安全研究。克罗德兹杰认为，无论是现实主义、自由主义、新自由制度主义，还是建构主义的安全研究的理论范式，都存在着不同程度的缺陷，都难以对不断变化和发展的全球化时代的现实具有足够的解释力。为此，他强调国际安全研究的未来应该是实现各种范式之间的“融合”，并进行形成更具实证意义和经验检验作用的安全范式。但安全研究的核心问题永远是如何理解为什么要“增加或者减少暴力”的问题。❷ 很显然，克罗德兹杰教授的看法依然保持了安全研究的“美国主义”，而不是布赞和汉森想要竭力倡导的“欧洲主义”。

而让读者能够深入地区分和甄别国际安全研究的“美国主义”和“欧洲主义”，恰恰是布赞和汉森这本书最重要的学术价值之一。正如该书自序中所说的，“这样一部思想史记载着不同学术视角如何相互影响、彼此吸纳和不断交锋，……一部思想与科学社会学史能帮助国际安全研究者更好地了解不同的理论从何而来，为何不同，它们之间的哪些争论事实上将整个安全研究领域链接在一起”。

国际安全研究起步于冷战阶段。那个阶段的安全研究的核心话题是在经历了两次人类惨不堪言的世界大战之后，如何避免世界再度悲剧性地进入新的大国战争。受到整个冷战的挤压，无论是美国还是欧洲，安全研究只有一个压倒一切的命题，那就是如何抵制苏联集团的意识形态扩展、

❶ Edward A. Kolodziej, *Security and International Relations*, Cambridge: Cambridge University Press, 2005; Ersel Aydinli and James N. Rosenau, eds., *Globalization, Security, and the Nation State: Paradigms in Transition*, Albany: State University of New York Press, 2005; Terry Terriff, Stuart Croft, Lucy James, and Patrick M. Morgan, eds., *Security Studies Today*, London: Polity, 1999; Ronnie D. Lipschutz, ed., *On Security*, New York: Columbia University Press, 1995.

❷ Edward A. Kolodziej, *Security and International Relations*, p. 318.

如何防止在经济和军事能力上和西方集团并驾齐驱的苏联集团战胜西方“自由世界”。在这样的背景下，安全研究绝对就是“国家安全”—以增强西方国家应对苏联威胁的能力建设和战略制定为核心，辅之以有效的政策实施和资源动员。国际安全研究的唯一主体是国家，国际安全研究就是围绕着国家在权力竞争中究竟如何能够得以生存的研究。虽然这一时期的安全研究也具有如何防止内部威胁的讨论，但其焦点都是围绕着国家如何防止遭受各种其他国家施加的“外部威胁”的争论。

冷战时代的安全研究的支配性范式，显然是现实主义。现实主义理论不仅带来了各种国家主义安全研究的强有力的理论解释系统，安全研究也成了现实主义理论成长和发展最重要的实证来源。其结果，传统的国际安全研究确定了国家作为主体、武力使用作为关注核心、外在风险作为威胁的基本来源、国家的军事能力建设和危机管理与应对为主要政策措施、实证主义和理性主义为认识论基础的安全学说。

80 年代开始后，冷战逐步进入美苏两大超级大国之间的“缓和时期”。被冷战阴霾长期压得喘不过气来的国际学术界终于开始可以同“生存”的沉重主题拉开一些距离，转而寻求对冷战教训和各种问题的反思。国际关系研究出现了明显的“多元主义”的趋势。1991 年的冷战结束更是国际关系历史进程中划时代的事件。国际关系理论的各种多元主义争论，最终汇集成为对现实主义研究范式的颠覆性批判。以“哥本哈根学派”为代表的欧洲安全研究发起了对继续坚持传统主义安全研究议程、继续强调理性主义方法论的“美国主义”安全研究发起了强大的挑战。而美国的安全研究，继续保持传统，强调安全研究就是“军事的、政治的、外交的”，和安全研究存在着重大关联度的“战略研究”则永远是探讨如何“打赢战争的艺术”。[1]

80 年代末以来，国际安全研究的“美国主义”与“欧洲主义”的争论，让国际安全研究进入了新的繁荣发展期。其学术成就，远远超越了冷战时期的“威慑理论”“均势理论”“霸权稳定”“理性决策”“安全合作”“军控和裁军”“战略研究”等分支。布赞和汉森在本书中概括了国际安全研究的 11 个分支，它们分别是：“常规建构主义”“批判建构主义”“哥本哈根学派”“批判性安全研究”“女性主义安全研究”“人的安全”“和平研究”“后殖民主义安全研究”“后结构主义安全研究”“战略研究”，以及“新现实主义安全研究”。这些安全研究中的不同学派，为我们呈现了不是单纯从国家与主权角度，而是更多地从社会的角度对国际安全问题的剖析和思考。这些分支和学派很多显示的是社会科学研究的“解释功能”，构成了“知识驱动型”的理论、而非“政策指导型”的理论，但这些色彩斑斓、各有学术依据的安全思想，真正为我们提供了安全认识的全息画卷。

---

[1] Richard K. Betts, “Should Strategic Studies Survive?” *World Politics*, Vol. 50, No. 1 (1997), pp. 7 – 33; Stephen M. Walt, “The Renaissance of Security Studies,” *International Studies Quarterly*, Vol. 35, No. 2 (1990), pp. 211 – 239.

三、布赞和汉森版的国际安全研究的思想史：特色和长项

该书最大的特点并非系统地阐释了“欧洲主义”的国际安全研究学说，而是，布赞教授集40年安全研究的知识积累，高屋建瓴地对国际安全问题在进入范式多元化时代的国际安全研究提出了系统的学科史总结，站在一个全球的视野上透视今天安全研究的演化，并希望在国际安全研究的学术领域，廓清时代特征条件下的未来安全研究议程。显然，对安全研究的学术成长来说，布赞和汉森的这一力作具有重要的学术价值。

例如，他们提出的国际安全研究的四类问题——是否应该把国家作为研究的优先指涉对象，是否应该同时将内部与外部的威胁纳入安全的考虑范围，是否应该将安全扩大到军事领域与武力使用之外和安全是否必然与威胁、危险和紧急事态相关联，可以说集中和生动地概括了今天国际安全研究中的多种视角和竞争性的范式。

此外，布赞和汉森对于安全概念的解释在本书中也颇具新意。例如，两位教授认为，为了很好地解释安全的概念，必须引入三组和安全概念相关联的概念。首先，对安全理解的补充性概念，即必须将安全引入更加具体和更加具有限定性的问题之中，例如，威慑、战略和遏制等；其次，必须考虑和安全概念具有重叠性的平行性概念，如权力、主权、认同等；最后，必须参考和安全概念存在着替代性的竞争性概念，如和平、冲突防止、风险控制与合作等。将安全的定义作这样的分析和解释，显然对于读者理解“安全”究竟是什么，以及掌握安全与一系列相关的概念——如权力、和平，以及战略研究等——的联系与区别，显然是非常重要的。例如，在当代国际关系学科中，安全与和平似乎在内在逻辑上密不可分，“安全研究”与“和平研究”却完全是独立的两个领域。“安全研究”在强调权力为手段、国家为主体的分析语境中，生存和防止遭受不可承受的暴力是核心问题。但“和平研究”则是一种以世界主义的和平价值为导向的研究。“和平研究”的主体常常是“人民”而不是“国家”，其更重视对实现停火、危机控制和冲突预防的技术性操作。[1]

布赞与汉森对安全概念所提供的这一分析结构，对于澄清国际关系领域内安全研究与国际关系中其他核心概念之间的关系，具有非常重要的启示性作用。

为安全概念的清晰化提供分析结构，是90年代以来国际安全研究的努力方向。例如，在分析安全时，学者们认为，“谁的安全”（whose security）是一个中心话题。[2] 因为对于不同的安全主体有着不同的安全理解和安全需求。为此，从80年代开始，布赞教授的研究就提出安全不仅是“国家的”“国际的”，也是“社会的”。如果社会结构中的个体——人民不能享有安全保障，国家安全的内在崩溃一定会导致国际不安全的根源。[3] 冷战结束之后，“人的安全”（ human security ）成为安全概念扩展的重要方向，联合国强调安全的定义

[1] David P. Barash, ed., *Approaches to Peace: A Reader in Peace Studies*, Oxford: Oxford University Press, 2000.

[2] David A. Baldwin, “Security Studies and the End of the Cold War”, *World Politics*, Vol. 48, No. 1 (Spring 1995), pp. 117 – 141.

[3] Barry Buzan, *People, States and Fear: The National Security Problem in International Relations*, Brighton: Wheatsheaf, 1983.

“不仅要让人民拥有和平，更重要的是要让人民不虞匮乏和免于恐惧”。安全讨论的范围开始延伸到“国内”，安全的主体也由国家延伸到了“人民”。其经典的案例是“失败国家”（failed state）。如果国内政治与社会秩序的崩溃，人民无法得到经济生活领域内的可靠保障，那么，这样的国内混乱就一定会成为恐怖主义、极端主义等暴力组织滋生与繁衍的温床。与此同时，这些“失败国家”的国内失序，也必定在一个全球化的时代将暴力威胁持续散发到国际领域。

与此同时，一系列后冷战时代安全因素的革命性变化，如全球金融与经济安全、气候变化与节能减排、全球公共卫生安全、网络安全等，为安全研究提供了新的分析结构。安全不仅是“人的安全”“国家安全”，同时也是“区域安全”与“全球安全”。这四个层次的安全同时又是相互重叠但各有区分的扁平状的四个独立领域。

布赞和汉森所提供的三个相互关联的安全概念的分析结构，是一个学术意义上的安全研究，而非现实世界的安全议题的分析结构。这一结构不是旨在准确勾勒安全议题的范畴和层次，而是旨在说明国际关系学中的安全研究领域，可以同其他的国际关系理论的中心概念建立起一种什么样的相互关联。

然而，这一点恰恰又是《国际安全研究的演化》一书非常富有学术开放性，但又有挥之不去的学术模糊性的一面。两位作者特别强调国际安全研究与国际关系研究相互重叠，又始终在努力想要清晰地划出这两个领域之间的界限。他们的看法是，区别国际安全研究与国际关系研究的基本因素是“国际安全研究开始更加聚焦于安全的前提假设和安全概念的争论”。这些争论可以拓展国际安全研究的疆域，因为国际关系研究不是国际安全研究的唯一学科来源。冷战时期，政治学理论、经济学中最早使用的博弈论、政治和社会心理学、国际政治经济学等，都为国际安全研究中的各种分支理论如威慑理论、认知理论等的创立和发展发挥了重要作用。因而两位作者断言，国际安全研究没有明确的“边界”，但有“边疆地带”。

这样的分析方式，用一个更通俗和更好理解的表达是，任何学科领域内的研究范式和理论学说都有“主流”和“非主流”。国际安全研究当然有其特定的“疆域”，构成了这一研究领域内的“主流阵地”；而“边疆地带”则并非是争议最大的地区，而是对争议提出“学术批评”的“非主流阵地”。问题是，在今天的国际安全研究中，“欧洲主义”恰恰是“边疆地带”，但本书并不愿意接受这是一个“非主流”的领域而已。

然而，和其他更多地否定安全研究的国家中心主义的“欧洲学派”相比，布赞和汉森教授在本书中就安全研究的各种观点和学说所做的归类和划分，是一种谨慎的、平衡的折中主义。这也可以说是本书的又一大特色。

在后冷战时代的国际安全研究中，“欧洲学派”又被称为“国际政治社会学”（International Political Sociology）。它综合了三大分支，分别是“哥本哈根学派”（Copenhagen School）、“巴黎学派”（Paris School）和“阿博利斯维斯学派”（Aberystwyth School）。这三大学派虽然有各自的研究侧重和研究方法，其成员也非简单地侧重在欧洲，但都是建构主义、非现实主义和欧洲价值导向的学者。它们拥有一个共同点，那就是它们的安全研究都不同于国际关系领域内的安全研究，而是侧重在研究不同的安全主体、社会结构为安全的决定要素，人的安全与“人类解放”（emancipation）、安全与“安全化”（security and securitization）的复杂性，以及拒绝安全研究的“国内”与“国际”的两元分裂❶。这些学者中，走得更远的，是完全沉醉于用欧洲的“后现代主义”来批评和解构传统的安全话语。他们批评的，不是简单的现实主义范式主导下的权力和国家中心主义的安全语境，而是根本否定国家为安全的主体的转向以“人类中心主义”、“批判理论”为认识论核心的安全观念。他们的方法论，是“福柯式的后现代主义”、赫德利·布尔的“国际社会”学说和形形色色的政治理想的产物。❷其理论特色是不再承认安全研究是国际关系研究的一个分支，而是要强调所谓在安全研究中安全“去边界化”（Debordering）。

之所以有这样的安全研究的“欧洲学派”，是因为这些欧洲学者相信，无论是国际关系还是国内政治，都是人类政治生活的组成部分，这两者并不存在难以逾越的鸿沟。打破“国际”和“国内”的认知差异，是欧洲主义的国际安全研究的认识论基础。然而，传统的国际关系研究者坚持认为国际关系与国内政治研究是两个完全不同的学科。国际关系学者坚信，国际系统完全不同于国内系统，因此，国内政治和国际政治是两个虽有一定关联、但互不隶属的两大研究领域。但欧洲主义的学者坚信，人类的政治活动是一个整体，“国内”和“国际”是不能分拆的。这是“欧洲主义”的安全研究竭力颠覆传统上以现实主义国际关系理论所主导的、“美国主义”的安全研究的重要武器。从认识论的角度来说，一旦人类政治生活没有了“国际”和“国内”的区别，那么，安全研究就不能单纯停留在“民族国家体系”的层面，而需要更多地关注人类日常生活更为广泛和频繁的国内政治领域。国际安全研究的“国内威胁”也就自然成为将比国家间竞争和冲突更重要的“学术疆界”。❸

布赞教授和汉森教授显然并不完全接受这种“泛疆域化”的安全研究。布赞教授在1998年曾提出，他并不拘泥于安全研究中的“国际与国内两分法”，因为许多的案例研究所显示的“不安全状况”并不是“国家主导”的。但他认为，国际安全研究还是有其独特的“研究议程”的，“构成国际安全议题的通常都是对安全的政治与军事解读”。❹

在该书中，布赞和汉森显然对此作了进一步的解释。一方面，他们在该书第二章中坚持认为，国际安全研究存在着“经典政治理解”以及“规范主义”方法论的“二元论”。国际安全研究就是在这一二元语境中“建构安全选择的倾向”。正是

---

❶ Paul D. Williams, *Security Studies: An Introduction*, London: Routledge, 2008, p. 117.

❷ 这方面的典型作品，参见：Ken Booth, *Theory of World Security*, Cambridge: Cambridge University Press, 2008.

❸ 这方面的经典论述，参见：Didier Bigo and R. B. J. Walker, “Political Sociology and the Problem of the International”, *Millennium*, Vol. 35, No. 3 (2007), pp. 725 – 739; Keith Krause and Michael C. Williams, eds., *Critical Security Studies*, London: UCL Press, 1997; R. B. J. Walker, *Inside/Outside: International Relations as Political Theory*, Cambridge: Cambridge University Press, 1993.

❹ Barry Buzan, Ole Wæver and Jaap de Wilde, *Security: A New Framework for Analysis*, Boulder: Lynne Rienner, 1998, p. 21.

在这样的观念支配下，该书保持了布赞教授安全研究的基本立场，那就是在“美国学派”和“欧洲学派”之间争取最大的平衡点。为此，两位作者一方面通过考察中世纪以来经法国大革命一直到今天人类政治生活进步的本质，强调界定国家与公民——人民或者社会个体的自由与安全是一切政治理论认识的前提，突出“国家安全”之外必须存在着“个体安全”与“群体或者社会安全”。他们认为，这不仅是由于“不安全”有时是国家本身造成的，还由于保障个体安全是减少国际冲突的重要来源。另一方面，在批评传统主义的安全研究中现实主义范式弊病的同时，布赞和汉森并不否认传统主义的安全研究议程的重要性。他们承认，现实主义所津津乐道的权力政治解释是现实世界中“物质要素分配”的决定性因素，因此，推动国际安全研究演化的五大驱动力之首，就是人类社会中永远挥之不去的“大国政治”或者“权力政治”。

正因如此，《国际安全研究的演化》一书强调不管人类社会和学术界在“规范主义”或者“后实证主义”的研究范式中展示了多么强大的思辨魅力和人文精神，“国际安全研究推进的核心是超级大国的对抗”；“9·11”事件之后“国家安全的回归”不仅由于恐怖主义组织这样的非国家行为体的暴力威胁，更重要的是“中国崛起”，并由此带来的国际安全影响。原因之一是“从20世纪90年代起，华盛顿一直坚持一个根深蒂固的观点：从长远来看，中国是美国独享超级大国地位的主要威胁”。中美关系的复杂性，让布赞和汉森在该书中承认，尽管后冷战时代国际安全在范围和研究方法上都有了巨大拓展，但传统的安全议题在“惊人地延续”。

四、国际安全研究的演化：认识安全问题的科学视角

对中国读者来说，《国际安全研究的演化》一书最大的魅力，是向我们提供了多元化的安全理解和安全研究议程。在这些既联系但又常常对立的安全理解和安全研究议程的背后，不是简单的看法不同、或者对现实的安全世界的认识不同，而是社会科学研究从认识论到方法论的多元化。《国际安全研究的演化》一书准确、有力地总结和介绍了究竟是什么样的不同认识论和方法论带来了竞争性的安全认知和安全主张。这不仅让我们得以客观和细致地了解国际安全研究学科发展的科学动力，同时也让我们生动地触摸到社会科学研究进步的真实魅力。这些分析和介绍，在两位大师级的学者深厚的学术素养的炮制之下，对于急切在21世纪实现民族复兴的中国人来说，提供了难得的分析工具和理性的认知方法。

布赞和汉森接受冷战时期国际安全研究为现实主义以及后来的新现实主义理论范式所主导的事实，但认为（新）现实主义国际安全理论研究范式“在解释安全现实的同时也在向人们灌输和创造着自己所一味认定的现实”。但这个安全分析的现实主义现实过于“政治化”，它可能延续着安全研究的“国家安全逻辑”或者对于民族国家来说安全永远是针对“外来威胁”的假设，然而，这种拘泥于单纯一种范式来探讨安全问题的学术努力和认知方式本身就是片面的。即便新自由主义的“理性选择”学说将国家视为“理性行为体”，且不说国家的“理性”常常采取其实是过分

的安全感，即便“理性选择”的新自由主义的安全假设，也常常更多地注重物质力量的作用，而忽视规范、观念、认同等认知（ideational）因素的作用。

在该书中，布赞和汉森强调他们在安全研究的文献梳理中所采用的“后库恩主义的科学社会学”（Post－Kuhanian sociology of science）认识论。这种“后库恩主义”的认识论，坚持托马斯·库恩（Thomas Kuhn）所强调的观点：人类的社会科学知识，并不简单来自对人类社会的科学研究和发现的积累，也来自认识人类社会生活的知识系统的创新与发展；而衡量和判断不同知识系统的重要标志是其“核心的假设和逻辑体系”——范式（paradigm）。因此，库恩认为，在单一的“范式”领域内，人类的科学知识永远难以进步。与此同时，布赞和汉森也批评库恩主义中的“实证主义研究至上”的论断，否认安全研究的知识体系只来自于经验和事实。他们认为，人类社会的分析，并不能单纯依靠经验和事实，更需要坚持“规范主义”（normative）的勇气和决心。他们主张，80年代后社会科学研究中许多新的方法论，如“批评理论”、后现代主义、后结构主义、女性主义等“后实证主义”方法论，同样可以使得学者们将对安全思考进行“归纳性”研究和“推论性”研究的结合。而这一点构成了两位作者所说的他们写作本书时的“认识论立场”（epistemologist footing）。具体来说，布赞教授和汉森更相信社会科学研究中的“科学社会学”，而不是新现实主义和新自由主义所强调的“理性主义”。

在这一基础上，两位作者认为，安全的基本认识只有包括三个部分才是综合全面的。这就是“客观安全”（objective security）、“主观安全”（subjective security）和“话语安全”（discursive security）。“客观安全”是指“缺乏或者存在以能力为基础的威胁”；而“主观安全”则是“对威胁的感知或者主体的感觉决定了是否存在什么性质的威胁和多大程度上的威胁”；“话语安全”则是认为“安全议题”是由政治、历史和社会性因素所决定的，安全说到底是“一种言语行为”，并不能真正用客观标准来衡量。为此，“安全”永远只能是特定政治议程中自我指涉的“问题”，产生这样的安全事实的本质力量并非“物质性”的，而是各种行为者之间“主体间性”（inter－subjective）的观念互动过程。

但是，布赞和汉森并非是90年代后欧洲国际关系研究中狂热地追求“去国家化”的“政治社会学者”（political sociologist）。他们强调，国际安全研究领域中“理性主义”与“规范主义”、物质力量和非物质力量都是不可忽略、不可简单回避的话题。因此，在他们提出的国际安全研究的五大驱动力中，“理性主义”和“规范主义”妥协性地并存。这五大驱动力既有“权力政治”“技术因素”和“制度化”，又有“国际事件”和“学术争论的内在动力”。前三大动力显然都是属于“理性主义”范畴，而“学术争论的内在动力”更多强调认知因素、话语因素和规范主义分析因素对安全研究的作用。“国际事件”可以介于这两者之间。因为“国际事件”的发生和影响常常是“物质主义”的，但对其的解读和反应，毫无疑问，又常常是“观念性”的、“话语性”的。布赞本人的研究显然更倾向于把安全既不是解释成“客观的”也不是单纯“主观的”，而是更符合他所提出的“话语安全”的特征。在1998年出版的《安全：新的分析框架》（中文的另一译名为《新安全论》）一书中，布赞教授提出，总的来说，安全是一种“自我指涉的活动”，因为安全的观念和紧迫性，都受到特定的政治日程的左右。[1]

如果知识永远是人类医治偏执和躁动的良药，那么，通过阅读本书，我相信不仅将引导更多的学生和学者客观、公正地从事安全和国际问题研究，更重要的是，将会减少中国式“愤青”群体的数量，让中国的读者真正了解国际安全研究不仅仅涉及国家之间“安全困境”等传统意义上的权力争夺，更重要的是，安全研究的学术努力，在于不断从不同的角度、立场和价值出发，通过有竞争性的安全问题探讨，力图超越单纯的“国家”和“民族”本位，而将安全在理论的定位和现实出路的探索进程中置于一个更加宏大和符合人类社会进步本质的维度上。这可能对于在现实的国家环境中早已经耳熟能详各种国家间竞争和对立主导安全认知的中国读者来说，无疑是一种灵魂的挑战。

然而，读一本学术精品书籍能让灵魂受到挑战，这恰恰是知识的最大魅力。

---

[1] Barry Buzan, Ole Wæver, and Jaap de *Wilde*, *Security*: *A New Framework for Analysis*, Boulder: Lynne Rienner, 1998, p. 27.

试论国际安全研究的一种新路径及其启示

——小议《国际安全研究的演化》

陈锴*

【摘要】《国际安全研究的演化》预示着未来国际安全研究的发展方向，具有十分深远的学术价值和现实意义。本书的理论贡献之一在于，采取多元的理论视角，结合结构、层次的分析方法，系统地呈现了国际安全的一种新研究路径。分析这一研究路径及其启示，有助于国际安全研究的深入发展。

【关键词】安全研究，研究路径，非国家行为体，决策者

《国际安全研究的演化》是国际安全研究领域的两位重量级学者巴里·布赞教授和琳娜·汉森教授合著的一部上乘之作。该书堪称一部里程碑式的著述，因为该书最先系统地梳理并阐析20世纪40年代以来国际安全研究的演化。❶ 不仅如此，该书是首部全面考量国际安全研究的著述，填补了国际安全研究的重要空缺。❷ 布赞和汉森基于对60多年来国际安全研究文献的解读，"揭示不同的理论流派如何在国际安全研究争论中表明其立场"❸，并剖析了国际安全研究的演化规律。

该书的理论贡献之一在于，采取多元的理论视角，结合结构、层次的分析方法，系统地呈现了国际安全的一种新研究路径。正如布赞和汉森所言，该书"不是总结出国际安全研究中最好的或唯一的理论，也不是合成国际安全研究中所有不同的文献以形成一种'成熟理论'"。这两位学者期望其方法"作为一种分析建构路径对其他学者有所帮助，或可激发他们形成自己的研究方法。"❹ 阐析这一新研究路径及其启示，具有重要的理论和现实意义。

一、新研究路径呈现的主要特征

概括而言，该书提出的国际安全研究路径主要呈现出以下三方面特征：

---

* 陈锴：浙江大学公共管理学院在站博士后，浙江大学非传统安全与和平发展研究中心研究员。

❶ Burgess, J. Peter. Editor's Note. Security Dialogue, Dec 2010; vol. 41: pp. 587 – 588

❷ Biersteker, Thomas J. Interrelationships Between Theory and Practice in International Security Studies. Security Dialogue, Dec 2010; vol. 41: pp. 599

❸ ［英］巴里·布赞、［丹］琳娜·汉森：《国际安全研究的演化》，余潇枫译，浙江大学出版社，2011年版，导读一。

❹ 同上书，中文版自序。

（一）开放的安全研究议程

布赞和汉森提出的这种研究路径具有明显的开放性，对国家安全的主要分析层次与构成国际安全研究的主要议题均有较为深入的理解。

从纵向层面来看，布赞和汉森采用“人、国家和体系”的层次分析方法，即国际安全研究的指代对象向下延伸至个人，向上延伸至国际体系，由此构建了一种纵向的安全分析框架。这种分析框架强调，结构层次的分析与单位层次分析相互关联，对其中任何一个层次安全的深入理解在一定程度上取决于对其他层次安全的认知。为了避免将国际安全或国家安全还原、简化为个人安全，布赞和汉森在安全的“指涉对象”上采取中间立场，既不像国家中心主义那样偏向于“国家安全”，也不像传统和平研究和批判安全研究那样偏向于个人安全。

从横向层面来看，布赞和汉森构建的国际安全新路径对跨领域的诸多积极、消极因素给予高度关注。布赞和汉森阐明了有关安全的三组概念（补充性概念、平行性概念和竞争性概念）结构，不仅使安全概念更具整体性，而且进一步将国际安全研究的诸多相关理论和分析联系在一起，拓展了安全研究的范畴，为国际安全研究中的扩展与深化路径提供了进一步支持。

（二）多元化的认识论与方法论

国际安全研究是一种多种理论、路径并存的领域。“国际安全研究的驱动力很大程度上是在认识论、方法论和研究重点选取上的学术争论。”国际安全研究之所以不断扩展，正是不同的理论相得益彰的结果。

布赞和汉森认为，不同的理论、路径之间存在通约性（commensurable），因而秉承多元的学术视角，不仅借鉴了新现实主义和建构主义的研究方法，还将各种理论置于历史进程中进行分阶段的对比，籍此探究国际安全研究诸多理论、路径的交点，同时试图令新的研究路径成为不同理论、路径彼此沟通的平台。考虑到“国际安全研究的大多数论文并没有尽力讨论它们在分析性、规范性、哲学和认识论层面的诸多假设”，[1] 布赞和汉森在该书中从认识论和方法论两个层面凸显了国际安全研究的多种路径的“综合化”。

在认识论层面上，强调“客观安全”“主观安全”和“话语安全”的差异。客观安全概念往往驻足于物质层面，认为一国威胁他国或威慑敌人的可能性基于其物质能力；主观安全概念通常强调历史和规范、恐惧心理以及与此相关而形成的人际关系（朋友、中立者、对手、敌人）的重要性；话语安全则强调安全是自我指涉的实践，是一种“言语行为”（speech act），是“安全威胁”的话语建构。

在方法论层面上，布赞和汉森坚持具有规范性、历史性以及哲学性的论述，同时强调社会学、历史学、哲学及法学对国际安全研究的重要性，促进不同理论之间的相互解释和补充，旨在构建一种结合多元方法论和认识论，又具有历史、哲学内涵的国际安全研究路径。“话语安全观一直是扩展路径的核心部分。后结构主义者、女性主义者、后殖民主义者、批判建构主义者和哥本哈根学派之间虽然有些

[1] ［英］巴里·布赞、［丹］琳娜·汉森：《国际安全研究的演化》，余潇枫译，浙江大学出版社，2011年版，第23页。

不同，但都倾向于把安全视为一种话语，通过这种话语，认同和威胁被建构起来，而不是把安全作为一个客观的、物质的条件。”

（三）将非传统安全研究路径置于逻辑框架之中

布赞和汉森高度关注非传统安全研究路径，他们意识到自身的视角是“一个更多地与非传统安全议题相联的欧洲视角，也正是这一视角成就了该书的特点。无论何种变化塑造了国际安全研究的前景，国际安全研究中的扩展与深化现象不可能逆转。”❶

这两位学者从“整合性”“批判性”“复合性”“规范性”“政治性”“发展性”六个分析维度，阐述了非传统安全研究的七种理论路径，即建构主义、哥本哈根学派、批判安全研究、女性主义、人的安全、后殖民主义和后结构主义。不仅如此，布赞和汉森通过五种驱动力（即大国政治、技术、事件、学术争论、制度化）及分析其对国际安全研究演化的影响，这也是该书的主要理论创新之一。他们认为五种驱动力“各自相互独立，每一种驱动力都能建构不同的视角与解释形式，但是并非所有的驱动力在全时段都同等重要，五种驱动力之间的互动与影响随着时间也在发生着变化”。

值得注意的是，托马斯·比尔斯特克（Thomas J. Biersteker）在评价《国际安全研究的演化》时指出，布赞教授与汉森教授在书中提出的五种“驱动力”并非源于某种社会学理论。无可否认，他们对这种研究方式具有非同寻常的期许。但是，这五种特定的“驱动力”是如何选定的？这些驱动力是否可以有所增减？有关这些问题的答案尚不明确。❷托马斯·比尔斯特克进一步指出，布赞和汉森未能明确地探究五种驱动力之间复杂、深刻的相互关系。“这五种驱动力的范畴并不具有排他性。比如，美国首次使用原子弹轰炸日本广岛，究竟算是事件，还是技术发展？显然，两者兼具。”❸

二、新路径给予的启示

任何分析框架都不可能穷尽问题，或者完全适用于所有的情形或现象，因此任何框架都不可避免地遭遇现有理论无法解释的现象。或许是限于本书的篇幅和构建国际安全新路径的限制，布赞和汉森尚未对其提出的诸多问题展开深入的论述，或给予系统、明确的答案。随着威胁的变化，国际安全研究必需针对既定的议题而做出诸多回应。书中的部分未尽之处，在一定程度上亦是新的研究路径给予的有益启示。

（一）关注“跨国行为体”

“9·11”事件以来，跨国行为体在全球范围内日益活跃，而跨国行为体在国际安全研究文献中被讨论的比重也随之增加。在许多国家和地区，追求本体安全的个体通过跨国行为体来影响安全

❶ ［英］巴里·布赞、［丹］琳娜·汉森：《国际安全研究的演化》，余潇枫译，浙江大学出版社，2011年版，中文版自序；第292页。

❷ Biersteker, Thomas J. Interrelationships Between Theory and Practice in International Security Studies. Security Dialogue, Dec 2010; vol. 41: pp. 600

❸ Biersteker, Thomas J. Interrelationships Between Theory and Practice in International Security Studies. Security Dialogue, Dec 2010; vol. 41: pp. 600

事务，而跨国行为体对于国际安全和国家安全的潜在影响已对现有的国际安全研究提出了新的挑战。不仅如此，与跨国行为体相关的诸多非传统安全问题（例如跨国犯罪、人口贩卖、轻小武器扩散和国际恐怖主义）与目前国际安全研究议程的契合程度仍有待商榷。跨界行为体虽然被视为一种指涉对象，但是有关"跨国行为体"的安全需求和安全应对，却时常在国际安全研究中被置于失语状态。迈克尔·威廉姆斯（Michael C. Williams）在评论《国际安全研究的演化》时，建议在布赞和汉森的研究范畴中加入公共安全和私人安全问题，例如分析国际安全分析面临的新现象，包括跨国的非国家暴力和安全私有化。❶ 在最近数十年，这一领域呈现迅速扩展的趋势，例如，私人军事企业（private military companies）涉及战斗、训练和物流，商业安全企业（commercial security firms）则在决策、危机分析和警戒中日益发挥显著的作用。❷

布赞为了完善其"世界社会"的研究，用分析层次的观点将不同行为体重新加以界定，区分出包括国家、非国家行为体与个人三者层次所构成的社会型态组合。布赞教授认为，世界社会的三种构成要素：国家、跨国行为体和个人。与此相对的三种社会类型分别是国家间社会（inter-state）、跨国社会（transnational society）和人际社会（interhuman society），任何一种国际社会与世界社会都是以上三种不同形态的混合体。由跨国行为体形成的世界社会则与由国家组成的国际社会十分相像，呈现出一种社会型态。这三种分析层次（国家、个人、跨国行为体）中的任何一种都不能主导其他两种，而且彼此之间能够相互作用。❸ 但是，布赞尚未对跨国行为体层次的社会加以明确的界定。❹

沿着布赞的理论思路，"跨国行为体"既是安全威胁的来源之一，也是安全的主体之一。强调"跨国行为体"在国际安全研究中的重要性，不是用跨越国家边界的行为体（如跨界民族）的安全去取代国家安全，而是从广义角度将"人的安全"扩展为"那些遭受贫困及其自身所在国迫害之威胁而被边缘化的人群的安全"，同时又能将贫困、不发达、饥饿和其他威胁人类存续的安全议题进一步纳入国际安全的研究进程。将国际安全研究在非国家行为体层次上展开，无疑会增强国际安全研究路径的扩展与深化。"有时国际安全研究随着内容或重点的变化而使其整体得以改变，有时国际安全研究又在不同的地方以不同的方式演化着。"❺ 至于传统意义上国家在安全研究中的主体地位，应取决于不同研究层次和不同理论命题的具体需要。

不过，有关"跨国行为体"的国际安全研究仍有诸多问题尚待解决。例如，跨国行为体及跨国社会在不同特定形态的国际社会中的表现和作

❶ Williams, Michael C. The Public, the Private and the Evolution of Security Studies Security Dialogue, Dec 2010; vol. 41; pp. 623.

❷ 同上书：pp. 628.

❸ Buzan, Barry. *From International to World Society? English School Theory and the Social Structure of Globalization*, Cambridge: Cambridge University Press, 2004. xvii – xviii

❹ 同上书，pp. 118 – 128，135 – 6

❺ ［英］巴里·布赞、［丹］琳娜·汉森：《国际安全研究的演化》，余潇枫译，浙江大学出版社，2011 年版，第 42 页。

用如何？再比如，布赞建构的国家间社会、跨国社会与人际社会仍有待融入大量的历史素材，籍此论述不同层次社会在不同历史阶段的形成、发展和变化。

（二）将国内社会变量纳入国际安全研究

国际安全研究的主要作用在于，依据历史发展呈现的不同特征，针对不断变化的国际安全态势，深入地展开分析并提出对策建议。布赞和汉森提出的研究路径可以深入发展下去，譬如探究理论与政策实践的相互关系。❶ 鉴于《国际安全研究的演化》的研究“主要是追溯和解释国际安全研究作为国际关系的一般次领域的演化，所以我们并不想以任何更具体的方式穷尽国家变量。”❷因此，布赞和汉森尚未在该书中将国内社会变量纳入国际安全研究的范畴。对此，托马斯·比尔斯特克认为，“在大国产生影响时，其他强大的社会动力也在发挥其作用，诸如革命运动和生态改变。应透过不同的分析范畴，对它们给予与大国因素同等的关注”。❸

但是，从理论角度来看，国内社会变量之所以重要，是因为其缺乏相应的理论化，而以往关于国内社会变量的研究，往往将其视为是理所当然的概念，忽视对概念本身的详尽讨论。这一缺失终究会影响国际安全研究的整体性。因此，在国际安全研究中，应当引入将国内社会变量（例如文化因素和决策者因素）纳入国际安全研究之中，进一步探讨文化因素和经济因素在国际安全研究中应处于怎样的地位？倘若理论与实践各自处于离散的范畴，那么事件、学术争论和制度化之间的相互关系就会变得模糊。❹

以决策者因素为例。作为一种国内社会变量，决策者对于安全的认知偏差或决策者自身利益因素的干扰，都会在一定程度上影响安全政策的合理性。现实中，决策者因素是国际安全研究中的一种“过滤器”，许多特定的安全问题通过决策者的取舍而被赋予不同的意义，并在不同的话语中建构相应的安全政策。国际安全研究与安全决策者之间的互动，在很大程度上体现为国家对复杂利益的协调与取舍。至于调和国家行为体与跨国行为体的安全需要则是更为困难的事，决策者因素的引入显得更为迫切。

在驱动力的框架中，政策与政治家通过制度化（借助智库及国家对大学和特定机构的投资）和大国政治产生作用。许多事件受到政策决策的驱动。因此，我们期待探究政策是否具有更高的解释性地位。❺

理论与政策实践在整体上及相互之间均有相关性。一般而言，政策实践者运用简化的框架，以一系列直接和间接的方式诠释、证明和/或使外

---

❶ Biersteker, Thomas J. Interrelationships Between Theory and Practice in International Security Studies. Security Dialogue, Dec 2010; vol. 41: pp. 605

❷ ［英］巴里·布赞、［丹］琳娜·汉森：《国际安全研究的演化》，余潇枫译，浙江大学出版社，2011 年版，第 51 页。

❸ Biersteker, Thomas J. Interrelationships Between Theory and Practice in International Security Studies. Security Dialogue, Dec 2010; vol. 41: pp. 600.

❹ 同上书。

❺ Buzan, Barry, Hansen, Lene. Beyond The Evolution of International Security Studies? Security Dialogue, Dec 2010; vol. 41: pp. 665

交决策具有合法性，无论其是否自我意识到这种实践。❶ 背景不仅包括共同的历史事件和经历、文本之间的参照，以及参与者和理论家的个人经历，还包括参与者和理论家用以界定、描述和诠释事件的制度安排。❷

布赞和汉森在其研究框架中，将部分有关个人经历的因素引入了“制度化”的探讨，尤其是学者研究的资金来源等。但是，其他有关个人经历的重要因素却尚未被涉及，例如，学者在政府或国际组织工作经历的影响，知识分子对特定领域发展的影响，或者学者在反对战争或不公的社会运动中发挥的作用，这些因素并未被系统地纳入布赞和汉森的分析框架中。❸ 虽然布赞和汉森在其分析中很好地整合了文本之间的不同要素，但是他们尚未明确地强调理论家的个人经历问题。国际安全研究的学者共同经历了部分事件并具有相同的历史体验，比如第二次世界大战或冷战的终结。❹ 对此，布赞和汉森撰文予以肯定，表示他们分析“主要基于国际安全研究产生的文本。对于文本、个人历史和主要研究者的网络的探究，能够从更为清晰的视角大致把握动机、冲突和边界设定”。❺

（三）基于历史哲学思辨构建非西方路径

透过布赞和汉森在书中的论述，呈现出国际安全研究持续发展所面临的两个困境。其一，缺乏与国际安全研究相关的历史、哲学探讨。尽管国际安全研究领域涌现了大量检验、采用或否定各种新的安全概念化的概念性、分析性研究文献，但是多数国际安全研究领域内的著述并未对国际安全研究的主题进行相关的哲学探讨，而局限于概念层面的阐释。❻ 其二，“国际安全研究面临着如何摆脱西方中心主义的现实困境”。❼ 尽管本书的内容也涉及了亚洲和其他非西方国家和地区的安全问题与安全议题，但涉及非西方的安全研究文献仅占总体文献的一小部分，西方的国际安全研究尚未更多地纳入非西方的安全思考与学术研究。可以说，如何将国际安全研究置于非西方的情境中，是学界亟待解决的一个问题。唯有将非西方的世界纳入到国际安全的研究视野，国际安全的历史叙述才会趋于完整。

可以说，构建非西方国际安全路径或理论的最终目的并非实现国际安全理论的多元化态势，而是形成独特的认识论、方法论内涵❽，基于非西方的历史、哲学研究来验证相应的研究路径或视角的特殊性，籍此与当前国际安全理论进行有意义的对话，以非西方化的历史与哲学作为发展普遍化理论的基础。

---

❶ Biersteker, Thomas J. Interrelationships Between Theory and Practice in International Security Studies. Security Dialogue, Dec 2010; vol. 41: 601 页。

❷ 同上书，第 601 页。

❸ 同上书，第 600 ~ 601 页。

❹ 同上书，第 603 页。

❺ 同上书，第 662 页。

❻ ［英］巴里·布赞、［丹］琳娜·汉森：《国际安全研究的演化》，余潇枫译，浙江大学出版社，2011 年版，第 10 页。

❼ 同上书，导读一。

❽ 例如，以《易经》为代表的“类比取象”观察“自我”与“他者”的关系如何体现“阴阳之道”，这种整体论的研究路径有助于消除“自我”与“他者”的对立，而不局限于无政府状态逻辑下的“自我”和“他者”之间的二元对立。

对于中国学者而言，应当进一步考量安全理论与实践之间的复杂关联，将理论架构与历史、哲学探讨结合起来，从中国历史与哲学思想中探究具有中国特色的安全研究路径。要实现这一目标，必需形成某种具有自觉且持续成长的国际安全研究学者群体，以免学术研究流于离散的态势。中国学者应将中国的历史、哲学理念体现于国际安全研究之中，清楚地解释中国国际行为。唯有如此，才能与国际安全学界进行不断的对话，在国际安全的众多议题中表达中国的路径和视角，从中强化自身的论述基础，从而令理论与实际能够相互佐证，彰显中国学者回应不同安全议题和加入理论探讨的余地。随着未来国际安全研究与新的安全关切的同步发展，中国学者势必会开辟出新的路径，对国际安全结构做出一般性的解释，并兼顾本国的安全政策与公共安全议题的研究。

从安全分析路径来看，考虑到科学的实证路径与哲学、社会学、历史学的建构路径分别代表了传统安全研究与非传统安全研究的不同理论视角，因此两者皆不可偏废。对于致力于使用定量分析方法的研究者来说，可以最大限度地利用国际学界广泛使用的已有数据库，根据研究目的和问题选择最合适的数据，尽可能使用不同数据来检验假设并证实观点。

三、结语

该书是一次宏大的跨学科探讨，预示着未来国际安全研究的发展方向，具有十分深远的学术价值和现实意义。布赞和汉森不仅总结了多年来国际安全研究领域的进展，还为国际安全研究提出了新的路径，不仅有利于国际安全研究的深入拓展，而且很有可能成为国际关系研究的新路径。

人的安全：非传统安全的价值基点

——《人的安全：概念与应用》书评

余潇枫[*]

（一）

人的安全这一概念最先于联合国《人类发展报告》（1993年、1994年）中使用，之后引起了学界的广泛讨论，我国学者从21世纪初开始对这一概念给予了诸多关注，《世界经济与政治》最早对国外的相关论文进行了译介❶。但是，目前尚未有作品对该概念及其政策应用进行系统的引介，这也是促成我们组织翻译该书的动力之一。

这里首先需要说明的是，human security究竟如何翻译更合适，存在着异见和争议。国内已经发表的文献中，主要的翻译是人类安全、人的安全，也有极个别学者使用“人本安全”❷，而日本有学者将之翻译成“人间安全”。各个译法都有其特定的语境和亮点，人类安全最早出自对联合国《人类发展报告》的翻译，突出“人类”的整体性，我们认为这样翻译是合适的；“人本安全”突出的是“以人为中心”的安全的内核理念；“人间安全”在中文看来更体现的是一个“物理场域”。所以，从human security这一概念本身强调的“人”是相对国家而言的，该概念所指涉的“人”既包括作为个体的人，也包括作为“类”的人来看，我赞成本书译者所采用的“人的安全”这一译法。

究竟什么是人的安全？这个概念具备哪些实质性的理论意义和政策操作性？概念层面的争论有：之于人权研究，人的安全是否是新瓶装旧酒？之于安全研究，人的安全与其之区别与联系在哪里？与亚洲提出的综合安全、合作安全等概念相比较，人的安全又是否是一种类似的称呼而已？或者说，人的安全是否是一个新的和必要的概念？以及人的安全是否因其内涵太宽泛而不具备分析的意义？政策层面的质疑在于，人的安全是否过

---

* 余潇枫：浙江大学非传统安全与和平发展研究中心主任，浙江大学公共管理学院教授、博士生导师，浙江大学非传统安全管理博士点负责人。

❶ 参见：阿米塔夫·阿卡亚著，李增田译：《人类安全：东方对西方》，载：《世界经济与政治》，2002年第5期，第57～62页；保罗·埃文斯著，汪亮译：《人的安全与东亚：回顾与展望》，载：《世界经济与政治》，2004年第6期，第43～48页；巴瑞·布赞著，崔顺姬、余潇枫译：《“人的安全”：一种“还原主义”和“理想主义”的误导》，载：《浙江大学学报》，2008年第1期，第6～7页；松下和夫著，李佳译：《论“人的安全”与“环境合作”》，载：《浙江大学学报》，2008年第1期，第29～38页。

❷ 参见：刘志军：《“人本安全”的价值论争》，载：《浙江大学学报》，2008年第2期，第116～125页。

于宽泛而难以操作，甚至会沦为政治领导者的政治口号？将其作为政策框架的利弊分别是什么？除此之外，亚洲的学界和政策层还质疑，人的安全是一个西方概念，体现的是西方在人权、政治自由方面的偏好，而亚洲真正需要的是实现社会的顺利运行和经济的发展。

在我看来，人的安全是非传统安全的价值基点。非传统安全带来的整个安全观的转型的重要贡献之一，便是把安全研究以国家安全为重心转向了同时以人的安全、社会安全和国家安全为重心。而我认为，之中的价值基点，便是人的安全。也就是说，人的安全，是安全的底线和核心，应该成为安全研究的价值基础，使得人拥有“免于恐惧”和“免于匮乏”的自由。这一价值基点也标示着安全研究的历史转型，标示非传统安全与以保障国家主权与政权安全为核心的传统安全的基本分界。

自然，智者见智，仁者见仁。关于人的安全，学界和政策界有种种质疑与批评，各类争论至今依然存在。争论即是价值。人的安全作为一个新的概念框架，可以说是一个方生方成的“思想实验”和“政策理想”，因此要面对各类质疑、批判甚至围攻亦是再正常不过。甚至可以预期，在中国，它或许将经受更大的质疑和挑战。尽管如此，我们依然满怀信心和希冀地将该书进行翻译引介，反对抑或赞同，对国内学界和政策层来说，都将是激活思想的马刺。

（二）

对“人的安全”的主要批评包括：“人的安全”类似于热空气，好听但缺乏可持续性；这一概念太宽泛以致无从分析；这一概念的危险性在于会沦落为政治领导的政治口号，而无法从实践上去真正落实；人的安全关注的是个人层面，但是没有国家参与的安全可能存在吗？将个体“安全化”（securitization）是否是解决全球化进程中国际社会所面临的挑战的最好路径？

在诸多批评者中，我想着重论及的是——安全研究的代表性人物、哥本哈根学派创始人之一——巴里·布赞（Barry Buzan）的观点，他的批评也具有典型性。

布赞不赞成在安全研究中使用“人的安全”这一概念，认为将其作为一种分析框架在国际安全研究中缺乏理论价值。他指出：“事实上，‘人的安全’这一概念的广泛使用（由此还制造出了诸多相应的概念），并无多少新的内涵以助于理论的分析，也无多少与人权讨论的区别以体现实际的价值。而产生的问题恰恰是把对国际安全的理解推向了一种“还原主义”（reductionism）的视角，即把个人构建为最终的安全指涉目标；同时还强化了另一种错误的倾向——把国际安全的理解推向一种‘理想主义’（idealism）的立场，即把安全问题理想化为某种可期望的终极目标。”❶

布赞指出“人的安全”概念的广泛使用会进入一种“还原主义”的误区，是有其理论来源的。在国际关系理论中有“还原论”和“系统论”之争。系统论者往往批判还原论只看细节不看全局，在研究局部时不把它放到整体环境之中。在安全

❶ 巴里·布赞：《“人的安全”：一种“还原主义”和“理想主义”的误导》，崔顺姬、余潇枫译，载：《浙江大学学报》，2008年第1期，第7页。

研究中，系统论在理论上更具有分析的优先性与优越性。因而从安全研究的系统角度来看，安全研究的主体，即定位“谁的安全”的问题是首要问题。在布赞看来，如果“人的安全”的指涉对象仅仅指“个体”，那么就割裂了“人的安全”的集体语境，陷入还原论的误区中；如果“人的安全”指涉的对象是“集体”，那么用“社会安全”概念会更具解释性。

布赞指出“人的安全”概念的广泛使用会进入一种“理想主义”的误区，其主要担心在于，作为关系范畴的安全研究会忽视“人的安全”以外的其他安全议程，或者会造成这样一种可能性：即混淆国际安全领域内性质各异的诸多议程之间的差别，混淆“社会安全”以及公民自由问题上性质各异的议程之间的差别，甚至混淆“国际安全议程”与“国内安全议程”之间关系与作用的某种区别与其间的合理张力。

同时，布赞也承认“人的安全”这一概念使用的某种价值上的合理性，他认为至少在讨论人权问题时，“人的安全”这一概念有可能加深政治考虑的复杂性与政治解决的周全性，但他又诙谐地强调这更多的是在“赶政治时髦”❶。

如何走出“人的安全”这种“还原主义”与“理想主义”的误区？布赞的观点非常明确，他认为“人权”的概念在日常政治生活中比“人的安全”的概念具有更大的适用性与解释力，既然人的安全关涉“个体”或“人类”的安全，应该说与“人权”的议程没有多大区别。因此，如果说“人的安全”的概念存在着把所有可能的安全指涉对象都引向个体、进而把安全看做是某种可期望的终极目标的危险的话，那么“人权”的概念则恰恰更好地体现出了“非安全化”（desecurtiization）的性质——即从“安全化”回到一种日常政治生活的状态，从而体现出了作为“可期望的终极目标”理念的现实可行性。❷

应该说，布赞的观点有其理论的独到性与分析的深刻性，但也必须指出，其分析也存在着某种缺陷。

首先，与“还原主义”倾向的不同解读是，人的安全是“人本主义”在安全领域的弘扬。以往的安全研究往往注重宏观上的安全维护，传统的“安全研究”将人的安全议程排斥在外，而以“和平研究”来容纳人的安全议程；但冷战后随着国际安全研究的转型，人的安全议程已经迅速上升到了安全研究的显著地位。事实上，“人的安全概念以它特殊的‘以人为本’的安全思想，对既往的安全研究提出了新的质疑。它要求我们把以往的安全和政策思想重新定位（reorient），把安全指涉的对象聚焦于个体或整个人类。因此，这一概念的挑战主要还是规范性的（normative），促使安全话语开拓出一个崭新的争论领域。”❸

其次，虽则“人权”与“人的安全”具有某种内容与实现方式的契合性，但人权议程的语境

---

❶ 参见：巴里·布赞：《“人的安全”：一种“还原主义”和“理想主义”的误导》，崔顺姬、余潇枫译，载：《浙江大学学报》，2008年第1期，第7页。

❷ 同上。

❸ 崔顺姬：《区域安全复合理论——基于“传统安全”和“人的安全”视角的分析》，载：《浙江大学学报》，2008年第1期，第20页。

长期以来已经被政治化了（也就是说政治性是其主要维度），不仅被用来影射某种政治制度的缺陷与提倡“反政府”，甚至还被霸权国家作为跨国干涉的理论依据与具有标榜性质的旗号，从而在某种程度上失落了“人权”概念在其实践运用中对“人”的问题的本然观照，其本质上是消极的。而人的安全，它包括政治、经济、社会、教育等多个维度，强调人拥有“免于恐惧”与“免于匮乏”这两个层面的自由。

再次，“冷战”结束后，大量的民族冲突凸显，国际恐怖主义兴起，诸多的非传统安全问题直接威胁到人的安全，“私人化战争”❶“人肉炸弹”等个体化的恐怖行为普遍增加；同时，人权问题变得更为复合与多维，人的权利的保障与实现也与更多的领域相互交叉与混合。在这样的语境下，国际安全理论越来越开始从“社会集体”（social collectivities）间的互动关系研究转向“个体”（individual）间的互动关系研究，因而从“人的安全”来观照人的生存安全与发展安全，更具有理论的合理性与解释的广泛性。

（三）

联合国发展署1994年发布的《人类发展报告》认为：人的安全有两大方面的内容，其一是拥有免于诸如饥饿、疾病和压迫等长期威胁的安全；其二是获得在家庭、工作或社区等日常生活中对突如其来的伤害性的骚扰的保护。该报告还提出了与此相应的“人的安全”的七大要素：经济安全（基本收入有保障）、粮食安全（确保粮食供应充足）、健康安全（相对免于疾病和传染）、环境安全（能够获得清洁水源、清新空气和未退化的耕地）、人身安全（免遭人身暴力和威胁）、共同体安全（文化特性的安全）、政治安全（基本人权和自由得到保护）。

应该说，“人的安全”概念的提出，突破了传统主权的限定与高政治（high politics）对安全问题的限定，因为“人的安全与人的权利是一个硬币的两面”❷，“人的安全概念的凸显意味着安全的核心将是日常生活的境况——食物、居所、求职、健康、公共安全和人的权利等，而不是国家外交政策与军事实力的专有物。”❸人的安全的提出其核心意义是凸现人自身的价值特别是人作为“个体”存在的价值。人类安全委员会的报告如此具体阐释人的安全：通过发展人类自由和实现人生价值来保护关涉人类命运至关重要的核心内容，保障人类的基本自由——自由是生命的精髓；保护人类免受严重的、普遍的威胁和危险情况的伤害，通过多种途径增强人类的能力和抱负，通过创造相应的政治、社会、环境、经济、军事和文化体系来建构人类的生存和尊严。

但不能否认的是，亚洲社会整体上缺乏将个人自由置于首位的自由和民主传统，亚洲社会本质上多为社群主义（communitarianism）的，国家或政府一直在安全中占主导地位。因此，可以说，

---

❶ 崔顺姬：《区域安全复合理论——基于“传统安全”和“人的安全”视角的分析》，载：《浙江大学学报》，2008年第1期，第20页。

❷ Muthiah Alagappa（ed.）：*Asian Security Order：Instrumental and Normative Features*：Palo Alto，Stanford University Press，2003，p. 536.

❸ 参见：Andrew T. H. Tan，J. D. Kenneth Boutin：*Non - Traditional Security Issues in Southeast Asia*，Select Publishing Pte Ltd.，2001，p. 2.

人的安全的概念对亚洲安全秩序的传统范式提出了挑战。所以，人的安全的研究对亚洲的安全拓展与深化具有特殊意义。

当然，人的安全在亚太地区的运用和实践已经使其具有了一定的影响与地位。从亚洲近十年来应对一系列跨国威胁（包括1997年经济危机、美国“9·11”事件发生以来的恐怖主义威胁、2002年和2003年发生在巴厘岛和印尼的恐怖主义爆炸事件、2003年SARS的爆发与2008年的甲型H1N1流感、2004年印度洋海啸等）的努力中，我们看到了亚洲地区对人的安全理念的支持。甚至一些倡导者已经将这一概念作为亚洲各国和国际社会回应跨国危险与安全治理的思维框架。那么，对于亚洲（包括中国）来说，追求人的安全是正确的选择吗？这是个极为重要但也依旧存在争议的问题。

首先，亚洲对人的安全的质疑有其历史渊源和现实基础：领土争端及其他形式的国家间冲突的存在、大多数亚洲国家有过殖民或半殖民历史，相对较新的独立实体地位使得国家主权具有绝对重要的优先地位；很多亚洲国家将集体安全或国家安全置于个人选择和自由之上；亚洲国家整体上处于民主相对缺失和非自由的政治制度中；“冷战”的持久影响和必须面对国际上竞争对手的威胁，至今仍分离的朝鲜半岛、中国大陆与台湾，以及各国之间的不断的主权争议与摩擦。

阿查亚在本书中认为，在国家安全占统治和优先地位的亚洲，人的安全若要融入亚洲的安全范式，必须注意国家安全与人的安全之间的平衡，不能因为后者利益而打破这一平衡。然而，阿查亚又从世界的视野分析指出，一些关键的长期发展因素将为亚洲安全秩序中的人的安全创造更大的空间。这些因素如下：

第一个因素是跨国挑战。如2001年印尼烧芭引起的大雾，“9·11”事件，巴厘岛恐怖主义爆炸事件以及SARS的爆发等，均标志出一个安全范式（即认为最严峻的安全挑战来自于入侵或暴乱）的极限，显示出政权安全在经历强烈的非传统安全危机时可能被破坏的程度。更进一步说，这些挑战使得人的安全在其各个方面都至关重要。

第二个因素是菲律宾、泰国和印度尼西亚等主要国家整体的民主化转向。这些国家和韩国、中国台湾一起，为人的安全的理念和策略创造了一个政治民主空间。这些国家支持人的安全理念，将之作为与独裁主义保持距离的方式，作为提高其国际合法地位和获取发展援助的途径。

阿查亚强调，人的安全在亚洲面临的挑战也是明显的，首先是在反恐旗帜下的“国土安全”时代所面临的挑战，只有在减少恐怖主义的恐惧和减少国家安全机器的恐惧的手段之间找到一个平衡点，才能解决这个问题。其次，人的安全的提升同样也受制于日益单极化的国际秩序，由美国领导的反恐战争主要是一个战略反应，而并非政治或人道主义反应，美国式的极端人道主义干预与以国家安全的名义进行的干预之间的界限依然模糊不清。

（四）

那么，人的安全，这一概念及其政策设定，对中国又意味什么？或者，我们可以如何看待其在中国的前景？

在中国古代的思想资源中，集体主义伦理学

资源丰富，个体主义伦理学资源相对缺乏，这就使得对作为个体的人的关怀、敬畏、尊重也往往缺乏。中国传统的历史文化对民众的生命权多表现出一种轻视，所以才有“命若琴弦”“草菅人命”“生命如蝼蚁”“生命如草芥”等说法；而百姓在官府面前自称“草民”、帝王死后的“殉葬”、史上的“焚书坑儒”，以致吴起、黄巢、张士诚、成吉思汗、忽必烈等在占领之后的屠城活动均表现出对人命的极大蔑视。屠杀、政治暗杀、政治恐怖、政治清洗等即便到了近现代中国的某些历史阶段也依然存在。

新中国成立特别是改革开放30多年以来，中国不断探索和拓展安全的内涵，首先在治穷脱贫、一心一意发展经济、保持社会稳定、普及义务教育的伟大实践中取得了举世瞩目的成就。之后，随着人的安全领域各类问题的爆发特别是以2003年SARS为标志，我国在与反恐行动相关的反恐合作以及与流行疾病（以SARS为标志）、环境问题、粮食安全、食品安全（以2008年三鹿奶粉事件为标志）等问题相关的人的安全维护方面表现出了前所未有的关注和努力。得益于SARS的经验和教训，在之后的禽流感、2009年的全球甲型HINI流感、新疆“7·5”事件中，我国都表现出了良好的处理经验和应对能力。这一过程促进了中国在安全领域两个方面的深入：一是人与安全的关系方面，即深化了对“人”为核心的新安全观的认知；二是体制与安全的关系，即对安全开始进行以“体制”为根源的深入反思，对安全的维护开始通过体制与法制途径进行。与此同时出台了一系列法律法规，如《突发公共卫生事件应急条例》（2003）、《中华人民共和国传染病防治法》（2004）、《中华人民共和国突发事件应对法》（2007）、《中华人民共和国食品安全法》（2009）。

如果说人的安全是所有安全问题的核心，那么人的安全在中国的语境中就是一种“以人为本”的安全视域的确立。有学者指出：“人”的安全具有与国家安全本质上不同的属性，即“人”的安全要求更多关注个人及群体的生活、价值和尊严；“人”的安全观不同于传统安全观的对抗观念，重视国际合作；然而，“人”的安全危机与国家安全危机、“人”的安全与国家安全相互依赖而存在；“人”的安全的最大关切是生命的保障，摆脱由于饥饿、疾病、犯罪等带来的对生命安全的威胁。❶

可以说，经济的发展与民众生活条件的改善意味着中国在践行人的安全方面拥有了更多“免于匮乏的自由”，但同时，“免于恐惧的自由”依旧相对缺乏（各类暴力事件、三股势力频繁活动、国际恐怖主义的威胁等）。中国的安全范式也将依然和众多亚洲国家一样，依然是国家安全占主导，学界和政策界至今也很少使用“人的安全”这一术语。但是，人的安全的研究对中国具有特别的意义。

我国正在经历发展理念的重大转变，在提出“科学发展观”追求全面的科学发展的过程中，联合国的人类发展指数值得重视和研究。人类发展指数（HDI）的评判维度有三：人均GDP、人均教育水平、平均寿命，三项加权平均后得出人类发展指数。该指数较之GDP更能揭示收入水平的巨

❶ 胡薇薇：《“非典”挑战“人”的安全观》，载：《世界经济与政治》，2003年第8期，第64～68页。

大差异与全民的普遍状态，得分的高低表明发展程度的高低。应该说，科学发展观将以人为本作为其核心内容，我们的发展也将更多地重视与人的安全相关的指数而不是传统的单一的GDP。

那么，在中国，“人的安全”究竟应视为“国家安全”的题中之议，还是与“国家安全”并列的议题，抑或是置于“国家安全”之上的人类新议题？本人认为，人的安全是国家安全的终极目的。一个国家、地区内个人是否安全，是一个国家是否尊重民本、民生最直接的体现，甚至人的安全与尊严在某种程度上应超越政府的权力与国家的权威。人的安全的重点除了强调人的生存的需求，也强调人的解放与社会正义上，没有人的安全，社会不会和谐，世界难以平静。因此，将人的安全纳入安全研究，纳入的不只是一个新名词，更是一种新时期关于安全的新关注和新理念。对人的安全的重视，体现的是国家安全治理能力的提升；强调的是安全是发展的核心，人是安全的价值基点；凸显的是人的安全相对于国家安全和全球安全的重要意义。可以预见，伴随着中国在经济上取得的巨大成就以及政治上的进一步开放，人的安全的前景值得期待。

亚洲对安全化理论的解读与超越

——《安全化困境：亚洲的视角》书评

余潇枫 *

一、关于安全化理论

有学者认为“冷战”结束后的安全研究基本形成了有着重要观点差异的“正统派”“扩展派”和“全球派”三派。正统派强调“冷战”后对非传统安全问题的研究只不过处于从属的、边缘的和被支配的位置，因而安全研究的基调和主流不应有实质的变化，安全仍应该以国家间的、国家与非国家行为体之间的对军事威胁的使用、控制和管理的研究为主。扩展派则强调在保持传统安全研究的同时，要实质性地加强非传统安全在安全建设和安全观念中的比重和分量，要对安全的概念进行扩大的解释和理解，以便让安全研究可以涵盖日益凸显的非传统安全问题。全球派则强调要将安全研究和安全关注的重点彻底从传统安全转向非传统安全，认为国家间军事对抗的时代已经过去，应该将基于人类共同利益、共同价值和共同体之上的道德性的安全关怀，变成实质性的国家、组织和国际社会的共同行动。❶ 不管上述三种观点的差异如何，非传统安全上升为重要的安全议题的事实是共同的。哥本哈根学派比较早且颇有贡献地对非传统安全议题进行了理论研究，安全化理论是其突出的理论贡献。

安全化最早由奥利·维夫（Ole Wæver）提出，随后巴瑞·布赞进行了全面的阐述。1991年，布赞出版《人、国家与恐惧》一书，初步从理论上概括了传统安全和非传统安全问题，把整个安全领域分为“经济、环境、社会、军事、政治”五个方面，并把安全对象层次分为国际体系（international systems）、次国际体系（international subsystems）、单元（unit）、子单元（subunits）、个人（individuals）五个层次。在之后的《新安全论》一书中，“安全化”理论得以了重点阐述。布赞等认为“安全化”是这样一个过程：某个公共问题只要尚未成为公共争论与公共决策问题以及国家并未涉及它，这一问题就还被置于“非政治化”的范围，所以还不是安全问题。当这个问题

* 余潇枫：浙江大学非传统安全与和平发展研究中心主任，浙江大学公共管理学院教授、博士生导师，浙江大学非传统安全管理博士点负责人。

❶ 参见：朱锋：《“非传统安全”解析》，载：《中国社会科学》.2004年第4期，第144页。

成为了国家政策对象的一部分，需要政府的决心和考虑资源的重新配置，或者还需要一种不同以往的公共治理体制的介入，则它就被置于“政治化”的范围，成为了“准安全”问题。而当这个问题被政府部门作为“存在性威胁”而提出，并需要多方面采取紧急措施，甚至这些措施超出了政治程序的正常限度而仍然被证明不失为正当，则这个问题就成为安全问题了。所以从广义的角度看，安全化就是使得一种公共问题经过特定的过程（如权威机构“宣布为危险”）而成为国家机构涉及的安全问题。国家安全威胁的实质是经过“安全化”机制运作的国际、国内社会公共问题的政治升级与社会建构。为此，“安全化”不仅使“宣布或认定为危险”成为一个合理的施动过程，而且还能很好地解释为何不同的国家会有不同的安全重点，不同的历史阶段会有不同的安全重心。而且，真正的安全问题被“政治化”之后表明，“安全”自然“是超越一切政治规则和政治结构的一种途径，实际上就是一种所有政治之上的特殊政治”。❶ 所以在现实中，当任何问题被认可为“安全化”的对象时，就会形成新的安全领域。

安全化理论的贡献在于可以把诸多原属于低政治领域的非传统安全问题纳入既有的安全框架内进行考虑，或者非传统安全问题可能通过安全化的路径——反复强调的逻辑、特殊的修辞结构、特定的言语行为（speech act）、认同的文化建构等——成为重要的新安全议题，从而把国家安全与社会安全、人的安全、全球安全整合在一个思考的框架内，使得以往其间的鸿沟有可能得以消除，其间的基点有可能相融合，其间的影响有可能被强化，其间的方法路径有可能被借鉴和运用。安全化理论达成了安全研究的方法论突破，带来了安全议题界限的拓展，引入了建构主义的安全分析元素，使得“言语行为”成为了安全建构中的重要途径，把安全从客观安全拓展到主观安全再拓展到主体间建构安全的层面上，从而超越了传统的现实主义安全困境。但是在亚洲的语境中，安全化理论遇到了难题、受到了多方面的检验，该书便是基于亚洲的语境对安全化理论的某种考量，这也是该书的价值和意义之所在。

二、亚洲对安全化困境的解读

该书的几大章节均从不同的安全领域探讨了安全化困境、安全化理论的效度以及如何实现对安全化理论的超越。

彼得·乔克（Peter Chalk）在《亚太地区的疾病与复杂的“安全化”过程》一章中探讨了亚洲的疾病的安全化问题，他认为疾病的跨国传播是后“冷战”时代安全性质变化的重要标志之一，传染病在亚洲的大规模“轻松”传播，不仅冲击了以往的区域稳定、国家稳定和国际稳定理念，而且冲击了传统的以某敌对国为中心制定安全策略的范式。疾病跨国传播的安全化过程表现出了非传统安全与传统安全的重要不同：首先，强调社会公共秩序的社会安全与强调民众个体生存质量的人的安全，取代了原来的强调维护国家领土主权完整的国家安全；其次，没有外在敌人威胁下的无组织无预谋的疾病骚乱，取代了传统安全

❶ 巴里·布赞、奥利·维夫：《新安全论》，朱宁译，浙江人民出版社，2003 年版，第 32 ~ 37 页。

理念下的国家间的有组织有预谋的军事暴力；最后，应对非传统安全威胁的合作（个人或国家间）所取得的共赢结果，取代了应对传统安全威胁的国家间竞争的零和结局。但乔克指出，虽然因传染病跨国传播已上升为安全层面的挑战而使得其安全化已经迫在眉捷，但对亚太地区的疾病进行安全化的过程是“复杂”的。乔克强调，全球化已经到达地球的任一角落，现代医疗措施特别是抗生素的普遍大量使用导致了适应性和抗药性更强的疾病，日益加速又不可持续的城市扩张从多方面助长着传染病的传播，全球气温上升和气候变化引发多种灾害进而使受灾地区随时可能爆发传染病，特别是性滥交和静脉注射毒品等社会和人类行为方式的改变与增多，更使得艾滋病等传染性疾病“横行肆虐”。虽则传染病在亚太地区广泛传播导致的后果是严重的，但乔克认为大多数国家对这一非传统安全挑战的认知和表达均还停留于传统安全层面，其安全化努力仅仅关注到生物武器的袭击可能造成的大规模传染病，加上褊狭的政治范式、脆弱的评估体系、低效的防治措施、稀少的专业官员，因而疾病能否成功地在亚太地区被“安全化”并不肯定。

伊拉维尼尔·拉米亚（Ilavenil Ramiah）在《亚洲艾滋病问题的安全化》一章中强调对艾滋病问题的安全化是不容置疑的，但对安全化行为体的确认则是一个可以探索的新话题。拉米亚通过对中国、印度等国艾滋病传染途径的研究，以及对高危人群通过桥梁人群传染至普遍人群的机理分析，揭示了亚洲地区特别是东亚、东南亚和南亚地区艾滋病传染情况越来越加剧的现象，并且强调如此发展下去会在人的安全（死亡率上升）、经济安全（生产力下降）乃至军事安全（对军队和维和部队的影响）方面产生毁灭性后果。那么如何开展安全化策略研究？拉米亚颇有独创性地将安全化行为体分为启动行为体、催化行为体和实施行为体三类，并指出：承担首要责任的是启动行为体——中央政府；起关键作用的是催化行为体——国际机构和他国的中央政府；起特殊作用的是实施行为体——地方政府、非政府组织或政府组织、宗教组织、媒体、私人企业和工会。这些安全化行为体的不同范围和它们之间的相互作用和影响，使得安全化过程变得十分复杂。拉米亚指出了“言语行为”路径的局限性，因为“言语行为”的实施者即“安全化行为体”。拉米亚提出了艾滋病特有的安全化过程的四个步骤：一是启动行为体（中央政府）与广大群众之间发生交流，这是一个劝导、说服以及协商的过程；二是催化行为体与启动行为体（中央政府）之间的互动，这是一个沟通、劝导、协同、评估、援助，以及有条件地供给资源的过程；三是启动行为体（中央政府）与实施行为体之间的交流，这是一个表达、沟通、劝导、协调、资助、支持，以及有条件地供给资源的过程；四是实施行为体与更广泛人群之间的互动，这是一个讨论、活动、草根会议、说服、劝导、协商以及为“听众”提供大量资讯的过程。要实现如上安全化过程的劝导和协商机制，拉米亚认为要重视安全化关键性指标的建构。有效安全化的关键性指标有五个：第一个关键性指标是设立艾滋病相关政策形成和协调的权威机构；其次是建立一个推动所有伙伴结成联盟的全国性艾滋病行动框架；第三是将艾滋病议题归入全民发展议程；第四是建立全民协调与评估系统；第五也即是综合性指标的实现：将艾滋病感染率降低。拉米亚通过对艾滋病问题安全化的理论解读是深刻而有创见性的，甚至其对亚洲安全化困境的现实指出了超越性的路径。

三、亚洲对安全化困境的超越

从亚洲的语境看来，安全化理论有其不足之处，因而在亚洲对安全化理论研究的同时也伴随着对安全化理论的质疑和拓展。比如，当安全化的行为体或启动行为体不作为时，安全化如何达成？当治理的主体变得多元时，安全化路径如何进行有效的拓展？即使安全化对安全问题的解决有其效果，是否以去安全化（desecuritization）的路径作为长期的政治目标更为合理？

1. 对安全化行为体的建构与对安全化路径的拓展

拉米亚在《亚洲艾滋病问题的安全化》中所提出的安全化行为体集合的建构也是对安全化路径研究所作的拓展。正如其总结的那样，“安全化”概念有巨大潜力，安全化行为体分析也适用于更广泛的非传统安全问题，如果一个问题需要安全化，而启动行为体不重视的话，那么催化行为体、实施行为体会成为安全化的必需要件，“安全化过程将不仅涉及由某一行为体施加的单边信息，更涉及对社会和政策伙伴之间交流重要的更广范围内的劝导和协商机制”。我在《非传统安全概论》一书中曾对布赞通过“政治化”路径实现安全化进行了拓展性解释，强调了通过“社会化”路径实现安全化的重要性与可行性，而拉米亚则在他的研究中强调了还可以通过“国际化”和更广义的“社会化”路径实现安全化，以最终求得对安全挑战的有效应对。

鲍伯·哈迪威纳达（Bob Hadiwinata）的《贫困与印尼非政府组织在维护人的安全中的作用》，强调了非政府组织作为安全化主要行为体对亚洲安全化困境的超越。印尼政府未能在经济危机和危机后的政策调整中照顾到弱势群体，因而对贫困进行安全化的“政治化”路径空缺，因而哥本哈根学派所强调的解决非传统安全问题“要依靠紧急的政府行为和危机时政府出台的政策”在此受到挑战。哈迪威纳达在分析中指出，国家在维护人的安全的过程中担负主要责任，但是在一些情况下，国家本身就是造成人的安全问题的一部分。如在印度尼西亚，穷人们把导致自己贫困的原因归结为政府，并把官员称做“骗子”“诈骗犯”“投机者”。而与印尼政府一起不计后果地实施结构调整方案而使贫困率大幅上升的还有国际货币基金组织。当国家行为体未能履行保护贫困群体职责时，非政府组织会试图将贫困安全化，他们的目的至少有二：一是帮助贫困群体通过自我救助来解决自身问题，二是代表被忽视群体斥责那些威胁他们安全的社会和政府制度。这样，在贫困的安全化问题上，非政府组织成为行为体，贫困群体成为指涉对象。哈迪威纳达指出，非政府组织参与维护人的安全的动因是：人的安全问题被提上了议程，人的安全维护使非政府组织面对受益人、赞助人、政府和公众时享有良好声誉，人的安全也为非政府组织的存活和可行性提供了机遇。特别值得一提的是，一些印尼的非政府组织只是动员贫民展开自我救助活动，因而成功地避免了与意识形态对抗的直接联系。似乎哥本哈根学派未预料到，哈迪威纳达的论证表明，当国家出现问题或无法履行职能时，贫困等非传统安全问题的解决方案可以超越国家职能的界限之外。换句话说，贫困的安全化进程使得在对待非传统安全因素时，需要将国家以外的行为体（非政府组织）作为合法机构。

2. 对“去安全化”（desecuritization）研究的深化

“去安全化”是与“安全化”相对的一个范畴，它强调的是不要将公共问题上升为安全问题进行处理，认为安全化代表正常政治制度或机制处理问题的失败，因而不提倡将问题提升至安全领域进行处理，而认为应该将问题排除于安全领域回到公共领域进行处理。克劳迪娅·阿拉多（Claudia Aradau）曾在研究亚洲安全化问题时指出：“好”的去安全化行为获得的支持远远高于“坏”的安全化行为。书中，普里杨卡·乌帕德亚雅（Priyankar Upadhyaya）即从“去安全化”的视角研究孟加拉移民问题。他通过孟加拉移民问题，对亚洲安全化的困境以及哥本哈根理论的不足进行了评述。乌帕德亚雅认为在应对非传统安全挑战中，对安全化和去安全的良好理解与把握十分重要，特别是在非欧洲区域的研究更有其对安全化理论框架进行检验的价值。他指出，经济萧条、工业化水平低、社会动乱、人口激增、政局动荡、宗教影响、民族冲突等都是孟加拉移民现象的刺激因素，而对印度各州来说，孟加拉移民狂潮则是一个难以摆脱的存在性威胁，因而也引发了印度移民将压倒原住民的担忧与各州反孟加拉移民的排外浪潮。跨境移民问题作为南亚地区未来几年内一个有争议的难题，乌帕德亚雅认为对其作不同的解释就会有不同的安全应对，如果以国家范式至上的范式为参照，即按照安全化的路径进行考虑，跨境移民则是对移民接纳国的重大威胁；如果以生命至上的范式为参照，即按照去安全化的路径进行审视，则跨境移民可被解释为是“当地居民跨境寻求美好生活的人类长期问题”，因而它可能在变成国家安全问题之前就得到控制。乌帕德亚雅对这一议题的去安全化路径的具体构想是：放弃单一的主权至上的观点，控制移民的共有原因，在有迁移征兆之前解决或缓和局势，不是简单地关闭整个边界而是进行勘察，给从事某些特定工作的人发行身份证，加强地区级别的双边对话；更积极的做法是给移民发放工作证，让其有序进入、合法工作和暂住；或者承认已经进入印度的孟加拉人为阿萨姆社会的一部分，实施同化政策，等等。乌帕德亚雅指出安全化路径也有其效用，但去安全化更应当被视为一个长期的政治目标，是“一种解决问题的美好愿景”。

廖庆永（Joseph Chinyong Liow）的《马来西亚处理印尼劳工的方法：安全化、政治化，还是宣泄?》，对安全化理论提出的分析框架进行了运用与检验，指出了其适用性与缺陷，特别是考察了政治与安全问题间的某种张力。廖庆永认为安全化理论的贡献在于拓展了安全议程与安全指涉对象，并将安全化过程从政治化过程中区分出来；正是得益于安全化理论，移民劳动力问题被作为了普遍性威胁的安全问题来进行分析——马来西亚境内规模庞大的无证印尼劳工导致就业竞争激烈、犯罪率提高、外来移民劝诱当地人改变宗教信仰等，增加了马来西亚人对社会结构断裂和恐怖主义活动的担忧，最终“他们对国家安全构成了威胁”。21 世纪初，马来西亚政府对外籍劳工进行过大规模驱逐，并实施“最后雇用印尼劳工”政策（只实行了两周），这引发了一系列骚乱，造成了政治及外交影响。廖庆永认为，马来西亚政府对印尼劳工的“安全化”所造成的影响不仅局限于使建筑业摇摇欲坠、使马来西亚的国际声誉受损，而且还暴露了安全化概念本身的模糊不定。此中的关键点是安全的指涉对象是谁？如果是印尼劳工，那么他们在危及马来西亚社会安全的同时亦有利于马来西亚的经济安全，况且印尼移民中有一部分拥有马来西亚出身证明却没有身份证的人，还有一些确实是为摆脱迫害从动乱的北苏门答腊省逃出来的政治难民。由是可以看出，“安全远非一个普遍的价值，而是一个复杂的概念”，很多情况下会出现琳娜·汉森所说的“沉默者的安全”（一些群体无法表达、没有权利表达或没有渠道表达其安全诉求），安全化的“言语行为”在此失去效用。廖庆永特别指出，在欧洲的社会政治背景下，政治领域与安全领域是相对区分的，而在同时决定政治与安全话语的国家强权下，公众舆论只是“相关观众”或“无助观众”，因而，在关于非法印尼劳工问题的讨论中，公众舆论的批评不被政府接纳也没有出现在国家控制的媒体中是不足为怪的。而事实是，安全化在印尼很大程度上只是一个“符号行动”，双边管制是临时的，紧急措施的执行是低效的，非法印尼劳工背后存在着大量腐败问题，政府各部门之间也存在不同意见而相互攻击。由此可以看出，安全化理论在亚洲语境下缺乏解释力之处在于：移民问题本身是复杂的、不清晰的，甚至充满争议的，安全化不能给予其确定的边界；政治领域与安全领域的区分在消除非法印尼劳工构成的安全威胁中没有体现，相反对非法印尼劳工的安全化被置于正常的政治范围内，而不是被排除在政治程序外；再者，脱离政治领域的环境背景或行为体的话语是不能被建构的，试图利用安全话语来处理非法印尼劳工问题难以成功。为此廖庆永得出的结论是：安全的话语表达固然重要，但安全化理论对“言语行为”认识论的依赖只有当它与行动能力相结合时才具有具体现实意义。

非传统安全相关学科研究综述

非传统安全集对分析的研究综述

赵克勤 *

【摘要】综述到目前为止的集对分析在水安全、空气安全、地质与土地安全、风险评估、矿山安全、企业安全生产、食品安全、航天航空安全、电力系统安全、网络与信息安全、军事安全等非传统安全研究中的应用，说明集对分析对多种非传统安全问题研究和分析的适用性和合理性之根源，在于各种非传统安全问题的防治和化解都与认识和处置这种或那种不确定性有关，而集对分析恰好是处理综合不确定性的一种新的系统数学理论，其特点是把研究对象中的各种不确定性关系与确定性关系作为一个不确定性系统处理。鉴于不确定性在非传统安全问题中的普遍性和重要性，建议在更多的非传统安全问题研究中应用集对分析。

【关键词】非传统安全，不确定性，集对分析，联系数

1. 非传统安全与集对分析的关联

非传统安全是指区别于传统安全的，来自经济、社会、环境、生态、文化、信息等更宽泛领域的各种安全威胁的一个统称。但余潇枫教授在文献［1］指出："要清楚明确地给出一个非传统安全定义，却并不是一件容易的事。确切地说，非传统安全目前仍无公认的严格定义与权威说法，就非传统安全范畴本身的问题还存在众多的争议，主要集中在：传统安全与非传统安全的划分标准难以确定，非传统安全的主体（是国家、社会、个人、全球还是并重）难以确定，非传统安全问题的研究对象与领域边界难以确定"等等。从中看出：无论是非传统安全的概念，还是非传统安全问题的研究对象与研究内容的确定都存在不确定性；从技术层面看，各种非传统安全问题的孕育、发展、出现与防治和化解也都与认识和处置这种或那种不确定性有关，这说明非传统安全问题从一开始就是一个与各种不确定性高度相关的问题。

集对分析（Set pair Analysis，SPA）是处理不确定性的一种新的系统数学理论，其特点是把研究对象中的各种不确定性关系与确定性关系作为一个不确定性系统处理。基本思路是在一定的问题背景下，分析集对中两个集合的确定性关系与不确定性关系并做同异反分类和联系数刻划，得

---

* 赵克勤：浙江大学非传统安全与和平发展中心集对分析与非传统安全研究所所长，诸暨市联系数学研究所所长。

到集对的特征函数，再利用特征函数及其伴随函数做进一步的建模和运算，由此去研究和解决不确定性系统中的有关问题。集对分析由笔者于1989年提出，已在许多领域得到应用，例如到2011年11月底，在中国知网（www. cnki. net）上用关键词“集对分析”精确检索，就有1300多篇文献。

集对分析的主要数学工具是联系数，其一般形式为：

$$\mu = a + bi + cj \tag{1}$$

式（1）中的 a、b、c 依次称为所论两个集合在给定问题背景和某个分析过程中的同一度、差异度、对立度，a、b、$c \in [0,1]$，$a + b + c = 1$；j 一般取 -1，i 是 j 的函数，若取 $j = -1$，则 i 在［-1，1］区间视不同情况取不同值，是一个需要进一步分析的不定数；称 μ 为联系数，代表等式右边的那个结构函数。

式（1）有以下一些等价函数：

$$\mu = a + bi \text{（同异式，或不确定式）} \tag{2}$$

$$\mu = a + cj \text{（同反式，或同一对立式）} \tag{3}$$

$$\mu = bi + cj \text{（异反式）} \tag{4}$$

还有以下一些伴随函数：

$$f(\mu) = \sum_{k=1}^{n} a_k + i\sum_{p=1}^{m} b_p + j\sum_{q=1}^{o} c_q \text{（多元联系数）} \tag{5}$$

$$\partial\,\mu = \frac{a}{a+b} + \frac{b}{b+c}i + \frac{b}{a+b}i + \frac{c}{b+c}j \text{（偏联系数）} \tag{6}$$

$$\zeta\mu = \frac{a}{b}i + \frac{b}{c}j \text{（邻联系数）} \tag{7}$$

$$Shi\mu = a/c \text{（势函数）} \tag{8}$$

$$\psi\mu = \begin{cases} a > b > c \\ a > b = c \\ a > b < c \\ \cdots \end{cases} \text{（态势函数）} \tag{9}$$

$$\beta(\mu) = \begin{cases} \mu' = r(\cos\theta + i\sin\theta) \\ r = \sqrt{a^2 + b^2} \\ \theta = \arctan\dfrac{b}{a} \end{cases} \text{（复联系数）} \tag{10}$$

等等，以及这些伴随函数的反函数。

联系数和它的等价函数以及它们的伴随函数和反伴随函数，用数学的语言构划出一个内容丰富的不确定性系统理论（详见文献［2～3］），其核心思想是把事物的确定性关系与不确定性关系看做是一个不确定性系统，从而使得集对分析在非传统安全问题的研究中有广泛的应用（可参见文献［4］），本文仅对到目前为止的各种非传统安全问题集对分析阶段性成果作一综述，并对进一步的研究作一展望。

2. 非传统安全集对分析的阶段性成果

2.1 水安全集对分析

2.1.1 区域水安全集对分析

（1）北京、上海、天津及全国的水安全评价

卢敏博士等在文献［5］中把集对分析用于北京、上海、天津及全国的水安全评价，评价指标值和评价特征值见表1，评价结果见表2。

表1　北京、天津、上海及全国的水安全评价指标值和特征值

指标		水资源			生态环境			社会经济		
		人均水资源量/m^3	水资源利用率/%	防洪标准/a	城市人均绿地面积/m^2	污径比/%	污水处理率/%	人均GDP/元	城市化水平/%	平均受教育年限/a
指标特征值	最差值	10		1	0.01	1	20.0	800	1	0
	及格值	1700	40		9	0.04		24000		
	最优值		10	1000			100		100	16
实际指标值	北京	272.8	168.5	50	14.91	0.6	42	17336	77.54	10.3
	全国	2171.0	19.9		6.8	0.02	36.4	6840	36.2	7.8
	天津	138.9	121.4	50	7.542	2.09	61.2	15824	71.99	9.2
	上海	183.63	10.85	500	6.503	0.6451	62	17328	88.31	9.5

表2　北京、天津、上海及全国的各项水安全指标的联系度平均值

联系度平均值	北京			天津			上海			全国		
	a	*b*	*c*	*a*	*b*	*c*	*a*	*b*	*c*	*a*	*b*	*c*
水资源$\overline{\mu}_1$	0.070	0.600	0.330	0.040	0.620	0.330	0.520	0.480	0.000			
生态环境$\overline{\mu}_2$	0.570	0.440	0.000	0.450	0.210	0.330	0.360	0.380	0.000	0.660	0.340	0.000
社会经济$\overline{\mu}_3$	0.710	0.290	0.000	0.650	0.350	0.000	0.490	0.270	0.000	0.370	0.630	0.000
综合联系度$\overline{\mu}$	0.447	0.442	0.111	0.382	0.396	0.222	0.624	0.376	0.000	0.594	0.406	0.000

表2细致地刻划出北京、上海、天津及全国由“水安全要求”与“水安全现状”这两个集合之“关系”的“结构”。由表2中联系度*a*，*b*值的比较可知，上海水资源安全程度最高，但人均水资源拥有量低于北京，最少的是天津；在生态环境方面，水安全程度从高到低的排列顺序为全国、北京、天津、上海；在社会经济方面，从优到劣的排列顺序为北京、上海、天津、全国；从综合联系度值μ来比较：上海水资源较为丰富，但生态环境建设方面不如北京和天津，如不注重生态保护，上海将面临水质型缺水的威胁；北京由于水资源量少，所以投入了足够的资金加大生态环境保护；而天津虽然也极为注重生态环境保护，但因为本身水资源缺乏加上污染严重，所以水安全程度最差。这些均与有关文献中采用函数曲线评价模型得到的结果一致。另外，表2还显示，上海的水安全状况不如北京，表明尽管天然水资源量是水安全程度的决定因素，但从长远来看，只有注重生态环境的保护，才能保证水资源的安全和可持续利用。说明生态环境保护是水安全极为重要的因素。

（2）黄河健康评价集对分析

王慧等在文献［6］中把集对分析中的五元联系数用于黄河健康评价，先通过专家咨询、确定评价指标及其权重，并把各评价指标的“河流健康”等级标准分为1 ~ 5级，分别对应于“很健康”“健康”“亚健康”“不健康”和“病态”5个级别，再根据文献数据作综合评价，结果显示当前的黄河处于亚健康状态，从子系统看，河流生态、形态和水环境均处于严重“病态”阶段，亟待结合各段实际情况治理解决。

（3）巢湖流域水安全集对分析

金菊良教授等人在文献［7］中用集对分析建立了我国巢湖流域的基于联系数的流域水安全评价模型（CN - AM），该模型既可测度流域水安全整体状态的高低程度，又可识别影响流域水安全状态的重要指标和重要子系统，模型显示当年的巢湖流域水安全系统处于临界安全状态，为此建议流域周边地区大力推广节水技术、控制城市人口增长，提升流域的经济和科技发展水平、保障该流域水的安全。

（4）新疆水资源开发利用的集对分析

新疆位于内陆干旱区，水资源主要由降水、高山冰雪融水补给，由河流经山区排泄到平原，通过水循环，蒸发消耗消失于沙漠之中。降水主要是来自大西洋的盛行西风气流，其次是来自北冰洋的冷湿气流，全疆平均年降水量仅145mm，为中国平均值（630mm）的23%，在全球同纬度各地中，新疆几乎是最少的，产水模数仅为5.3亿m^3/平方公里，只有全国平均值的18.1%，从自然生态角度来看，新疆属缺水地区，水资源能否合理开发利用是新疆实现可持续发展的关键。秦萌等在文献［8］中以2007年新疆水资源利用数据为基础，对新疆各项水资源开发利用指标进行分析，并采用集对分析法对新疆水资源的开发利用程度进行了评价，结论是新疆水资源利用现处于初级水平，但同时又表现出了一定的不协调性，主要为用水结构和管理的不协调，其中又以东疆和南疆较突出。

（5）南京市水资源安全的集对分析

尹志杰博士等在文献［9］针对南京市水资源利用现状，提出了南京市水资源安全综合评价指标体系，引入集对分析理论构建南京市水资源安全综合评价模型，计算了不同层次水平上的水资源安全多元联系数，将多指标问题转换为一个综合指标，评价结果为临界安全。

（6）吉林东丰县水资源安全集对分析

郭元利等在文献［10］中结合吉林东丰县的实际情况，在专家咨询和调查研究的基础上综合考虑影响水资源安全的各方面因素，采用集对分析模型对东丰县水资源安全状况进行综合评价，得出东丰县水资源安全状况为一般的结论。

（7）湖北漳河灌区水资源集对分析

王富强等人在文献［11］中基于集对分析原理，选取区域水资源短缺风险程度的风险率、脆弱性、可恢复性、重现期和风险度为评价指标，建立了基于集对分析的区域水资源短缺风险评价模型并用于湖北漳河灌区水资源短缺风险的评价；得到该灌区处于较低风险水平的评价结果，该结果与灌区现状的开发利用程度和缺水量相符，模型具有可操作性和实用性，为该区域水资源规划和水安全管理提供了决策依据。

还有其他一些文献也把集对分析用于区域水安全集对分析，因篇幅原因从略。

2.1.2　湖库水体富营养化评估的集对分析

水体富营养化是当代诸多国家和公众最为关

注的水安全问题之一。王栋博士等在文献［12］中把集对分析用于我国邛海、洱海、博斯腾湖、于桥水库、磁湖、巢湖、甘棠湖、蘑菇湖、杭州西湖、南京玄武湖、武汉墨水湖、广州东山湖12个代表性湖库Chl－a、TP、TN、COD、SD等评价指标实测浓度与富营养化评价标准的对照建模。评价结果与调查结果相符，也与单一模糊模式识别结果基本相符，较好地反映了待评湖库水体的营养化实际；其中南京玄武湖、武汉墨水湖、广州东山湖都是全湖出现水华，属于重富营养，严重影响养殖和观瞻。

高军省博士在文献［13］中依据集对分析理论建立了湖泊富营养化评价的五元联系数模型，利用置信度准则来确定富营养状态等级，避免了不确定系数 i 的取值。利用模型对2005年8月至2006年7月洪湖不同区域的富营养化状态进行评价。结果表明入湖区、养殖区、开阔区、保护区及全湖的富营养化状态依次为轻富营养、轻富营养、中营养、中营养和中营养，与模糊数学评价结果一致，说明五元联系数模型用于湖泊富营养化评价可行，结果可信。

2.1.3　地表水环境质量评价的集对分析

王国平等人在文献［14］中依据国家地表水环境质量标准GB 3838—2002（表3）把集对分析中的五元联系数用于大运河苏州段5个监测点位的监测数据（表4）的综合评价。

表3　地表水环境质量标准 GB 3838—2002

分类	污染指标				
	溶解氧	化学需氧量	氨氮	挥发酚	氰化物
Ⅰ类	7.5	15	0.15	0.002	0.005
Ⅱ类	6	15	0.5	0.002	0.05
Ⅲ类	5	20	1	0.005	0.2
Ⅳ类	3	30	1.5	0.01	0.2
Ⅴ类	2	40	2	0.1	0.2

表4　大运河苏州段5个监测点数据

点位	污染指标				
	溶解氧	化学需氧量	氨氮	挥发酚	氰化物
横瑭	7.04	4.78	0.611	0.008	0.007
大庆桥	4.61	8.77	1.073	0.023	0.005
化工厂	3.29	9.27	2.218	0.089	0.003
宝带桥	3.26	9.67	2.195	0.070	0.003
尹山	6.95	4.53	1.091	0.009	0.002

得到的结果是$\mu_{尹} > \mu_{横} > \mu_{大} > \mu_{宝} > \mu_{化}$，不仅与其他方法的评价结果一致，还同时指出评价对象处于何种水平等级，如$\mu_{横}$与$\mu_{尹}$的集对态势同为同势7级，由于$e=0$，则a大优于a小，即$\mu_{尹}$优于$\mu_{横}$；$\mu_{化}$与$\mu_{宝}$的集对态势同为同势18级，由于$e \neq 0$，$\mu_{宝}$的集对势大于$\mu_{化}$的集对态势，因此是对该类地表水安全评价方法的改进和创新，且思路清晰，计算简便，结论可靠，可以用于其他类似水环境安全与否的评估。

2.1.4 地下水环境质量评价的集对分析

刘慧等在文献［15］中较早把集对分析用于地下水环境质量评价 。

（1）邯郸市化工区地下水水质集对分析

孟宪萌博士等在文献［16］中：针对水质评价中各评价指标的不确定性，将集对分析理论应用于水质综合评价。先通过计算评价样本与评价指标之间的联系度对样本做初步分类，再对样本做进一步的同一、差异、对立的集对分析以判断评价样本的等级。在确定各评价指标的权重时，将信息论中的熵值理论引入该模型，运用信息熵所反映实测数据的效用值计算各评价指标的权重，使权重的分配具有一定的理论依据。最后运用蒙特卡罗法构造算例，讨论了实测过程中的随机观测误差对评价结果的影响。以邯郸市化工区地下水水质资料为实例分析，通过与其他综合评判法的比较，表明基于熵权的集对分析模型的评价结果合理、客观。

（2）黑龙洞泉域地下水水质评价

邱贵江等在文献［17］中，考虑到泉域地下水评价指标数达33项，计算量过大，为此把评价指标先作归类，把规范值差异很小的指标归为一类，则33项指标可归为A、B、C、D和E五大类：A类指标Cl^-、SO_4^{2-}、NO_3-N、COD_{Cr}、有机磷，cj0分别为7、7、0.3、4、0.005mg/L；B类指标NO_2-N、CN、Mo、Be、Hg，cj0分别为0.1、0.1、0.1、0.005、0.02μg/L；C类指标色度、TDS、氟化物、碘化物、酚、NH_3-N、HDS（硬度）、Fe、Mn、可溶性固体，cj0分别为0.5、30、0.05、0.01、0.0001、0.0002、15、0.01、0.000 5、30mg/L；D类指标COD_{Mn}、Se、As、Zn、Cd、Co、Ba、Cu、PB、Ni、C_r^{6+}，cj0分别为0.2、0.001、0.001、0.002、0.000004、0.0002、0.0004、0.0004、0.001、0.001、0.001mg/L，细菌总数10×104个/L；E类指标浑浊度，cj0为0.2mg/L。由于划分的A、B、C、D和E五大类指标中，同属一类指标的同级标准规范值差异很小，因而可以将它们的各级标准规范值的平均值作为该类的分级标准（表5）

在此基础上给出基于指标规范值的地下水水质评价的集对分析法并应用于黑龙洞泉域地下水水质评价，得出的评价结果与属性识别理论方法和加权优序法的评价结果基本一致（表6），表明该方法应用于地下水水质评价具有简单、实用的特点。

表 5　各类标准值

类别 Class	指标 Index	级别/灰类（l） Level/Gray class（l）				
		1 级（灰类 1）	2 级（灰类 2）	3 级（灰类 3）	4 级（灰类 4）	5 级（灰类 5）
A 类/X_A	Cl^-、SO_4^{2-}、$NO_3^- - N$、COD_{Cr}、有机磷	0.1890	0.2778	0.3513	0.4030	0.4470
B 类/X_B	$NO_2 - N$、CN、Mo、Be、Hg	0.1151	0.2625	0.3362	0.3937	0.4415
C 类/X_C	色度、TDS、氟化物、碘化物、酚、$NH_3 - N$、HDS、Fe、Mn、可溶性固体	0.2303	0.2639	0.3231	0.4151	0.4409
D 类/X_D	COD_{Mn}、Se、As、Zn、Cd、Co、Ba、Cu、Pb、Ni、Cr^{6+} 细菌总数	0.1609	0.2599	0.3615	0.4292	0.4552
E 类/X_E	混浊度	0.2708	0.2708	0.3219	0.3912	0.4318

表 6　黑龙洞泉域地下水水质评价结果

监测点	HDS		SO_4^{2-}		CI^-		$NO_3^- - N$	
	c_j	x_j	x_j	x_j	c_j	x_j	c_j	x_j
南鼓山水源地	558.0	0.3616	283.4	0.3701	139.0	0.2989	4.89	0.2791
磁山镇	282.7	0.2936	22.8	0.1181	11.0	0.0452	3.44	0.2439
固镇	291.3	0.2966	103.9	0.2698	19.5	0.1025	5.36	0.2883
二里山水厂	396.3	0.3274	109.3	0.2748	25.5	0.1293	6.03	0.3001
黑龙洞泉水	381.5	0.3236	110.3	0.2757	18.0	0.0944	3.83	0.2547

监测点	可溶性固体		F^-		多种方法评价结果		
	c_j	x_j	c_j	x_j	属性识别理论方法	加权优序法	基于规范值的集对分析法
南鼓山水源地	882	0.3381	0.3	0.1792	Ⅲ级	Ⅲ级	Ⅲ级
磁山镇	287	0.2258	0.1	0.0693	Ⅰ级	Ⅰ级	Ⅱ级
固镇	398	0.2585	0.3	0.1792	Ⅱ级	Ⅱ级	Ⅱ级
二里山水厂	468	0.2747	0.3	0.1792	Ⅱ级	Ⅱ级	Ⅱ级
黑龙洞泉水	379	0.2536	0.3	0.1792	Ⅱ级	Ⅱ级	Ⅱ级

2.1.5 南水北调中线水源区与海河受水区旱涝遭遇的集对分析

南水北调中线工程水源区与受水区的旱涝遭遇性是跨流域水资源调配与管理运行的重要依据。张利平教授等在文献［18］中利用我国近500a旱涝等级历史资料和近几十年的实测雨量资料，进行了南水北调工程水源区与海河受水区历史旱涝特征分析，采用集对分析法对水源区与海河受水区的旱涝遭遇进行了研究。结果表明：南水北调中线水源区与海河受水区历史上旱涝灾害频发，持续性旱涝灾害严重，近三个世纪以来旱涝灾害发生次数和程度都呈现出增加的趋势。水源区与海河受水区旱涝的联系度很低，两个区域的旱涝状态同步性比较差，旱涝遭遇情况对工程调水有利的概率为56.7%，对工程调水不利的概率为24.88%。因此，要使南水北调工程发挥最大效益和价值，还需要其他水利工程配合调控。

2.1.6 海洋水环境安全的集对分析

随着我国沿海经济高速发展，海洋污染和生态破坏也在不断加剧．近几年的《海洋环境质量公报》显示，我国河口和近岸海域的污染形势严峻，营养盐失衡、河口产卵场退化、生境丧失或改变、生物群落结构异常，赤潮频繁发生，使海洋水产养殖业蒙受了巨大损失，海洋水环境安全与否成为人们普遍关注的焦点。为此，李明昌等在文献［19］中提出基于非线性隶属函数的集对分析综合评价方法并用于评估渤海湾某工程海域的水环境，该文选择渤海湾内某工程海域21个站位的COD、DO、无机氮、磷酸盐、石油类、汞和镉7个指标，检验集对分析方法的有效性和可行性，结果表明集对评价法所得结果与神经网络法基本一致（表7）；但集对分析法具有简洁和易操作等优点，非线性隶属函数能更好的描述评价指标的等级归属程度，评价结果具有比其他方法更高的可信度。

表7 两种评价法的评价结果

站位	评价结果	
	集对评价法	神经网络法
1	Ⅰ	Ⅰ
2	Ⅳ	Ⅳ
3	Ⅰ	Ⅰ
4	Ⅲ	Ⅲ
5	Ⅳ	Ⅲ
6	Ⅰ	Ⅱ
7	Ⅰ	Ⅰ
8	Ⅲ	Ⅲ
9	Ⅳ	Ⅳ
10	Ⅱ	Ⅱ
11	Ⅳ	Ⅳ
12	Ⅰ	Ⅰ
13	Ⅰ	Ⅰ
14	Ⅰ	Ⅰ
15	Ⅳ	Ⅳ
16	Ⅳ	Ⅳ
17	Ⅳ	Ⅲ
18	Ⅰ	Ⅰ
19	Ⅰ	Ⅰ
20	Ⅱ	Ⅱ
21	Ⅰ	Ⅰ

王文圣教授等在文献［20］中把集对分析用于海洋冰情预测，建立了基于集对分析的组合预测模型，步骤是：（1）把海洋冰情的实测值集合A与单个预测模型的计算值集合B组成集对$H(A, B)$，分析集合A和B的同异反程度，其同异反准则按绝对预测误差或相对预测误差的大小给定，得到集对$H(A, B)$的特征函数$\mu(A, B)=a+bi+cj$，再根据a，b，c的大小对各单个预测模型定权重，由此得到基于集对分析的海洋冰情组合预测模型，用

此模型作我国某海洋 1970～1993 年冰情预测，预测精度比单个预测模型的精度都有所提高，是一种直观、简便、通用、稳健的组合预测。

2.1.7　人水和谐的集对分析

赵春霞博士等在文献［21］中把集对分析中的五元联系数用于郑州市人水和谐度评价研究，评价涉及到20 个指标（包括人文系统16 个，水系统4 个）和研究区中 30 个集对的分析，利用五元联系数确定待评系统与不同级别的评价标准之间的联系数，按照博弈辨识结果确定各单指标的权重，通过确定和谐度计算的指标体系及标准构造集对和确定单指标联系分量、确定综合联系数和联系分量系数，得出评价结果，该结果与用 SMI－P 法结果整体接近，但个别年份有较大差别；结果显示：郑州市 2000～2005 年的和谐度等级分别为Ⅳ级、Ⅲ级、Ⅳ级、Ⅳ级、Ⅳ级、Ⅳ级，即除 2001 年为较不和谐外，其他年份都是较为和谐。

2.1.8　水资源突发事件应急管理与可恢复性评价集对分析

程瑶等在文献［22］中提出了“洪水灾害可恢复性评价”的概念，建立了基于集对分析的水资源突发事件应急管理与可恢复性评价指标体系（表 8），评价模型采用五元联系数，并用于某区域洪水灾害可恢复性评价数据（表 9）的处理，得到该区域洪水灾害可恢复性较强的结论。

表 8　区域洪水灾害可恢复性评价等级标准

可恢复性等级	灾害发展状况			用于恢复的资源状况			灾害所处环境状况					
	洪水流速/($m\cdot s^{-1}$)	淹没深度/m	洪水历时/h	人员保障率/%	资金保障率/%	设备保障率/%	人口密度/(人·km^{-2})	基础设施脆弱性	人均GDP/10^3万元	经济密度/(万元·hm^{-2})	植被覆盖率/%	平均坡度/(度)
1	>40	>2.5	>30	<10	<10	<10	>500	>0.9	>50	>900	<6	>16
2	30	2	24	30	30	30	400	0.7	40	700	12	14
3	20	1.5	18	50	50	50	300	0.5	30	500	18	12
4	10	1.0	12	70	70	70	200	0.3	20	300	24	8
5	<5	<0.5	<6	>90	>90	>90	<100	<0.1	<10	<100	>30	<4

表 9　某区域洪水灾害可恢复性评价数据

基础设施系统（权重为0.45）								社会经济系统（权重为0.35）								生态环境系统（权重为0.25）							
灾害发展状况			用于恢复的资源状况			灾害所处环境状况		灾害发展状况			用于恢复的资源状况			灾害所处环境状况		灾害发展状况			用于恢复的资源状况			灾害所处环境状况	
洪水流速/($m\cdot s^{-1}$)	淹没深度/m	洪水历时/h	人员保障率/%	资金保障率/%	设备保障率/%	人口密度/(人·km^{-2})	基础设施脆弱性	洪水流速/($m\cdot s^{-1}$)	淹没深度/m	洪水历时/h	人员保障率/%	资金保障率/%	设备保障率/%	人均GDP/m^3万元	经济密度/(万元·hm^{-2})	洪水流速/$m\cdot s^{-1}$	淹没深度/m	洪水历时/h	人员保障率/%	资金保障率/%	设备保障率/%	植被覆盖率/%	平均密度/(°)
22	0.7	10	0.76	0.08	0.58	210	0.66	22	0.7	10	0.68	0.62	0.54	7	740	22	0.7	10	0.45	0.38	0.36	16	14

2.1.9 水安全评价方法的集对分析

高军省博士等在文献［23］指出，到目前为止，尽管对水安全的描述各种各样，而且还没有统一公认的定义，但对水安全状态的评价已经成为水安全研究方面的热点之一，其研究内容包括水安全评价指标体系的构建，水安全评价标准的确定和水安全评价方法的研究等。就评价方法而言，从不同的基础理论出发进行评价，就形成了不同的水安全评价方法或评价模型，如模糊优选模型 、遗传投影寻踪模型、综合指数模型和集对分析方法，实例应用表明集对分析用于水安全评价的可行性和科学性。

此外，郭彦等在文献［24］中建立了基于集对分析的区域需水量组合预测模型。

由上综述可见：水安全涵义丰富，涵盖面广，水洪致灾，水缺致贫，水少致困，水污致病，都属于水安全范畴，都可以应用集对分析。但事物处在不断的变化和发展之中，如何把集对分析与概率统计等成熟理论有机结合，作各种水安全现状的变化和发展趋势分析，仍有待深入系统地研究。

2.2 空气安全的集对分析

2.2.1 集对分析法在大气环境质量评价中的应用

郭绍英等在文献［25］中指出：“目前对大气环境质量评价的方法有很多，如层次分析法、模糊评价法 、灰色聚类法 、人工神经网络法等。但这些方法都有其自身优点和不足，层次分析法无论是建立层次结构还是构造判断矩阵，人的主观判断、选择、偏好对评价结果的影响极大；模糊数学方法不能解决评价指标相关造成的信息重复问题，评价精度一般较低 ；灰色聚类法需要构建隶属函数或白化函数，无法精确描述级别区间内的变化特征；人工神经网络法则一般需编制较复杂的计算机程序而有可能导致评价错误。基于大气环境是一个多因素多水平耦合作用的复杂不确定系统，因此，采用处理不确定问题的集对分析法来评价大气环境质量”。并具体地用四元联系数评价了武汉市的大气质量，在所用的 8 个测点数据上的评价结果与改性属性识别法所得结果相对照，在 6 个测点数据上的评价结果相同，通过对两个不同评价结果的测点数据的具体分析，认为集对分析法评价结果比改性属性识别法所得结果更合理，由此，文献［25］认为：“集对分析法突破了以相关系数、隶属度和灰色关联度单一表征关系的传统框架，采用四元联系度有效地解决了大气环境质量综合评价中的不确定性问题。作为大气环境质量综合评价的新方法，该方法具有独特的优势：将定性分析和定量分析相结合，评价模型严谨，计算简便，可手工或用 Excel 电子表格计算；评价过程直观，信息利用率高；评价结果合理、精细、稳定。当然集对分析法运用于大气环境质量综合评价也存在一些不足，诸如如何更加科学地计算联系度，如何更合理地对差异系数 i 进行取值等问题，尚需进行更深入的研究和完善”。

2.2.2 基于遗传集对分析的空气环境质量评价

邬敏等在文献［26］中将遗传算法应用于联系数表达式中 i 值的优化求解，使得联系数确定化，并用于某地 6 个测点的四种空气污染物监测数据的空气环境质量综合评价，评价结果与用其他方法评价结果一致，说明了把遗传算法与集对分析结合是优化求解联系数表达式中 i 值的一条可行途径。

2.2.3 室内空气质量的集对分析

亢永博士在文献［27］中把集对分析用于室内空气质量评估，其思路是：室内空气质量会随着建筑物使用时间、装修、用途等原因而发生改变，进而威胁到人的呼吸安全。通过定期的空气质量检测及与国家标准比照，可以掌握室内空气是否被污染以及污染程度。利用集对分析方法进行室内空气质量污染程度的评价时，从安全出发，以国家标准及检测分析出的最低检出限为依据，将检测点各指标的含量划分为未检出（低于最低检出限）、检出（高于最低检出限）、超标（高于评价标准），由此，用集对分析联系度表述为：a 相当于未检出率，b 相当于检出率，c 相当于超标率。a 值越接近于1，说明空气质量越好，b 值越大，说明空气质量已经不好，有被污染的迹象；c 值越大，说明空气已被污染，且程度较高。

2.2.4 城市空气污染预报的集对分析

诸晓明，王国强在文献［28］中把集对分析用于城市空气污染预报，思路是根据集对分析（SPA）把不确定性和确定性作为一个动态的同异反系统处理的思想，动态地分析和处理每次预报中因子作用的变化，即每次预报前，先对因子进行态势判别和同异反分析，然后使可能干扰预报的弱势因子的作用受到有效抑制，使有助于预报的强势因子的作用得到充分发挥，从而实现了因子作用大小在各次预报中的动态变化，取得较为满意的效果，说明在预报模型中增加不确定性处理有助于提高预报准确率。

2.2.5 基于集对分析的沙尘暴预报模型

王繁强、郭大梅在文献［29］中基于概率统计分析和参考文献［28］的工作，从 SPA 的同、异、反分析出发，用联系度公式导出解决沙尘暴预报中合理地使用预报因子的方法，实现预报模型因子结构的动态优化，增强模型预报机制的合理性，达到提高模型预报能力的目的。在以往对沙尘暴研究成果的基础上，以强风、热力和沙源三大影响因子为着眼点，结合2001～2003年的沙尘暴天气个例，对沙尘暴天气进行了分类，分别选取预报因子，建立基于 SPA 的沙尘暴预报模型。于2004年春季进行了短期（24h）预报试用，结果表明，这一方法具有较好效果。

2.3 地质灾害与土地安全的集对分析

（1）地质灾害评估集对分析

中国地质调查局地面沉降研究中心秘书长龚士良博士在文献［30～31］中指出：我国是地质灾害高发的国家，人员伤亡严重，经济损失巨大。地质灾害易发区范围达600多万平方公里。约占全国总面积的65%。至2005年，全国共有地质灾害隐患点22.92万处，威胁3500多万民众，威胁财产安全超过万亿元，防灾形势严峻。以2008年5月12日四川汶川八级强震为例，该次地震引发地质灾害15 000多处；崩塌滑坡形成坝高超过10米的高危堰塞湖33座；潜在隐患点10 000多处，仅四川极重灾区新增的地质灾害隐患点就达2782处，为震前的2.38倍：地震次生地质灾害直接造成的人员死亡估计约2万人。而在现有的认识水平和技术条件下，由于地质灾害的内在机制与作用过程尚有诸多不确定性，而地质灾害防治本身也是一项涉及面众多的系统工程。因此，借助集对分析理论与方法，无疑是一条研究地质灾害新的重要途径。为此，龚博士把集对分析关系式 $\mu = a + bi$

$+cj$ 的内涵作了新的解释：其中：μ 为联系度；a 为承灾体状态标量；b 为地质灾害状态标量；C 为致灾体状态标量；i 为不确定性标度；J 为对立性标度。承灾体状态标量 a 表征地质环境容量与灾害承载力等指标，a 值越大，地质灾害的防御与承受能力越强，稳定性较高；地质灾害状态标量 b 表征孕灾过程的发展态势，b 值越大，灾害特性越趋明显，b 值越小，N 趋向稳定。b 值可认为是地质灾害的过程状态量，其增长即是灾害的孕育与发展过程的刻画，其最大值即灾害的临界状态，在其附近则可视为灾害预警区间。因此，b 值也可作为地质灾害预警预报的阀值指标；致灾体状态标量 c 表征灾变要素的活动强度，c 值越大，越促使地质灾害的形成与发展，破坏性和灾害后果也越强。并依据有关数据将我国地质灾害风险性初步划分为 5 个区域，即极重度分布区（Ⅰ区）、重度分布区（Ⅱ区）、中度分布区（Ⅲ区）、轻度分布区（Ⅳ区）、微度分布区（Ⅴ区），5 个区域的集对态势分析表达式经归一化处理后具体为：

“（极重度分布区）$=0.056+0.444i+0.500j$；代表性区域有

（重度分布区）$=0.188+0.375i+0.437j$；

（中度分布区）$=0.303+0.333i+0.364j$；

（轻度分布区）$=0.500+0.286i+0.214j$；

（微度分布区）$=0.692+0.231i+0.077j$。

以上各区在中国的分布情况见下图：

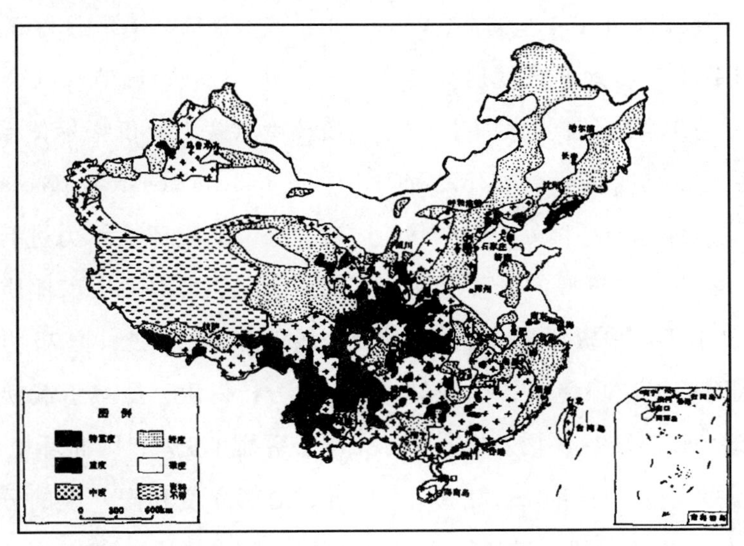

图 1　全国自然灾害程度图

由图看出，我国地质灾害风险性较高的地区大多集中在中西部的云贵高原和四川盆地等地区。那里地质构造活跃、岩土体疏松，地形差异显著，山地地质灾害集中且高发；且处冷暖气流交汇地，气候瞬息万变，暴雨等灾害性天气频发，从而也加剧了地质灾害发生的可能性与危险程度。其是地质灾害防治的重点区域。华南地区岩溶广布，岩溶塌陷是主要的地质灾害类型。而滨海平原地区以地面沉降等缓变型地质灾害为主。地质灾害风险分区及其各个区域的集对态势量化表达式，将有助于地质灾害的分析研究，可为地质灾害防治提供技术支持，并为灾害风险管理提供重要借鉴。

龚士良博士还进一步在文献［32］中提出地质灾害防治集对论优态共存准则：其基本思想和主要内容是：地质环境状态可分为优化、弱化、劣化、恶化4个状态，与之对应的灾害形态则分别为没有威胁、有潜在威胁、有间接威胁、有直接威胁。直接威胁是典型的危险状态，而生存优态则是真正的安全状态。由此，地质灾害防治应追求行为体间的优态共存，这是地质灾害防治中环境安全一个新的思考视角。首先，优态是安全指向的对象，表征的是行为体可持续发展的生存境况，标示出安全所要达到的更深远的价值目标是发展与安全；其次，共存是安全获得的条件，唯有相互协同才能和谐共处，使地质环境系统处于安全态势，降低环境危机的威胁 。由此，若将地质环境所具有的资源属性作为同一度，将地质环境同时具有的灾害属性作为对立度，将人类对地质环境的开发利用强度作为差异度，则要确保地质环境处于安全状态而不引发地质灾害，必须使对资源的开发利用处于有效控制状态，既要小于可采资源量，也要小于致灾的开发强度。从而使地质环境系统呈现健康稳定的同势状态，而避免或减弱容易诱发地质灾害的反势状态。地质灾害防治是守业经济，减灾就是增效。其突出特点就是“以负换正、减负得正、负负得正”，通过防灾投入“负”效益的影响作用，来减少灾害损失，而减少的部分就是正效益。用集对分析同异反的辩证观点，就是减小对立度，也即相应地增大了同一度，从而使系统态势的同一性即稳定度得到了提高。而防灾措施的实施，也使不确定度得以有效降低，并促进同一度增加和对立度减小，综合效益得到显现。地质灾害具有不可逆性，而灾害的孕育过程通常较为隐蔽而易被忽视并使人麻痹，而一旦致灾则难以逆转，危害充分凸显，治理难度骤增。因此，未雨绸缪、防患未然是地质灾害防治的关键和首要。防灾减灾工作是持续性的，防治工程应体现风险最小、效益最大的最优化原则，从而构建灾害综合防御与风险管理体系 。

（2）城市地质环境承载力的集对分析

随着全球城市化进程的不断加快，城市地质环境正在承受前所未有的影响与压力，为了科学地指导城市地质环境规划，有效提高城市地质环境的调控手段，需要对城市地质环境承载力进行系统综合的研究。为此，姚治华等人在文献［33］中，在对地质环境承载力概念内涵分析的基础上，从资源、环境、调节和社会经济四个方面构建地质环境承载力评价指标体系；用基于熵值－AHP（The analytic hierarchy process）法的集对分析模型对大庆市地质环境承力进行评价。研究表明：肇州、肇源是当前大庆市地质环境承载状况较差的区域，需重点保护；据20世纪80年代和现状数据对比分析得出，虽然承载状况呈转好趋势，但环境子系统却变差，因而环境保护尤为重要。另外，通过对对立度和同一度的分析，提出了改善地质环境承载力的具体策略。

（3）滑坡变形动态建模的集对分析

工程地质中的滑坡是一个确定—不确定动态系统，其变形表现出复杂的非线性演化特征，变形分析是工程中的主要技术难题之一，用现有的力学理论彻底解决有关变形问题至今仍然有很大难度。为了克服传统分析方法在处理滑坡变形系统不确定性方面的不足，刘晓博士等在文献［34］

中将集对分析法（SPA）引入岩土变形监测分析领域，并结合层次分析法（AHP）提出了滑坡变形动态预测模型，给出了基于概率论的最优预测算法，提出并证明了集对论中最大同一度在等势条件下存在极限解，据此提出位移势的概念。在位移势的基础上，进行 SPA 二次建模，提出了基于 SPA 的滑坡变形与水库蓄水过程相关性动态分析模型。运用上述预测模型对新近发生的刘家沱滑坡进行变形监测定量分析，实践证明：最优预测值具有良好的短期预报精度；位移势能够表征系统当前状态下位移所能达到的最大潜力，可作为短期预测的上限值，其变化能够反映系统宏观层面上的演化特征，对滑坡演变加速预警具有指导意义；运用集对分析方法进行滑坡变形响应滞后效应的定量研究是一条可行的新思路，反演结果与实际情况吻合；该方法在岩土监测分析和工程安全领域有良好的应用前景。该文对联系度中的式中的不确定系数 i 取值作了创造性的研究，提出在等势条件下存在最大同一度极限解并用于滑坡位移量的预测，其思路如下：

设存在初始联系度（μ）$=a+bi+cj$，a、b、c 均为非负实数，且满足归一化条件：$a+b+c=1$，通过不确定系数 i 的顺势取值法，在保持集对势 shi（H）$=a/c$ 值不变的情况下，将 b 分解为 $b=b(a+b+c)=ab+b+bc$，式中：ab 为差异度 b 中倾向于同一的部分，归入同一度部分；bc 为倾向于对立的部分，归入对立度部分；bb 为保留下来的差异度。这样构成新的联系度（）$=+ab)+bEi+(c+bc)j$，满足归一化条件，且集对势保持不变。经上述变换，宏观不确定量变为 b，大大减小了不确定程度。在此基础上反复使用顺势取值法 k 次，则当 $k\rightarrow\infty$ 时，得到最大同一度，这一“最大同一度”是给定集对系统所能达到的最大潜力值的量化，是定量评价联系度的一个重要标志，再结合具体的滑坡因素算得最大同一度条件下的滑坡位移量。

（4）农业土壤安全的集对分析

葛康等在文献［35］中把集对分析用于土壤重金属污染评价，基本原理是：首先将土壤中各种污染因子指标的实际值与参考标准值构成一集对，就这一集对做同异反决策分析，利用三角模糊数构造其差异度系数 i，然后基于三角模糊数确定联系数，并结合评价指标权重来综合评价土壤重金属污染状况，本文将土壤重金属综合评价等级分为清洁（I）、尚清洁（II）、轻污染（III）、中污染（IV）和重污染（V）五级，设等级界限值分别为 s_1、s_2、s_3、s_4、s_5，按集对分析理论可知，可将评价样本指标值符合 I 级标准的定义为同一度 a，相应的同一度系数看作为 1，符合 V 级标准定义为对立度 c，相应的对立度系数 j 取 -1，而将符合 II、III、IV 级标准定义为差异度。进一步细化，由五元联系数定义，设将符合 II 级标准定义为偏同差异性，符合 III 级标准定义为中差异性，符合 IV 级标准定义为偏反差异性，相应地 i_1、i_2、i_3 分别称为偏同差异度系数、中差异度系数、偏反差异度系数［10］。因为相邻等级之间的差异度系数存在极大的模糊性，本文利用三角模糊数来表示差异度系数的模糊性，即采用分析取值法确定标准等级分割点处的差异度分量系数，即将等级界限值 s_2、s_3、s_4 处的差异度系数分别取作 $i_1=0.5$，$i_2=0$，$i_3=-0.5$。该文实例选用华东某地区 10 个区域的土壤环境作为评价对象，选用了 6 个评价因子：Cd、

Hg、Pb、Cr、Cu、Zn，其权重参考有关文献设为 $w = \{0.339, 0.213, 0.110, 0.087, 0.103, 0.148\}$，评估结果与他方法结果基本一致。

2.4 风险评估集对分析

2.4.1 自然灾害风险度综合评价的集对分析

自然灾害风险度综合评价是一种影响因素较多的、复杂的系统工程，王文圣教授等在文献［36］基于集对原理提出了自然灾害风险度评价新方法——集对分析法（SPAM）。SPAM 考虑标准分类的模糊性，避免直接确定联系度中差异度（分量）系数。SPAM 概念清晰，结构简单，计算简洁，评价结果可信。以全国各省自然灾害资料为例（表 10），探讨集对分析法在自然灾害风险度评价中的应用，研究表明，SPAM 是可行而有效的。评价结果显示在各省区的综合结果中：北京市自然灾害风险度为 4 级（高风险），内蒙古，由于 $h_1 = f_1 = 0.7 > 0.55$，所以内蒙古自然灾害风险度为 1 级（极低风险），四川省由于滑坡、泥石流、山洪频发，地质结构复杂多变，自然灾害风险为高风险较合理，“5·12”汶川特大地震是一个例证；至于上海，洪水、台风的危险度较大，考虑其经济发达，人口密度大，承灾体的易损性强，因而自然灾害风险评价为较高的级别也是合理的。其他省区的风险级别见表 12 和图 2。

表 10 各省自然灾害统计表

分类	地震 z	地质 d	洪水 h	台风 t	危险性指标 x_1	平均国内生产总值 g/（亿元）	平均固定资产投资 q/（亿元）	经济易损性指标 x_2	人口总数 r/（万人）	面积 s/（10^4km^2）	社会易损性指标 x_3
北京	3	3	2	0	0.8	1504	783	0.77	1383	1.68	0.82
天津	3	1	3	2	0.9	989	395	0.72	1004	1.1	0.91
河北	3	2	3	2	0.9	3035	1039	0.83	6699	19	0.35
山西	3	2	1	1	0.6	1095	336	0.73	3272	16	0.21
内蒙古	1	1	1	0	0.3	873	259	0.7	2377	118	0.02
辽宁	3	2	2	2	0.8	2818	849	0.82	4194	15	0.28
吉林	1	1	2	1	0.5	1168	348	0.73	2691	19	0.14
黑龙江	1	1	2	1	0.5	2084	535	0.79	3811	45	0.09
上海	1	1	2	2	0.6	2675	1320	0.83	1614	0.6	1
江苏	3	1	3	2	0.9	5199	1682	0.88	7355	10	0.74
浙江	1	2	3	3	0.8	3571	1376	0.85	4613	10	0.46
安徽	2	1	3	2	0.8	1954	499	0.78	6328	14	0.45
福建	3	2	3	3	1	2269	676	0.8	3440	12	0.29
江西	1	3	2	2	0.7	1291	304	0.74	4186	17	0.25

续表

分类	地震 z	地质 d	洪水 h	台风 t	危险性指标 x_1	平均国内生产总值 g/（亿元）	平均固定资产投资 q/（亿元）	经济易损性指标 x_2	人口总数 r/（万人）	面积 s/（10^4km^2）	社会易损性指标 x_3
山东	3	1	3	2	0.9	5156	1451	0.88	9041	15	0.6
河南	2	1	3	1	0.7	3113	859	0.83	9555	17	0.56
河北	1	3	3	0	0.6	2595	790	0.81	5975	19	0.31
湖南	1	3	3	2	0.8	2271	1250	0.82	6596	21	0.31
广东	2	3	3	3	1	4993	2071	0.89	7783	18	0.42
广西	1	3	2	3	0.8	1407	389	0.75	4788	24	0.2
海南	3	2	3	3	1	337	163	0.62	796	3.4	0.23
重庆	1	3	2	0	0.5	1520	533	0.76	3097	8.24	0.38
四川	3	3	2	0	0.8	2955	882	0.83	8640	48	0.18
贵州	1	3	1	0	0.5	648	208	0.68	3799	18	0.21
云南	3	3	1	0	0.7	1250	421	0.74	4287	39	0.11
西藏	3	3	1	0	0.6	69	35	0.46	263	123	0.002
陕西	3	3	2	0	0.8	1051	366	0.73	3659	21	0.17
甘肃	3	3	1	0	0.6	633	212	0.67	2575	45	0.06
青海	3	2	1	0	0.5	170	80	0.55	523	72	0.007
宁夏	3	2	1	0	0.5	171	82	0.55	563	6.6	0.09
新疆	3	2	1	0	0.5	836	345	0.71	4876	160	0.03

表 11　主要省区的评价结果

类别	北京	内蒙古	重庆	黑龙江	江苏	上海	山东	四川
f_1	0.0	0.7	0.4	0.7	0.0	0.133	0.0	0.023
f_2	0.0	0.27	0	0.0	0.0	0.267	0.0	0.277
f_3	0.15	0.03	0.36	0.03	0.0	0.0	0.0	0.0
f_4	0.506	0.0	0.24	0.27	0.0	0.0	0.0	0.356
f_5	0.344	0.0	0.0	0.0	1	0.6	1	0.344

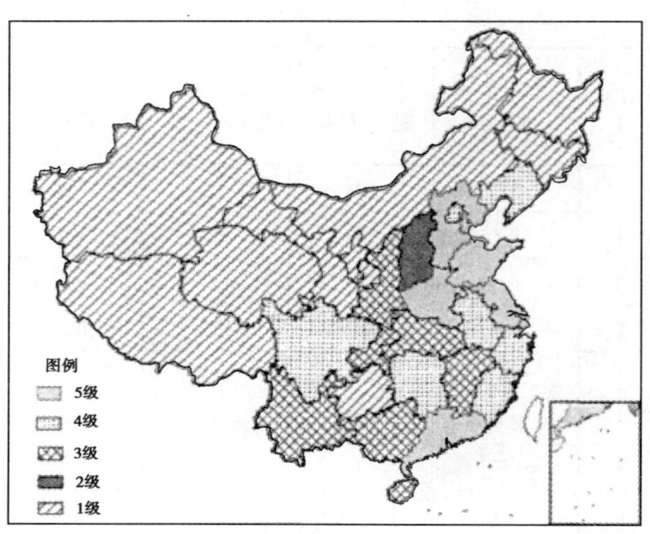

图 2　全国自然灾害风险等级分布

表 12　各省区风险级别的综合评价结果

行政区	风险度/级（集对分析法）	文献［3］		行政区	风险度/级（集对分析法）	文献［3］	
		风险度/级	*F* 值			风险度/级	*F* 值
北京	4	4	0.71	湖北	3	3	0.45
天津	5	5	0.82	湖南	4	4	0.6
河北	5	4	0.69	广东	5	5	0.81
山西	2	3	0.41	广西	3	3	0.55
内蒙古	1	1	0.18	海南	3	4	0.66
辽宁	4	3	0.59	重庆	3	2	0.38
吉林	1	2	0.33	四川	4	3	0.57
黑龙江	1	2	0.33	贵州	1	2	0.34
上海	5	3	0.58	云南	3	3	0.46
江苏	5	5	0.81	西藏	1	2	0.29
浙江	4	4	0.65	陕西	3	3	0.54
安徽	4	4	0.63	甘肃	1	2	0.37
福建	4	4	0.74	青海	1	2	0.27
江西	3	3	0.49	宁夏	1	2	0.29
山东	5	4	0.77	新疆	1	2	0.31
河南	5	3	0.59				

2.4.2　城市自然灾害风险的集对分析

张明媛博士等在文献［37］中，从风险具有的不确定性和复杂性入手，将城市灾害综合风险看做是基于危险性和易损性的不确定系统。通过判断风险确定的和不确定的影响因素，基于集对分析思想，建立了城市灾害综合风险评价模型。利用客观的降维方法——投影寻踪确定了因素的权重，降低了风险分析问题的复杂性。重点研究了集对联系度中差异性系数的客观量化方法，将其偏向性和偏向程度加入风险不确定性的计算中，得到了风险阈值的范围，进而得出了风险不确定性的大小。利用该方法对某市做了动态风险分析评价和趋势预测，并得出该市处于中度风险的可能性为52%的结论．该方法解决了以往灾害风险分析中多需要历史灾害数据或大样本数据的问题，为更多的目标物风险分析提供了可行方法。

2.5　*矿山安全的集对分析*

（1）煤矿瓦斯危险源风险评价集对分析

煤矿生产系统是一个由人、机、环境组成的复杂系统，存在着能量载体或危险物质，物的故障、物理性环境因素，以及组织管理因素等各种危险源，可能发生瓦斯煤尘爆炸、突水、井下火灾、顶板事故、瓦斯突出、机电事故等。各种危险因素具有动态性、随机性和模糊性。对煤矿事故的控制，归根到底就是对煤矿存在的各类危险源进行辨识、评价和控制。为此，田水承教授等在文献［38］把集对分析用于煤矿瓦斯危险源风险评价：将危险源及系统安全保障体系这两个集合作为一个集对，用联系数表示三类危险源，用专家打分法确定联系数，应用集对理论分析方法，结合危险源理论对安全—事故集对联系数进行同、异、反分析，指出安全—事故集对处于反势时，应控制好表征第二类、第三类危险源的不确定项 *bi*，进而使表征危险物质和危险结构等第一类危险源的 *cj* 项得到有效控制，使系统趋于安全状态。

（2）煤与瓦斯突出综合预测的集对分析

卢宏伟在文献［39］中应用集对分析方法，建立了预测煤与瓦斯突出的集对模型。从应用实例中可以看出，采用集对分析方法预测煤与瓦斯突出是可行的。对某煤矿10个工作面的瓦斯突出情况进行预测，精度达到90%。与其他方法相比，集对分析法计算过程简单，是分析、预测不确定性问题的有效方法。

（3）冲击地压危险性的集对分析

冲击地压是聚积在矿井巷道和采场周围煤岩体中能量的突然释放，动力将煤岩抛向巷道，同时发出强烈声响，造成煤岩体振动破坏、设备损坏和人员伤亡等。冲击地压还会诱发其他矿井灾害，尤其是瓦斯、煤尘爆炸，火灾以及水灾，干扰通风系统，严重时造成地面震动和建筑物破坏等。因此，冲击地压是煤矿重大灾害之一，目前，人们虽然对冲击地压有了一些预报和预防措施，但由于地下煤岩体结构的复杂性，人们对其发生的机理还不十分清楚。因而，远没有达到有效的预报和预防。目前对于冲击地压危险性评价和预测包括很多方面，概括起来主要有：现场监测的实时预测、监测数据的拟合预测、区域性的危险性评价预测等。实时预测通过对某些指标的现场监控获取监测数据，比如钻屑法、微震法、电磁辐射法等，然后分析这些监测数据的变化规律，比较危险状态与实际状态间的差别，从而实现对冲击地压的预测，这类预测方法的关键和困难是临界指标或阈值的确定；拟合预测则是对监测数据的未来趋势和变化规律进行预测，从而掌握冲击地压的发展状况，使预测过程更加主动和有效，但建模非常困难且准确性不足。为此，张志镇等人在文献［40］中针对煤矿冲击地压危险性综合评价指标的不确定性和不相容性，基于集对分析方法，将多个指标合成为一个可反映冲击危险级别的联系度参数，建立了煤矿冲击地压危险性预测评价的集对分析模型。将该模型应用于富力煤矿276工作面和华亭煤矿回风顺槽掘进工作面，选用开采深度、煤层上方坚硬岩层距煤层距离、构造应力集中指数、顶板岩层厚度特征参数、煤的单轴抗压强度和煤的冲击能量指数等6项指标，分别对其冲击危险性进行了预测评价。计算结果与工程实践符合，表明所建立的集对分析模型能够合理评价区域冲击危险等级。

（4）尾矿库安全集对分析

尹君等在文献［41］中，从尾矿库安全管理面临的决策需求出发，通过对尾矿库危险源进行分析，建立了尾矿库安全评价预测指标体系，详细探讨了差异度和集对势在尾矿库安全评价和预测方面的应用。分别应用模糊层次分析法和集对分析理论对尾矿库进行安全评价和预测，确立了尾矿库的安全等级，反映尾矿库安全管理水平，分析尾矿库安全状况发展趋势，探索了一条安全评价与预测相结合的新途径，为尾矿库的安全管理和运行提供有效支持。

2.6 企业安全生产集对分析

（1）石化企业安全投资集对分析

石油化工企业的安全事故频发和职业危害严重，不仅造成重大经济损失，而且对社会造成不良影响，不合理的安全投资是造成这种状况的主要原因之一，对企业现有安全投资状况进行评价是合理进行安全投资的前提和基础。为此，孙宝铁高工等人在文献［42］中把集对分析与马尔可夫链结合，建立了基于集对分析的石化企业安全投资状况的动态评价模型，为安全投资状况评价工作提供了一个新的实用方法。并以某石油化工企业为例，通过对该企业2006～2009年这四年安全投资状况进行动态评价分析，预测出2010年该企业的安全投资状况。评价结果表明，将集对分析和马尔可夫链理论用于石化企业安全投资状况的动态评价与预测，起到了非常好的效果，能够为企业科学合理地作出正确决策提供理论依据。

（2）火电厂综合安全评价集对分析

李冲等在文献［43］把集对分析和模糊层次分析法和系统功能论集于一体，构建了一个适用于火电企业的综合安全评价模型，不但考虑了影响火电厂安全的关键因素，而且可对火电厂安全因素之间的相互作用的协调性做量化分析，并将其结果构造系统优势函数，以解决系统安全功能大于各子系统安全功能之和的问题。实例表明该综合安全评价模型能够整合火电厂中各安全因素内在联系和非线性影响，使安全评价趋于合理，为企业安全生产管理提供科学的依据。

（3）油库安全系统评估集对分析

郑贤斌博士等在文献［44］中把集对分析用于油库安全系统评估和比较，已知待评判的四个油库数据如表13所示，从安全状况好转趋势角度评得油库3最好，油库2次之，油库1再次，油库4最差；但从不确定性的角度看，油库1的不确定性（潜在的非安全性）大于油库2的不确定性大于油库4的不确定性大于油库3的不确定性．因此，油库安全管理人员从分析结果既可以看出所分析的4个油库的安全现状（次序），也可以窥视到潜在的不确定性（次序），这对于辨证地评价和改进这4个油库的安全工作，不断提高这4个油库的安全程度具有重要意义。郑文最后认为集对分析法从一个全新的角度对待评系统进行安全分析，系统地认识安全系统所处的态势及差异性等。该方法能有效地克服只强调某些方面而忽略另一些方面而带来的片面性，考虑了安全系统中的确定与不确定因素，从而实现定性与定量相结合的评价。

表13　待评油库系统及计算结果

所评油库	评价指标																				
	办事效率(0.15)			安全教育(0.15)			安全规章制度(0.10)			主要作业程序(0.20)			事故管理(0.10)			事故预案演练(0.10)			人员素质(0.20)		
	高	中	低	好	一般	差	好	中	差	好	中	差	好	中	差	好	中	差	高	中	差
1	0.5	0.3	0.2	0.2	0.4	0.4	0.4	0.3	0.3	0.5	0.2	0.3	0.4	0.4	0.2	0.2	0.6	0.2	0.5	0.3	0.2
2	0.4	0.4	0.2	0.2	0.6	0.2	0.2	0.2	0.6	0.6	0.2	0.2	0.4	0.2	0.4	0.6	0.4	0	0.6	0.3	0.1
3	0.7	0.1	0.2	0.2	0.6	0.2	0.4	0.2	0.4	0.4	0.5	0.1	0.4	0.4	0.2	0.6	0.2	0.2	0.7	0.1	0.2
4	0.6	0.2	0.2	0.4	0.4	0.2	0.3	0.3	0.4	0.6	0.3	0.1	0.2	0.4	0.4	0.4	0.2	0.4	0.2	0.4	0.4

（4）建筑施工安全评价集对分析

赵聚红工程师在文献［45］中，对河北省1997~2001年建筑企业事故作了分析，在这期间，河北省建筑施工共发生伤亡事故117起，其中死亡142人。其分布如下：高处坠落死亡63人，占44.37%；坍塌死亡27人，占19.01%；物体打击死亡17人，占11.97%；触电死亡13人，占9.15%；机械伤害死亡7人，占4.93%；中毒死亡7人，占4.93%；火灾死亡7人，占4.93%；起重伤害死亡占0.7%。为此应用集对分析对该市的三家建筑公司作了建筑施工安全综合评价，结果是三建>二建>一建。三建和二建属于评价等级中的一级，一建属于二级。通过各等级联系度的对比，二建确有需要改进的地方。结论是：将集对分析用于施工现场的安全评价中，可以有效的利用数据，避免人为因素的干扰，结果可靠性较高。该方法不仅能从总体上进行有效的评价和对比，同时，可针对每一家建筑公司的某一方面的实际情况进行评价。对于综合评价较高的建筑公司，也会指出其存在的不足，有效的进行评价及整改工作。该方法简洁、准确，将建筑施工现场的安全评价量化，是建筑施工管理中不可多得的方法。

2.7　我国乳产品供应链质量安全的集对分析

张智勇等在文献［46］中建立了基于集对分析模型（SPAM）的乳产品供应链质量安全风险控制体系，综合分析乳品供应链系统中的不确定性与复杂性因素，实现对其质量安全风险控制体系的综合评估，并以此为依据提出乳品供应链的质量安全控制策略，评估程序见图3，其5个一级指标和22个二级指标见图4，评估结果联系数见表14，最终评估结果见表15。

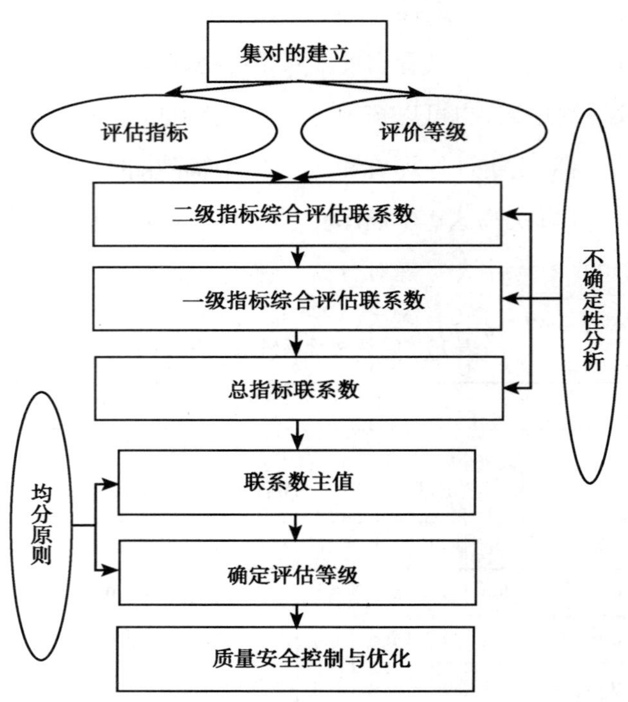

图 3　乳品供应链质量安全风险控制评估优化体系

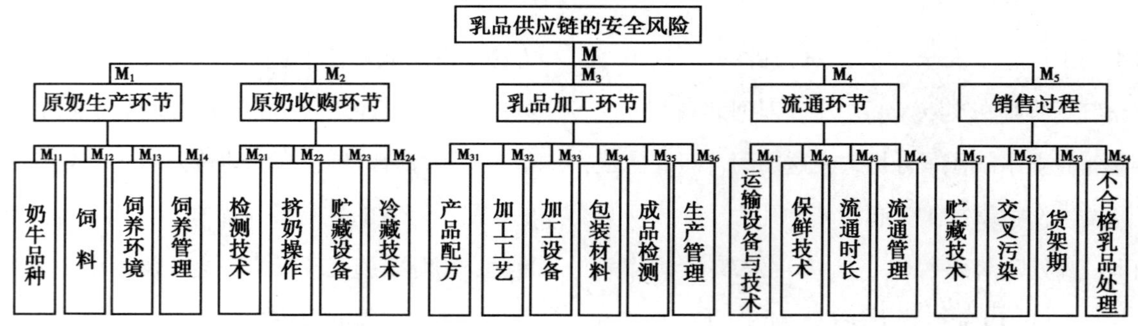

图 4　乳品供应链质量安全风险控制体系

表 14　乳产品供应链质量安全风险评估结果五元联系数

一级指标	综合评估五元联系数
原奶生产	$0.1675i_1+0.705i_2+0.1275i_3$
原奶收购	$0.1111i_1+0.5735i_2+0.2866i_3+0.0288j$
乳品加工	$0.3481i_1+0.4266i_2+0.2253_{i3}$
产品流通	$0.09+0.6642i_1+0.2458i_2$
产品销售	$0.1125+0.41i_1+0.4775i_2$

表 15　目前我国乳产品供应链质量安全综合评估结果

指标	指标的联系主值数	对应评估等级
原奶生产	0. 02	中
原奶收购	0. 12	中
乳品加工	0. 06	中
产品流通	0. 42	良
产品销售	0. 32	良
总体系	0. 10	中

由评估结果看出，我国目前的乳产品供应链质量安全总体状况处于一般水平，远没有到达安全水平。据此提出相对应的策略建议是：1. 建立乳产品供应链的 HACCP 体系；2. 杜绝供应链企业间的质量安全风险博弈；3. 增强供应链全体成员的质量安全风险控制意识；4. 全程控制并把安全控制过程公开化。

2. 8　航空航天安全集对分析

（1）飞机安全设计的集对分析

文献［47］认为集对分析在描述复杂系统方面有着独到的视角，其特点是立足于对元系统作系统分析，能够有效处理模糊、随机以及其他方法无法处理的中介不确定性这种现实中存在的实际问题。为此基于集对分析基本理论，对飞机区域内系统风险的联系度进行了计算，有效地发现危险来源，确定危险控制的关键项目，提高新老型号产品的区域安全性分析应用效果；实例证实了方法的有效性。

（2）飞机战伤抢修性设计评价方法的集对分析

张均勇等在文献［48］中在概括了抢修性评价的基本步骤和简要阐述试验统计法、专家评定法、模糊综合评价法、层次分析评价法、灰色关联评价法、计算机仿真评价法等各种抢修性评价的方法及其优缺点的基础上，提出了一种基于特征的飞机战伤抢修性集对分析评价法，可有效解决抢修性评价中的专家分歧和不确定性等难点问题，熟练掌握和运用这些方法，可为关注飞机战伤抢修性设计的各决策部门提供可靠的决策依据。

（3）火箭漏电故障诊断集对分析

赵刚博士等在文献［49］指出：在火箭（LV）测试和发射过程中，漏电是影响 LV 正常飞行的主要故障之一，排除故障是保证控制系统正常运行的必要前提。然而，由于漏电故障具有引发因素多、涉及面广、定位困难、危及成败等特点，因此，当电路上某点发生漏电时，与该电路相连的供电母线上的所有线路均表现为漏电，凭经验一时无法判断发生漏电的部位。LV 系统中一个关键位置出现差错会造成极大的影响和经济损失，甚至会出现毁灭性的结果。因此，LV 系统的漏电故障诊断问题受到了一些学者和专家的重点关注。目前，国内外针对 LV 系统的漏电故障诊断的研究成果见诸文献的很少。为了在这方面有所突破，以构建复杂系统故障影响因素的重要度模型，实现故障检测路径次序优化作为研究重点，先后基于概率论信息熵理论 、图论、多 Agent 理论 、灰色理论，建立了不同的故障诊断方法，并在 LV 漏电故障诊断的实际工程中取得了一定效果。然而，越来越多的实际工程应用表明，LV 系统的漏电故障诊断具有一定的范围，如漏电阻小于 3MΩ 为漏电，大于 10MΩ 为不漏电，处于两者之间存在一个中间状态。这个中间状态下对系统漏电有怎样的影响，如何准确描述这种影响，文献表明，到目前为止还没有一种合理的方法能够解决这个问题。很显然，目前已有的漏电故障诊断方法对于描述系统漏电现象具有一定的局限性，其最终评判结果可能并不符合实际要求。因此，为了解决上述问题，赵刚博士等在文献［89］中引入针对系统从可靠到失效存在中介过渡环节现象所提出的“中介可靠性”概念，采用集对分析（SPA）联系数理论，对LV控制系统漏电故障树进行定量分析，深入分析系统漏电故障原因的各种组合方式，并从同（漏电）、异（不确定性）、反（不漏电）三个侧面定量分析系统漏电状态，将系统或部件常介于故障与非故障之间的状态体现出来，并研究不同底事件对系统故障的影响程度，客观反映系统现实情况，有所侧重地对设备漏电情况进行管理和监测，以有效提高系统运行可靠性；该方法成功应用于某火箭控制系统漏电故障诊断的工程实例表明：该方法能及时诊断火箭系统的漏电故障原因，采取合理的措施有效地排除故障，具有良好的更新能力和应用前景。

2.9　电力系统安全集对分析

（1）配电系统可靠性集对分析

万官泉等在文献［50］中，在联系数运算和配电系统可靠性评估网络等值法的基础上，提出基于联系数的配电系统可靠性不确定性评估新方法。该方法用联系数表示原始参数和可靠性指标，通过联系数运算处理原始参数的不确定性，计算出具有确定项与不确定项的可靠性联系数指标。该方法与常规的可靠性评估方法相比，可反映各原始参数不确定性对可靠性指标的影响及不确定性情况，能更好地描述系统可靠性的真实程度；与区间分析法和未确知数法相比，该方法包含了前2种方法的所有特点，提供的信息量更大，更适合实际应用。算例表明了该方法的合理性和有效性。

（2）输变电工程风险集对分析

安磊等在文献［51］中指出：“十一五”期间，国家电网公司供电范围内的电力建设投资将近10 000亿元。由于输变电工程建设周期长、投资额巨大、技术要求高，且线长、点多、面广，有些项目横跨数省，自然环境恶劣，加之参加单位众多，管理水平参差不齐，协调难度大，不确定性因素众多，给输变电工程建设带来一定的风险，如何加强输变电工程的风险管理，提升风险防范意识，提高投资效益，降低风险具有重要的研究意义。为此，文献［78］就输变电工程风险发生的原因进行逐层分解、采用故障树法构建其风险评价指标，然后运用集对分析理论，推导集对故障树计算法则，并建立了输变电工程风险评估模型。算例表明，所构建的模型具有一定可行性，可为输变电工程提供一定的决策支持。

2.10　网络与信息安全的集对分析

（1）P2P安全集对分析

P2P安全是P2P技术中的关键问题。传统基于信誉度的投票选举方法能够很好地反映P2P网络中未知节点的表现，为该节点的可信度提供可靠依据，但该方法并未将P2P网络中的不确定因素考虑进去。为此，文献［52］把集对分析理论用于传统基于信誉度的投票选举方法的改进。提出了一种基于节点的不确定性的P2P网络信誉度安全机制，采用集对分析方法对信誉度进行了定量分析，研究表明：基于集对分析的P2P网络安全中的信誉度改进算法能够比较准确地反映出节点的可信度，易于定量计算和比较，并能够较好地解决投票者的虚假作弊问题。

（2）网络攻击模型BBF2PAN集对分析

任大勇等人在文献［53］中针对以双枝模糊决策和模糊Petri网为基础的攻击模型BBFPAN在描述网络攻击进展情况方面存在的问题，提出了一种BBFPAN双枝集对分析模型。该模型发掘了网络攻击模型BBF2PAN中对层次的集对关系，并对这些集对进行了双枝集对分析，用联系度表示攻击模型BBF2PAN中因素对网络攻击效果的支持程度，用贴近度表示决策分量与攻击和防御成功相对隶属度的接近程度，同时给出了BBFPAN双枝集对分析的基本步骤，为集对分析理论在攻击模型BBF2PAN的推理过程中的应用奠定了基础。

2.11　军事安全集对分析

（1）雷达信号分选算法集对分析

张秀辉等人在文献［54］中指出：随着新技术雷达的不断出现，雷达侦察接收机接收到的雷达信号更加密集和复杂，传统的分选方法已不能对其进行有效分选。为此，张秀辉等人将集对分析用于雷达信号分选算法研究，具体思路是把雷达脉冲信号与已知雷达的脉冲信号特征两两视为集对，应用集对分析算法，通过计算脉冲信号之间的关联度，实现信号分选。仿真结果表明，该算法不仅简单，易于编程，而且与传统分选算法相比，基于SPA的雷达信号分选不仅快速，而且高效，当有脉冲丢失时，对分选影响不大，对特殊体制雷达也能进行很好的分选；而且该算法实现中可由其他的高分选率算法替换CDIF算法，这样就可以进一步保障已知雷达知识库R的正确性，而且算法开始部分分选出雷达知识库R时所需脉冲数较少，即高分选率算法对整体运行时间影响不大。实时、高效地实现密集和复杂信号环境下的信号分选任务。

（2）导弹武器系统作战效能评估集对分析

吴杰等人在文献［55］中指出：导弹武器系统作战效能评估是一个多因素综合评估问题。在以往的效能评估中存在两方面的不足，较多考虑命中率这个重要指标而忽视其他重要指标；不同国家的同类别导弹的作战效能缺乏有效的比较方法，使获得的效能指标缺乏横向可比性。为解决上述不足，吴杰等人采用集对分析法评估具有典型意义的鸬鹚（德国）、捕鲸叉AGM－84A（美国）、空射雄风2（中国台湾）、飞鱼AM39（法国）、天王星空射X－35（俄罗斯）5种空舰导弹武器系统的作战效能，获得了较好效果。

（3）战场态势集对分析

陈绍顺博士等在文献［56］中以集对分析的同异反联系度和关联分析为基础，构造了现代战场态势的评估模型，其特点是把联系度中的b用某种关联函数表示，使得模型较好地符合现代战场态势。张琳博士等在文献［57］中则以集对分析的同异反联系度和距离测度为基础，构造了现代战场态势的分析模型，并用于一个实例分析。

（4）空中目标威胁评估集对分析

单鑫等人在文献［58］中针对空中目标威胁综合评估的不确定性和常权方法的缺点，提出了一种新的空中目标威胁综合评估模型，给出了具体操作步骤，实例应用表明该方法简单、准确、合理。

谭乐祖等人在文献［59］中，针对空中目标威胁判断指标属性权重与属性值均为区间数的多属性决策问题，利用连续区间数据有序加权平均（C－OWA）集成算子对区间数属性权重进行了处理；采用集对分析理论，将区间属性值转换成为联系数的形式，并通过联系数建立了目标威胁判断模型，充分反映了目标机动对威胁程度的影响。最后，通过算例表明模型合理、有效。

此外，冯志军等人在文献［60］中把集对分析用于作战仿真结果分析中的对应用。

（5）炮兵决策集对分析

于洋在文献［61］中把联系数 $a+bi$ 用于炮兵决策，实例应用表明：联系数模型能获得与其他方法一致的效果，而且能客观地反应出方案排序在不确定性作用下的变化，为武器的选优提供简单、实用的评价方法

赵磊等在文献［62］中针对传统目标排序方法忽略了现实中不确定因素和对立因素的缺点，基于集对分析理论建立了炮兵远程精确打击目标排序指标体系。从同、异、反 3 个方面研究打击目标的确定性与不确定性，运用联系度的概念从全局角度对目标排序问题进行集对分析，并以实例进行目标排序。结果表明，该方法简单易行、思路新颖、易于编程，适合处理大量数据，能较好解决定性分析时认识判读偏差的问题。

（6）综合防护集对分析

国防大学陈小青博士等在文献［63］中把集对分析用于综合防护（把进攻与防护集为一体）中的不确定性因素分析，通过把联系度中 b 的分解，使不确定性得到定量表达，用联系度的值表示赢得的效能；并以某防护工程口部的不同部位已受到 2000 磅、3000 磅半穿甲炸弹、5000 磅爆破炸弹冲击为例，说明了联系度的应用，该文献对联系度中的同一度、差异度和对立度采用函数形式表示，由此得到联系度函数的概念，这对其他领域应用集对分析有重要借鉴意义。

（7）机场目标毁伤效果集对分析

李大伟等在文献［64］中把联系数及其伴随函数偏联系数用于机场目标毁伤效果评估，针对机场目标机场目标是由飞机、跑道、油库等多种设施组成的系统的特点，仅考虑物理毁伤效果间的相互作用，提出效果选取原则，构建网络图评估模型，引入联系数对效果进行量化、计算，实现网络图与联系数的机结合，并利用偏联系数进行趋势分析，实现了对毁伤效果的累积、级联、多次等作用的合理整合，算例表明用联系数对毁伤效果进行量化、计算、分析，结果合理。

2.12　其他非传统安全集对分析

（1）钢混结构地震损伤的集对分析

钟延营等在文献［65］中，基于集对分析理论，选取整体损伤指数、最大层间位移角、滞回耗能循环次数和楼层能量集中指数作为评价指标（表 16），建立了钢混结构地震损伤评价的多元联系数集对分析模型。模型将多指标表示成一个能从总体上衡量损伤级别的 n 元联系数，用层次分析法确定指标权重，从主客观两方面定量计算地震损伤程度。将模型应用于对 4 种不同型式的结构进行分析（表 16～17），评价结果合理（表 18），而且评价模型严谨、分辨率高，是钢混结构地震损伤评价的有效方法。

表 16 评价指标

地震设防水准	小震		中震		大震
	1 级	2 级	3 级	4 级	5 级
损伤程度	基本完好	轻微损伤	中等损伤	·严重损伤	倒塌
整体损伤指数	0~0.10	0.10~0.30	0.30~0.65	0.65~0.85	0.85~1.00
最大层间位移角	0~1/450	1/450~1/300	1/300~1/150	1/150~1/50	1/50~1/20
滞回耗能循环次数	50~30（0~0.4）	30~20（0.4~0.6）	20~10（0.6~0.8）	10~4（0.8~0.92）	4~0（0.92~1.0）
楼层能量集中指数	1.0~2.073+0.046*n*	2.073+0.046*n*– 2.854+0.084*n*–	2.854+0.084n+ 3.346+0.113n	3.346+0.113n– 3.554+0.132n	3.554+0.132–6.0

表 17 4 种不同型式的结构参数

结构损伤指标	结构 1	结构 2	结构 3	结构 4
整体损伤指数	0.783	0.861	0.762	0.726
最大层间位移角	0.019	0.043	0.025	0.017
滞回耗能循环次数	0.7887	0.9544	0.9332	0.8785
楼层能量集中指数	4.201	4.616	5.334	4.238

表 18 评价结果

结构序号	结构 1		结构 2		结构 3		结构 4	
两种方法	传统方法	本文方法	传统方法	本文方法	传统方法	本文方法	传统方法	本文方法
1 级	–1	–0.4548	–1	–0.9463	–1	–0.7422	–1	–0.5911
2 级	–0.9719	0.0452	–1	–0.4631	–1	–0.2147	–1	–0.0370
3 级	–0.1799	0.5611	–0.9275	0.0369	–0.5438	0.2852	–0.2086	0.4172
4 级	0.9719	0.8598	0.3807	0.5377	0.8432	0.7909	0.9823	0.9538
5 级	0.1799	0.2967	0.9275	0.9447	0.5438	0.7308	0.2086	0.5179
评价等级	严重损伤		倒塌		严重损伤		严重损伤	

（2）辐射源威胁评估的集对分析

胡华强等在文献［66］中把集对分析用于辐射源威胁评估。辐射源威胁评估是指侦察机利用侦察到的辐射源参数（载频、重复频率、脉宽和方位）来综合评判辐射源的威胁大小程度，并根据辐射源威胁等级的高低，确定威胁辐射源干扰的优先等级。由于辐射源威胁等级综合评估受到信息的高度不确定性以及处理过程中主观因素的影响，从而使得威胁评估问题具有威胁等级评估的不确定性和评估方法的多样性等特点。对辐射源威胁评估，目前采用的方法有专家打分法、MADM 法、模糊评判法、贝叶斯网络法、神经网络法、基于支持向量机的方法，这些方法各有不足。由于对辐射源威胁等级评估的关键工作主要集中于从相对确定性和相对不确定性两个方面进行评估和合理确定权重。本文根据辐射源威胁等级评估作为多属性决策问题这一特性，利用集对分析中的联系度来处理威胁评估中各因素的确定不确定关系，采用信息熵的方法确定各因素的权重，从而建立基于集对分析的辐射源威胁评估模型。实例应用表明：该模型的计算结果与指挥员决策结果一致。

（3）堤防安全集对分析

刘亚莲等在文献［67］中针对堤防工程为防洪体系的重要组成部分，将信息熵与模糊集对分析理论相耦合，构建了基于熵权的模糊集对分析安全评价模型，以广东省北江大堤为例，计算了各评价指标的熵权，并集对分析了样本各指标的同一、差异、对立，根据计算的联系度按集对分析评价原则安全评价了各样本，为堤防工程安全评价提供了新途径。

（4）境外上市风险集对分析

随着全球经济一体化趋势的日益加强，国际金融市场的变化及中国相关政策的放开，越来越多的中国企业开始考虑利用境外上市这一融资途径，来解决企业发展中遇到的资金问题。在境外上市的过程中，一些企业上市成功，一些企业则因为盲目效仿铩羽而归，为此，杨伟娜等在文献［68］中，运用集对分析法对企业境外上市过程中的自身风险进行了客观评价，为企业境外上市风险管理提供现实、可行的决策依据。

3 展望和结语

以上是到2011 年为止的各种非传统安全问题集对分析文献的一个不完全综述，从中可以看出：尽管非传统安全的概念有争议、界限不明确，致使涉及的领域众多，内容各异，但并不影响集对分析在这些问题中的应用；其原因就在于不同领域中不同性质的非传统安全问题或多或少与这种或那种不确定性有关。而集对分析作为一种全新的处理不确定性的系统数学理论，与其他处理不确定性的系统数学理论相比，其理论特色是对不确定性采取“客观承认、系统描述、定量刻划、具体分析”，这一点集中体现在集对分析联系数的建模、运算和分析上；因其如此，才使得集对分析在非传统安全中得到广泛应用。

不过，从本文收集到的文献看，大部分文献中介绍的工作还主要集中在对非传统安全问题的综合评价分析上。但现实世界中的各种非传统安全问题一开始就是一个动态变化的问题，如何应对各种动态的、变化着的非传统安全问题进行集对分析，是一个需要深入研究的问题。2011 年 11 月合肥召开的第 11 届全国集对分析年会已提出集对分析发展的下一个阶段性目标是开展动态集对分析和非线性集对分析的理论和应用研究；另外，本文作者还在致力于传统概率论的集对分析研究，通过把传统概率的联系数化，有可能形成一种非传统的概率统计理论（见文献［3］，［69～70］），预计这种新理论在非传统安全研究，特别是一些突发性非传统安全问题的预防研究中将会有重要的应用；总之，随着集对分析理论和联系数算法的不断创新完善，可以在更多的非传统安全问题和更深入的研究中应用集对分析。

参考文献

[1] 余潇枫，潘一禾，王江丽．非传统安全概论［M］．杭州：浙江人民出版社，2006年11月：51.

[2] 赵克勤．集对分析及其初步应用［M］．杭州：浙江科技出版社，2000年3月.

[3] 赵克勤．集对分析中的不确定性理论及在AI中的应用［J］．智能系统学报，2006，1（2）：16-25.

[4] 赵克勤，米红．非传统安全与集对分析［C］．北京：知识产权出版社，2010年4月：1-218.

[5] 卢敏，张展羽，石月珍．集对分析法在水安全评价中的应用研究［J］．河海大学学报（自然科学版），2006，34（5）：505-508.

[6] 王慧，毛晓敏，尚松浩，董锋．五元联系数在黄河健康评价中的应用［J］．水资源与水工程学报，2010，21（1）：1-4.

[7] 金菊良，吴开亚，魏一鸣．基于联系数的流域水安全评价模型［J］．水利学报，2008，39（4）：401-409.

[8] 秦萌，王润峰．基于集对分析模型的新疆水资源开发利用评价［J］．地下水，2011，33（1）：46-49.

[9] 尹志杰，管玉卉．南京市水资源安全综合评价方法研究［J］．水电能源科学，2010，28（6）：16-18.

[10] 郭元利，房桂芝．东丰县水资源安全评价［J］．吉林水利，2010，30（11）：46-48.

[11] 王富强，韩宇平，汪党献，赵若．区域水资源短缺风险的SPA—VFS评价模型［J］．水电能源科学，2009，27（4）：31-34.

[12] 王栋，朱元生生，赵克勤．基于集对分析和模糊集合论的水体营养化评价模型的应用研究［J］．水文，2004，24（3）：9-13.

[13] 高军省．湖泊富营养化综合评价的五元联系数法［J］．人民长江，2010，41（21）：81-84.

[14] 王国平，杨洁，王洪光．五元联系数在地表水环境质量评价中的应用［J］．安全与环境学报，2006，6（6）：21-24.

[15] 刘慧，龚士良．地下水环境质量评价集对分析方法［J］．上海地质，2000，21（2）：21-23.

[16] 孟宪萌，胡和平．基于熵权的集对分析模型在水质综合评价中的应用［J］．水利学报，2009，40（3）：257-262.

[17] 邱贵江，李祚泳，李霞．基于指标规范值的地下水水质评价的集对分析法［J］．安徽农业科学，2011，51（4）：2209-2211.

[18] 张利平，秦琳琳，张迪，曾思栋．南水北调中线水源区与海河受水区旱涝遭遇研究［J］．长江流域资源与环境，2010，19（8）：940-945.

[19] 李明昌，张光玉，尤学一．海洋水环境质量评价的非线性隶属函数集对分析方法［J］．河北工业大学学报，2010，39（6）：81-86.

[20] 王文圣，李跃清，金菊良，丁晶．水文水资源集对分析［M］．科学出版社，2010年4月：142－143.

[21] 赵春霞，左其亭．基于五元联系数和博弈辨识的人水和谐度评价研究［J］．节水灌溉，2010（12）：74－78.

[22] 程瑶，陈安．水资源突发事件应急管理与可恢复性评价［J］．人民长江，2009，40（16）：13－15.

[23] 高军省，高绣纺，潘红忠基于集对分析理论的水安全评价方法研究［J］．长江大学学报（自然科学版），2009，6（3）：44－47.

[24] 郭彦，金菊良，梁忠民．基于集对分析的区域需水量组合预测模型［J］．水利水电科技进展，2009，29（5）：42－45，60.

[25] 郭绍英，张江山，郑育毅．集对分析法在大气环境质量评价中的应用［J］．环境工程，2009，27（4）：113－116，42.

[26] 邬敏，李祚泳，刘智勇，郭淳．基于遗传集对分析的空气环境质量评价［J］．环境科学与技术，2009，32（2）：168－171.

[27] 亢永．室内空气品质评价的集对分析方法［J］．工业安全与环保，2009，35（10）：56－57.

[28] 诸晓明，王国强．集对分析在城市空气污染预报中的应用研究［J］．应用气象学报，2006，17（1）：124－128.

[29] 王繁强，郭大梅．不确定性理论集对分析在沙尘暴预报中的应用研究［J］．中国沙漠，2006，26（2）：268－272.

[30] 龚士良．基于集对态势分析的中国地质灾害风险评估［J］．科技创新导报，2008，（34）：86－88.

[31] 龚士良．中国地质灾害风险评估集对态势分析方法［J］．安阳工学院学报，2008（2）：83－87.

[32] 龚士良．地质灾害防治集对论优态共存准则［J］．灾害学，2009，24（3）：16－21.

[33] 姚治华，王红旗，郝旭光．基于集对分析的地质环境承载力研究——以大庆市为例［J］．环境科学与技术，2010，33（10）：183－189.

[34] 刘晓，唐辉明，刘瑜．基于集对分析的滑坡变形动态建模研究［J］．岩土力学，2009，30（8）：2371－2378.

[35] 葛康，汪明武，陈光怡．基于集对分析与三角模糊数耦合的土壤重金属污染评价模型［J］．土壤，2011，43（2）：216－220.

[36] 王文圣，金菊良，李跃清．基于集对分析的自然灾害风险度综合评价研究［J］．四川大学学报（工程科学版），2009，41（6）：6－12.

[37] 张明媛，袁永博，周晶．城市自然灾害风险分析新方法［J］．大连理工大学学报，2010，50（5）：706－711.

[38] 田水承，王莉，李红霞．基于SPA模型的煤矿瓦斯危险源风险评价［J］．安全与环境学报，2006，6（6）：103－106.

[39] 卢宏伟．煤与瓦斯突出综合预测的集对分析模型与应用［J］．矿业安全与环保，2007，34（1）：3－5.

[40] 张志镇，高峰，许爱斌，刘冠男．冲击地压危险性的集对分析评价模型［J］．中国矿业大学学报，2011，40（3）：379－384.

[41] 尹君，王玉杰，吕林，陈先锋．基于模糊层次和集对分析的尾矿库安全评价及预测［J］．金属矿山，2010，45（10）：159－161.

[42] 孙宝铁，张福群，纪德香，王国胜．基于集对分析的石化企业安全投资状况动态评价［J］．中国安全生产科学与技术，2011，7（5）：113－117.

[43] 李冲，杨宗霄，宋磊．火电厂综合安全评价模型的构建与应用［J］．计算机工程与应用．2010，46（2）：230－233，242.

[44] 郑贤斌，陈国明．基于SPA安全综合评价方法及其应用［J］．哈尔滨工业大学学报，2006，38（2）：290－293.

[45] 赵聚红，基于集对分析的建筑施工安全评价研究［J］. 商业文化 . 2009（2）：193 – 194.

[46] 张智勇，张永裕，杨磊 . 基于集对分析的乳产品供应链质量安全风险分析与控制［J］. 黑龙江畜牧兽医，2011，(4) 下旬版：13 – 15.

[47] 颜春艳，诸文洁，孙有朝，车程 . 基于集对分析的区域安全分析研究［J］. 飞机设计，2010，30（1）：47 – 50.

[48] 张均勇，李武奇，刘晓新，孟宪峰，闻邦椿 . 飞机战伤抢修性设计评价方法的研究［J］. 飞机设计，2010，30（6）：71 – 74.

[49] 赵刚，黄大荣，黄席樾 . 火箭漏电故障诊断技术研究［J］. 兵工学报，2010，31（7）：916 – 921.

[50] 万官泉，张尧，汪穗峰 . 基于联系数的配电系统可靠性不确定性评估［J］. 电力系统自动化，2008，32（4）：30 – 34，.

[51] 安磊，王绵斌，谭忠富 . 基于集对故障树法的输变电工程风险评估模型［J］. 华东电力，2009，39（1）：12 – 18.

[52] 胡波，王汝传，王海艳 . 基于集对分析的 P2P 网络安全中的信誉度改进算法 . 电子学报，2007，35（2）244 – 247.

[53] 任大勇，黄光球 . 基于 SPA 的攻击模型 BBFPAN 双枝集对分析模型［J］，河北工程大学学报（自然科学版），2009，26（2）：86 – 88.

[54] 张秀辉，刘以安，曹宁生，李三全 . 基于集对分析的雷达信号分选算法 . 现代雷达，2010，32（2）：35 – 37.

[55] 吴杰，曹延杰，吴福初，贺英政，金红波 . 基于集对分析的导弹武器系统作战效能评估［J］. 战术导弹技术，2009（2）：11 – 14.

[56] 陈绍顺，宁伟华，张琳 . 防空战斗中的态势评估模型［J］. 空军工程大学学报，2004，5（4）：29 – 33.

[57] 张琳，陈绍顺 . 基于集对分析的战场态势分析模型 . 电光与控制，2005，12（3）：31 – 35.

[58] 单鑫，董文洪 . 基于变权 SPA 的空中目标威胁综合评估方法［J］. 现代防御技术，2007，35（5）10 – 13.

[59] 谭乐祖，杨明军 . 采用区间数的集对分析目标威胁判断模型［J］，电光与控制 . 2011，42（2）：73 – 76，84.

[60] 冯志军，薛青，邵秋峰 . 集对分析法在作战仿真结果分析中的对应用［J］. 装甲兵工程学院学报，2004，18（1）：10 – 12.

[61] 于洋 . 基于联系数 A + Bi 的区间多属性决策在炮兵中的运用［J］. 舰船电子工程，2011，31（2）：39 – 41.

[62] 赵磊，陈庆龙 . 基于集对分析和 AHP 的炮兵远程精确打击目标排序［J］. 兵工自动化，2011，30（1）：47 – 48.

[63] 陈小青，王可定 . 集对分析在综合防护研究中的应用［J］. 军事运筹与系统工程；2004，18（4）：7 – 12.

[64] 李大伟，赵文杰 . 基于网络图的机场目标毁伤效果评估 . 兵工自动化，2009，28（1）：47 – 50.

[65] 钟延营，杨娜，张勇 . 钢混结构地震损伤评价多元联系数模型［J］. 低温建筑技术，2010，(3)：32 – 35.

[66] 胡华强，石亮，陈游 . 应用集对分析理论的辐射源威胁评估与排序方法［J］. 第三届中国智能计算大会论文集，济南，2009 年 5 月 15 – 19：330 – 334.

[67] 刘亚莲，胡建平，周翠英 . 基于信息熵和集对理论的堤防工程安全评价［J］，水电能源科学 . 2010，28（10）：96 – 98，73.

[68] 杨伟娜，潘杰义 . 基于 SPA 的企业境外上市自身风险综合评价研究［J］. 工业工程，2007，10（1）：87 – 90.

[69] 赵克勤 . 二元联系数 A + Bi 在理论基础与基本算法在人工智能中的应用［J］. 智能系统学报，2008，3（6）：476 – 486.

[70] 赵克勤 . 联系数学的基本原理与应用［J］. 安阳工学院学报，2009（2）：107 – 110.

责任编辑：刘　爽

封面设计：Zdesign 书装设计　　　**责任出版：**卢运霞

图书在版编目（CIP）数据

非传统安全研究．总第 2 期 / 浙江大学非传统安全与和平发展研究中心、塔里木大学非传统安全与边疆民族发展研究中心编．—北京：知识产权出版社，2012.6

ISBN 978－7－5130－1251－5

Ⅰ.①非…　Ⅱ.①浙…　Ⅲ.①国家安全－研究－丛刊　Ⅳ.①D035．3－55

中国版本图书馆 CIP 数据核字（2012）第 066443 号

非传统安全研究

FEICHUANTONG ANQUAN YANJIU

2012 年第 1 期（总第 2 期）

浙江大学非传统安全与和平发展研究中心
塔里木大学非传统安全与边疆民族发展研究中心　编

出版发行：知识产权出版社

社　　址：北京市海淀区马甸南村 1 号	**邮　　编：**100088
网　　址：http：//www.ipph.cn	**邮　　箱：**bjb@cnipr.com
发行电话：010－82000860 转 8101/8102	**传　　真：**010－82005070/82000893
责编电话：010－82000860 转 8125	**责编邮箱：**liushuang@cnipr.com
印　　刷：三河市国英印务有限公司	**经　　销：**新华书店及相关销售网点
开　　本：889mm×1194mm　1/16	**印　　张：**12
版　　次：2012 年 6 月第一版	**印　　次：**2012 年 6 月第一次印刷
字　　数：262 千字	**定　　价：**28.00 元

ISBN 978－7－5130－1251－5 / D·1462（4131）